PRAISE FOR *THE PARTNERSHIP ECONOMY*

What people are saying:

"In the modern marketing age, trust is no longer a one-way street, with businesses telling consumers they are trustworthy and hoping consumers believe them. Consumers now drive this conversation, and they demand to know how a brand's external commitments align with their values. Consumers are looking for brands to show them—not tell them—they are trustworthy. In *The Partnership Economy*, **David A. Yovanno shares the context for how brand-consumer relationships have changed and actionable strategies for how to build authentic partnerships that will help your business thrive.**"

—Stefania Pomponi, founder of Hella Social Impact and author of *Influencer Marketing For Dummies*

"It's been said that great product never beats great go-to-market. And who could argue? With more than 15,000 SaaS applications in market, the best products no longer win on their own merit. Instead, the best customer experiences do. We've entered a new era, an era of partner ecosystems. And now, great go-to-market never beats great partner ecosystems.

"Welcome to *The Partnership Economy*, ushered in and documented for the first time ever by David A. Yovanno's **must-read for every partner leader and executive** in this new era. I've been complaining for years that there is no definitive work on partnerships and no book to reference. Thanks go to David for answering the call because ***The Partnership Economy* is the book I've been waiting for and that you must read now.**"

—Jared Fuller, host and producer, *PartnerUp: The Partnerships Podcast*

"If partnerships are the game changer of today's industry, then **this book is a must-read for anyone looking to create successful partnerships** that will give them an undisputed competitive edge. The concept of partnerships in advertising is not new, but *The Partnership Economy* really gets under the hood of what makes a powerful modern partnership and, crucially, how today's brands can use them to achieve customer acquisition and retention, drive sales, and establish a strong, long-term brand reputation.

"With real business examples presented in an accessible, conversational way, *The Partnership Economy* is **a remarkably engaging and captivating read** for anyone interested in furthering their knowledge of modern marketing."

—Julia Smith, founder and CEO,
The Digital Voice

"*The Partnership Economy* **is a great book for anybody interested in the wider universe of performance marketing.** As an industry that has previously been very focused on a narrow set of rules and tactics, focusing on a handful of metrics, it's great to read about the dramatic evolution that has transformed the space into a much more versatile and sustainable one to be a part of."

—Niamh Butler-Walton, staff writer,
PerformanceIN

"David A. Yovanno shares what all marketing leaders will soon know: Partnerships are the future of marketing. Dave and his team at **impact.com** have continually been at the forefront of using technology to transform the partnership industry, and *The Partnership Economy* **will show you a blueprint and case studies for success** in the brave new world of partnership marketing."

—Robert Glazer, CEO of Acceleration Partners and number-one
Wall Street Journal bestselling author of *Elevate* and
Performance Partnerships

"*The Partnership Economy* **will become required reading for anyone in revenue acquisition.** The adoption of cloud technologies and social media has accelerated the scale and speed of change in the partner landscape, and author David A. Yovanno offers a clear and cohesive path forward."

—Patrick McCue, board advisor and
former senior vice president,
Global Partners and Okta

THE
PARTNERSHIP
ECONOMY

DAVID A. YOVANNO

THE
PARTNERSHIP
ECONOMY

HOW MODERN BUSINESSES
FIND NEW CUSTOMERS, GROW REVENUE,
AND DELIVER EXCEPTIONAL EXPERIENCES

WILEY

Contents

Part III Get Started in Partnerships

Part IV Unleash Your Partnership Potential

Preface

How Modern Partnerships Were Born

Let's start with the end. The genesis—and rise—of the modern partnership economy came about as digital advertising imploded with the proliferation of email spam, unwanted pop-up ads, takeovers, intrusive retargeting, autoplay video ads, and other aggressive advertising tactics that have outright disregarded the consumer experience.

When information about products and services was scarce, consumers relied on advertising to fill their information gaps. But as the internet matured, search engines improved, and publishing became more democratized, consumers began to have a disruptive alternative to advertising: they could seek out the information on their own. Influencers, large publishers, bloggers, and even businesses, all with deeper, more authentic connections with consumers than before, served as guides that provided more information and trust than advertising ever could. They generated content that they knew their audiences would love—content that advised, informed, compared, reviewed, or recommended the products and services they felt would connect well with their audiences.

In addition to the shift in consumer behavior, Big Tech's action made the situation worse, agglomerating 90 percent of all new digital ad spend and then clamping down on digital advertising with privacy updates that eviscerated the ability to target, track, and measure display and mobile ads outside of their walled gardens. The writing was on the wall, and advertisers began to dump their ad budgets.

Quietly and relentlessly in its place, however, a new channel for business growth emerged, not conceived at Wharton or in Silicon Valley, but built by consumers themselves, equipped with unprecedented autonomy and jaded by years of marketing that ignored their needs.

A new user-powered way of communicating put first-hand information before impersonal data. Category experts and tastemakers established trust with their audiences. Consumers began engaging with publishers and content creators of all types as go-to sources of information. Much of the information they were seeking was commercial in nature, such as information about products, companies, and experiences.

Savvy brands began to tap in, publishers found ways to monetize, and the first modern partnerships were born: collaborative, customer-facing relationships that provide brands unique access to the consumer through the publisher's (influencer, creator, business, and others) circle of trust.

As a partnership management platform company, **impact.com** has a unique vantage point to this remarkable shift—and it comes from our clients' actions in response to what they are seeing with their customers. Brands like Home Depot, Target, Ticketmaster, Uber, and Walmart were building application programming interfaces (APIs), creating integrations, and referring business in entirely new ways. That was when we realized just how big the potential of modern partnerships as a channel had become; we had entered the era of Partnerships with a capital P. As a partnerships management platform that serves all constituencies in modern partnerships—the brands, their agencies, and the diverse array of partners they align with—**impact.com** has a deep, multifaceted understanding of this evolving ecosystem, how it operates, and its value. That's why it's time for this book. Business decision makers in every sector need to have at least a baseline understanding of this new consumer-centered ecosystem because there is no path to business growth today without a partnership intersection. For chief executive officers (CEOs), chief marketing officers (CMOs), entrepreneurs, and investors, partnership literacy and acumen are no longer optional.

My goal is for this book to provide both that basic fluency and the business case that leaders and marketing minds need to confidently make what can be a dramatic shift in mindset and strategy. *The Partnership Economy* shares the whats, the whys, and some of the hows of today's partnerships so that you can determine what opportunity they represent for you, both now and in the future. It is divided into four sections:

Part I, "Welcome to the Partnership Economy," provides an overview of today's partnerships and how they can be employed across your myriad extended customer journeys to drive customer acquisition, close more sales, and build customer retention and long-term value. It walks you through the six essential components of partnerships, and introduces the Partnership Design Canvas, a useful framework for designing today's partnerships.

Part II, "What Are Modern Partners?," offers an in-depth look at several partnership types, including influencers; mass media publishers; strategic business partnerships; coupon, cashback, and loyalty sites and apps; and partnerships designed around communities, associations, and causes.

Part III, "Get Started in Partnerships," provides an overview of the key components of a successful partnerships program along with proven suggestions for how to build the necessary organizational commitment to enable your partnerships program to get off the ground and reach its full potential. There's a chapter on designing your partner experience, and one on considering agencies as your partners in partnerships.

Part IV, "Unleash Your Partnership Potential," describes the steps that enterprises are taking to reach their full potential. The section concludes with a vision for what's next for partnerships—a deeper dive into partnerships ecosystems—and offers suggestions for how companies can prepare for the future by forming partnerships today.

You will also find a digital experience to accompany the book that includes planning worksheets that enable partnerships teams to turn concepts into results, interactive tools, resources that delve deeper into various partnerships maturation strategies, and more at **www.thepartnershipsbook.com**.

Modern partnerships have transformed thousands of businesses. My hope is that *The Partnership Economy* helps you gain the extraordinary growth and success that so many others have. The potential is there for everyone.

David A. Yovanno

Acknowledgments

Although this book has one author, in reality, it takes a team to write a book that defines a paradigm shift in both consumer behavior and how businesses need to respond. And what a fantastic book team I have had to work with on *The Partnership Economy*.

The spark and vision for what has become *The Partnership Economy* belong to Per Petterson. His tireless drive and tenacity to transform business through science and technology is inspirational to behold. His verve to get technology into the hands of brands, publishers, creators, and agencies, and then collaborate with them to solve their problems, has played an integral role in evolving modern business partnerships.

I am deeply grateful to my writing partner, Lisa Leslie Henderson, for her fresh eyes and her tireless and genius work—listening, questioning, identifying, synthesizing, articulating, and framing—which has expanded our collective understanding of the partnership economy—and for then translating this understanding into themes, chapters, and supplementary experiences for practitioners and educators.

Where would we have been without the brilliance of Jaime Singson, whose deep knowledge of modern partnerships, combined with his inquisitive and evaluative mind, enabled us to further expand, improve, and refine the concepts in this book? Inspired by both ideas and by putting those ideas into action, Jaime has been instrumental in bringing to life the concepts put forth in *The Partnership Economy* through myriad new **impact.com** initiatives that are already benefiting the industry.

Laura Dobbins, your way with words is truly a gift, as is your ability to shape a narrative, both of which are made manifest throughout *The Partnership Economy*. Equally valuable are your strong communication, problem-solving, and negotiation skills, which kept this book project progressing, and the team enthusiastic and productive.

Sarah Phillips, you are an exceptional organizer; your focus and attention to detail, thousands of details in fact, kept the team on track and organized. Knowing that you were always "on it" enabled the rest of us to be able to focus on what we all did best. Thank you.

Nora Wertz, your ability to transform complex ideas into simple visuals, often under very tight deadlines, has certainly enhanced the readability and understandability of *The Partnership Economy*, for which all of us are most grateful.

A resounding thank-you to the broader book creation team—Cristy Garcia, Jordan Dockendorf, Rich Cherecwich, Eileen Salzig, Katharine McAnarney, and Andrea Ferris—for their many contributions, and to Wiley's Richard Narramore, Deborah Schindlar, and Jessica Filippo for recognizing the importance of the emerging partnership economy and for committing their time and publishing expertise to making sure that the story gets told on a larger scale.

And where would we be without the many who have birthed and are now shaping the emerging partnership economy upon which this book is based? Thank you for pioneering this new way of doing and being for organizations. I would like to thank those who generously shared their time and insights specifically for this book: Christina Arango, Jamie Birch, David Bakey, Jenni Cassidy, Pete Christman, Stefan DeCota, Ellie Flanagan, Bob Glazer, Stephanie Harris, Jay McBain, Ryan McDermott, Siara Nazir, Reese Moulton, Kelsey Peterson, Keith Poshen, Jared Saunders, Lacie Thompson, Larry Weber, and Priest Willis, Sr.

Profound thanks to the **impact.com** executive team and employees around the globe. What a privilege it is to work together with you to transform the way enterprises manage and optimize all types of partnerships.

And finally, deep gratitude and appreciation to my wife, Susie, and two daughters, Alexis and Summer, for their inspiration, support, patience, and understanding over the years. I couldn't ask for a better "team" in life!

David A. Yovanno

PART I

Welcome to the Partnership Economy

CHAPTER 1

Unlock Unexpected, Lasting Growth with Modern Partnerships

Every so often a game changer takes place in the business world that causes a fundamental shift in how things are thought about and done. We've seen game changers in supply chains, production methods, and marketing strategies, to name just a few. Companies that see and embrace relevant change have the opportunity to understand, shape, and benefit from the disruption. Over time they generate new forms of competitive advantage that enable them to thrive when others fail.

Modern partnerships are today's game changer.

Partnerships of one sort or another have been around since the beginning of commerce, but today's partnerships are a game changer because they enable companies to achieve significant and sustainable growth in today's fast-changing, highly competitive, and consumer-led marketplace. By harnessing the talent, resources, and market presence of hundreds, if not thousands, of partners, enterprises are able to expand their capabilities far beyond what they can achieve on their own.

These are not just any partners. These are partners that share the same or similar target customers and are passionate about meeting those customers' needs and desires. Partners come together to create value for their customers and they do so in a collaborative, transparent, and mutually rewarding way. They ask themselves: How might we create experiences that will delight our shared target customers?

What can we create together that we couldn't do on our own? What information can we provide customers to add value to their daily lives?

Building on their combined understanding of the target customers, partners then translate these ideas into useful, interesting, and often remarkable products, services, content, and experiences. When these collaborations are truly a reflection of customer need and desire, the value these partnerships create is meaningful. They catalyze the reach, sales, and loyalty that companies need to generate significant and sustainable revenue growth.

Modern partnerships are making it possible for many of today's fastest-growing businesses, including Spotify, Uber, Airbnb, BarkBox, Harry's, Stitch Fix, and Casper, as well as established enterprises like eBay, Lenovo, and Walmart, to meet—and exceed—their revenue goals. Indeed, in a recent study Forrester found that companies with mature partnerships programs generate an average of 28 percent of their companies' total revenue through their partnerships efforts.[1] That is a fecund source of growth by any measure.

What's more, this is *real* revenue growth, not fluff. It's growth that comes from successfully reaching and converting new prospects into customers, expanding into new markets, increasing the lifetime value of customers, enhancing current value propositions and creating entirely new ones, and being able to quickly make strategic pivots that keep companies afloat during periods of market disruption (Figure 1.1). These are tried-and-true ways of making money; partnerships simply

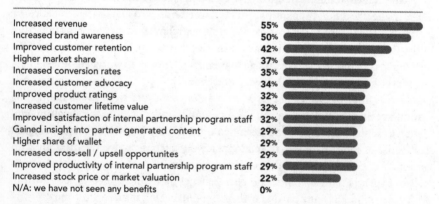

Top benefits from partnership programs include more revenue and better brand awareness

Increased revenue	55%
Increased brand awareness	50%
Improved customer retention	42%
Higher market share	37%
Increased conversion rates	35%
Increased customer advocacy	34%
Improved product ratings	32%
Increased customer lifetime value	32%
Improved satisfaction of internal partnership program staff	32%
Gained insight into partner generated content	29%
Higher share of wallet	29%
Increased cross-sell / upsell opportunites	29%
Improved productivity of internal partnership program staff	29%
Increased stock price or market valuation	22%
N/A: we have not seen any benefits	0%

Base: 454 global partnership, marketing, business development, and sales professionals who lead performance-based, nonreseller partnership strategies and programs.

FIGURE 1.1   Partnerships drive real growth, not fluff.

Source: A commissioned study conducted by Forrester Consulting on behalf of impact.com, April 2020. © 2020 Forrester. Reproduction prohibited.

enable enterprises to achieve these business goals with a much broader palette of resources—perhaps an infinite palette.

The magnitude and sustainability of this growth is why more than 75 percent of leaders from companies of all sizes, stages of growth, and business models, and in every industry and vertical, see partnerships as central to their sales and marketing strategies and to delivering their revenue goals.[2]

How do these percentages translate into absolute numbers? Consider that North American companies currently have an average of 173 partnerships in their portfolios[3] and the average partnerships program is forecasted to grow by 10 times over the next five years.[4] That means that over the next 20 quarters, the average North American company will build and manage 1,753 partnerships. Some companies are preparing to far exceed that goal. Salesforce, for example, is recruiting 250,000 new partners to meet its goal of doubling its business in four years.[5] Similarly, Microsoft is onboarding 7,500 partners a month to meet its growth goals; this is in addition to its 355,000 existing partners.[6] Partnerships are now more than a growth strategy for a handful of companies—they indicate the emergence of the partnership economy.

Modern Partnerships at Work

Partnerships as a concept aren't new. For some time, enterprises have built complex webs of partnerships to effectively develop, distribute, market, sell, and service their products. Their partnerships have included retailers, value-added resellers, exclusive dealers or agents, and managed service providers—think grocery stores and car dealerships. Under this reseller partnership model, partners typically transact directly with end users or downstream partners, acting as enterprises' indirect sales and marketing and customer service teams.

Today enterprises are increasingly moving toward a new partnership model, the referral partnership, otherwise known as nontransactional partnerships. This new type of partnership reflects the reality that more transactions are happening within enterprises themselves, rather than with resellers—think subscription and direct-to-consumer (D2C) approaches. Like the reseller partnership model, referral partnerships are customer-facing. However, rather than transacting directly with the buyer, in referral partnerships partners simply refer and recommend an enterprise's products to its target customers. These referrals and recommendations can take many forms. They can be a simple email to the enterprise's target customers recommending an enterprise and its offerings. Or, at the other end of the spectrum, they can be a mobile app or website integration that incorporates an enterprise's offering directly into a partner's own platform, creating a permanent and ongoing referral. Two actual referral partnerships that represent both of these options are explored next.

Sunbasket and Rastelli's Partnership: Several Thousand Percent Revenue Growth in One Week

Sunbasket is a leader in the $7.60 billion global delivery services market. The company's healthy meal kits, which provide all the ingredients necessary to create delicious, home-cooked meals, simplify people's lives by eliminating their need to plan meals and go to the grocery store. What's more, Sunbasket's meals are considered healthier than commercially prepared food, and can be configured for any dietary preference: paleo, gluten-free, diabetes-friendly, pescatarian, vegetarian, vegan, carb-conscious, and more. Its meats are antibiotic- and hormone-free; its seafood is wild-caught; its eggs organic.

The meal kit industry as a whole was on a roll, enjoying compound annual growth rates of 12.8 percent before the coronavirus pandemic outbreak in 2020.[7] As people's lifestyles changed during the pandemic, the demand for meal kits skyrocketed. Outbreaks of the virus at meatpacking plants further increased demand, as consumers facing empty meat coolers at supermarkets looked for other options. Sunbasket answered the call.

The company soon realized, however, that while it was providing families with three to four meals per week, it was not providing all of the food that a household needed. To help its customers access high-quality foods for the 15–20 other meals they ate in a week, Sunbasket worked with one of its long-time suppliers, Rastelli's, a purveyor and supplier of meats and seafood, to build awareness and interest for Rastelli's D2C protein delivery program.

Sunbasket referred its customers to Rastelli's and received a percentage of any sales that resulted (Figure 1.2). Within hours of Sunbasket making its first referrals, Rastelli's began to see a significant uptick in its website traffic. Within the week, Rastelli's had experienced several thousand percent growth in its business.[8]

A Taste of Modern Partnerships with Spotify and Ticketmaster

What happens when Spotify, the largest digital music streaming service in the world, partners with Ticketmaster, the number-one ticketing company in the world?

Here's Sam's story.

Inspired by a recent *Rolling Stone* poll that asked readers to vote for their favorite Billy Joel song, Sam, a dedicated Spotify user, swipes his way through several Spotify playlists to find his favorite Billy Joel song. This turns out to be a rather lengthy undertaking—one that Sam quite enjoys—as Joel is a prolific songwriter with many hits. Indeed, hours later when the poll would eventually close, *Rolling Stone* readers would name 70 different Billy Joel songs as their favorites.[9] At first Sam is sure

FIGURE 1.2   The Rastelli's and Sunbasket partnership generates extraordinary growth in revenue.

"New York State of Mind" is his favorite, but then there is "Uptown Girl," and "Scenes from an Italian Restaurant." Inspired by all the oldies—Joel hasn't released an album in more than two decades—Sam decides it would be fun to see Joel live. To make this happen, Sam simply glances down the screen on the Spotify app to view Joel's upcoming concert schedule (Figure 1.3). Madison Square Garden pops up, and two clicks later, Sam has two tickets to an upcoming concert. These are solid, Ticketmaster tickets, not tickets from an unfamiliar source. Pleased, Sam sits back and enjoys "Piano Man" in its entirety before deciding that it's his favorite.

Sam doesn't stop there, however. The same ability to purchase a Ticketmaster ticket is embedded in the personalized playlists that Spotify regularly curates for him based on his listening habits. Sam loves who the Spotify algorithm thinks he is—a bit more hip than he would have thought—and buys two more tickets, this time to hear Real Estate, that cool modern indie band Spotify recommended to him. His girlfriend—or so he's hoping—is excited about both concerts. In a quiet moment, Sam will tell you that the Spotify and Ticketmaster integration is changing his life.

Creating a more holistic music experience—embedding the ability to view upcoming concert schedules and purchase concert tickets directly in the Spotify app—is a game changer for Sam, Spotify, and Ticketmaster. Spotify subscribers

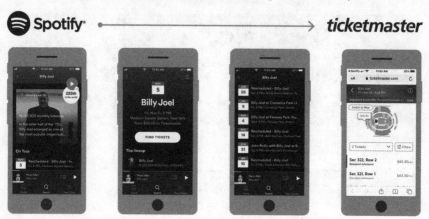

FIGURE 1.3 Together Spotify and Ticketmaster create a more holistic product experience—and generate 32 percent year-over-year growth.

like Sam put the new feature to use right away, generating buzz and ticket purchases. Continually enhancing the value Spotify brings its subscribers is important to the company; it's a proven way to build loyalty in the highly competitive music streaming industry. This new feature also creates a new revenue stream for Spotify, as it receives a cut of every ticket sold on its app. And in some ways it's even better: Spotify has created a better consumer experience through this partnership, increasing satisfaction, retention, and usage of its product. And of course Ticketmaster also wins: the company experienced 32 percent year-over-year growth thanks to partnerships like these.[10]

Who Are These Referral Partners?

As these two partnership examples illustrate, referral partners can take a variety of shapes and forms and they can span industries. Shared or similar target customers are the glue that brings enterprises and their partners together, and their satisfaction and delight is what ultimately makes partnerships successful.

Some of the most common referral partners include coupon and deal, cashback, and loyalty sites and apps; influencers, podcasters, and brand ambassadors; mass media publishers; and strategic business partnerships between brands, community groups, associations, and nonprofits and online marketplaces, descriptions of which can be found in Figure 1.4.

COUPON, CASHBACK, AND LOYALTY PARTNERSHIPS

offer discounts, cash back, and reward points to consumers for undertaking various activities, including making a purchase. Examples include Ibotta, RetailMeNot, Giving Assistant, and Chase Sapphire Rewards.

INFLUENCERS AND BRAND AMBASSADORS

are creators, writers, editors, podcasters, photographers, bloggers, community managers, experts, celebrities, and people just like us who have something to say and connect with others to talk about their shared interests. Examples include Oprah Winfrey and Richard Branson.

MASS MEDIA PUBLISHERS

are online and offline publishers and media companies that produce content covering a wide range of industries and formats (i.e., videos, podcasts, articles, infographics). Several of these partners have expertise in commerce content, employing storytelling as a conversion-driving strategy. Examples include Sports Illustrated, CNN.com, and BuzzFeed.

STRATEGIC BUSINESS PARTNERSHIPS

are brand-to-brand collaborations focused on creating joint value for two or more organizations (B2B, B2C, and B2B2C) and their shared customers and audiences made possible by leveraging both brands' strengths and credibility. Examples include Ticketmaster and Spotify and Sunbasket and Rastelli's.

COMMUNITY GROUPS, ASSOCIATIONS, AND CAUSE-BASED ORGANIZATIONS

comprise a subset of strategic business partnerships that are focused on a particular membership group of interest. Examples include GEICO offering special savings to alumni association members, faculty, and staff of selected colleges and universities.

ONLINE MARKETPLACES

are a type of ecommerce platform where multiple merchants' products, services, or experiences are offered by the marketplace operator, providing consumers with a wide array of options in one place. Sales conversions take place on the ecommerce platform and are fulfilled by the merchants directly. Some marketplaces provide a wide variety of goods, while others are customer or customer need focused. Examples include Amazon, Tencent, Taobao, and eBay.

FIGURE 1.4 There are many types of referral partners.

Why Do Referral Partnerships Work So Well?

There are several reasons for referral partnership success, which are explored in depth in the coming chapters. At the top of the list: referral partnerships reflect today's customer preferences and customer journeys; indeed, they were derived from them. Businesses are operating in an environment of consumer skepticism and lack of trust in their own media, advertising, and salespeople. With easy access to the internet, consumers are electing to conduct their own research when it comes to making decisions about what to buy and from whom. They construct and consult with their own circle of trusted resources—favorite writers, podcasters, publications, communications, and friends and family—to better understand their needs and desires, to identify their options for potential solutions, and to evaluate these options and eventually make a purchase decision (or choose not to). Referral partners are part of these trusted sources. This means that referral partners are able to generate and participate in conversations that enterprises cannot. As a result, when partnerships are conducted with integrity and authenticity, referral partners can make recommendations that generate demand for enterprise products, services, and experiences—over and over again. If enterprises don't have these relationships, they won't be found.

A second reason that referral partnerships are successful is because they enhance enterprise customer experience, today's primary source of competitive advantage. They do so in two ways: by increasing the effectiveness of enterprise customer engagement efforts, and by continually enhancing the value propositions of enterprises. As we have seen, referral partners can initiate customer and shopping journeys, and they can also drive consideration, close sales, and spur reengagement. Interjecting trusted sources across entire journeys builds trust and authenticity in these journeys, giving consumers what they are looking for: ready access to solid third-party recommendations with which they can make decisions quickly and confidently. When executed well, each of these interactions improves an enterprise's overall customer experience.

Similarly, continually enhancing the relevance and value of enterprise products, services, and experience is vital to excellent customer experience. Partnerships are able to help enterprises meet this need for constant innovation by bringing additional features, functions, and resources to the table to broaden and strengthen customer value propositions. Consider the positive impact of embedding Ticketmaster purchases into the Spotify app and of Sunbasket referring Rastelli's meat products to its customers during a time when it was hard for them to make these purchases from traditional channels.

A third reason that referral partnerships are successful is because they build business competitiveness with each of today's business models. They work effectively for companies operating with a business-to-consumer (B2C) model, a business-to-business (B2B) model, and a D2C model. Referral partners can direct interested customers to enterprise websites and mobile apps, to stores and online marketplaces, and to specific resellers in their home markets or most markets around the world. Further, these partnerships are highly cost-effective, often operating on a pay-for-performance basis, whereas enterprises only pay for results achieved. Referral partner content often creates synergies with enterprise marketing efforts, magnifying their impact and even reducing overall marketing spend. As enterprises scale their partnerships, they unlock even more sources of competitiveness. They build powerful skills and collaborative relationships that prove to be powerful barriers to entry for competitors. Scalability also enables enterprises to compete at a systems level by harnessing the knowledge, resources, and market presence of each of their partners. Referral partnerships: don't leave home without them.

Partnerships Go the Distance

Enterprises can generate revenue and achieve additional business goals, whether they are party to 10 or 10,000 partnerships. However, creating the conditions that enable their partnerships programs to expand and develop to their full potential is where the most value lies.

What does full potential look like? Companies operating at their full potential enjoy an optimal number of active and diverse partnerships that consistently create value for themselves, their collaborators, and their shared customers and audiences: a win-win-win. They do so by operating in a collaborative, transparent, and mutually rewarding way. And their efforts are supported by a strong and broad organizational commitment to partnerships as a growth strategy; a vision for how partnerships can enable them to meet their critical business goals and a solid strategy for realizing the vision; and a robust partnerships growth engine, the latter being the right combination of, and alignment among, the necessary people, process, and technology, to bring this strategy to life (Figure 1.5).

Is Operating at Full Potential a Pipe Dream?

Are companies reaching their full potential? Yes and no. Full potential is an ever-evolving concept. Yesterday's interpretation of full potential differs from today's, and most certainly from tomorrow's. That's part of what makes partnering essential and exciting. What really matters is that companies begin.

FIGURE 1.5 What does it take for an enterprise to reach its full partnerships program potential?

Once companies form their first partnership, they have taken the first step to realizing their full potential. They are moving forward, building the essential partnerships skills, capabilities, and experiences that will enable them to grow and meet their most critical business goals. They are learning and defining what it will take to thrive in the emerging partnership economy, even while they usher it in.

As enterprises gain traction, they reap greater rewards. Forrester found that companies that have the strongest partnerships capabilities, organizations they describe as having the highest level of maturity, significantly outperform companies that are in earlier stages of maturity.[11] They derive an average of 28 percent of overall revenue from partnerships, compared to 18 percent for companies that are just getting started. That's a difference of $162,000 in incremental partnerships revenue (Figure 1.6).[12]

In addition to deriving a greater portion of their overall revenue from their partnerships effort, companies with the most mature partnerships programs are driving 2.3 times faster revenue growth, are more profitable, and enjoy higher market valuations than their early-phase peers (Figure 1.7).[13]

Imagine What's Coming

We are in the early stages of modern partnerships. As Priest Willis, senior manager, global partnerships marketing strategist at the global technology company Lenovo, explains, "Partnerships can be a lot more than people thought in the past.

**Companies with high partnerships program maturity...
derive more of their overall revenue from partnerships**

LOW-
MATURITY
COMPANIES **18%**

AVERAGE-
MATURITY
COMPANIES **23%**

HIGH-
MATURITY
COMPANIES **28%**

A difference of $162K worth of incremental revenue

and enjoy greater revenue growth.

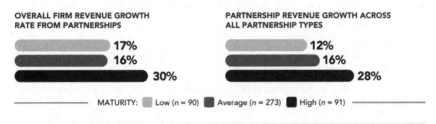

OVERALL FIRM REVENUE GROWTH
RATE FROM PARTNERSHIPS

17%
16%
30%

PARTNERSHIP REVENUE GROWTH ACROSS
ALL PARTNERSHIP TYPES

12%
16%
28%

MATURITY: Low (*n* = 90) Average (*n* = 273) High (*n* = 91)

FIGURE 1.6   Maturity pays off! Get up the experience curve!

Source: Adapted from a commissioned study conducted by Forrester Consulting on behalf of impact.com, April 2020. © 2020 Forrester. Reproduction prohibited.

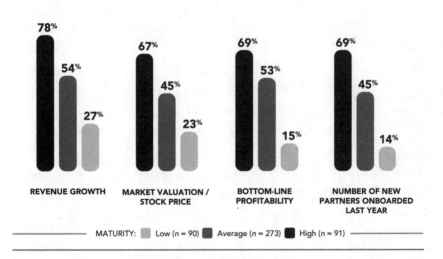

REVENUE GROWTH
78% 54% 27%

**MARKET VALUATION /
STOCK PRICE**
67% 45% 23%

**BOTTOM-LINE
PROFITABILITY**
69% 53% 15%

**NUMBER OF NEW
PARTNERS ONBOARDED
LAST YEAR**
69% 45% 14%

MATURITY: Low (*n* = 90) Average (*n* = 273) High (*n* = 91)

FIGURE 1.7   Companies with high partnerships program maturity are more likely to exceed expectations across multiple business metrics.

Source: A commissioned study conducted by Forrester Consulting on behalf of impact.com, April 2020. © 2020 Forrester. Reproduction prohibited.

We are starting to push the boundaries of what this role really means. It's fun and it's challenging at the same time."[14]

As enterprises become increasingly capable and comfortable expanding their organization's resources and borders with modern partnerships, we foresee partnerships becoming central to *every* company's ability to grow, achieve their business goals, and build competitive advantage. Imagine what will be possible when enterprises are able to tap an infinitely large set of resources to better understand their target customers and to embed that understanding into their products, services, and interactions. Consider how they might increase their revenue, expand their market share, enhance their customer loyalty and long-term value, and improve their customer experience. Imagine what is possible for their partners. And, most importantly, imagine what is possible for their shared customers and audiences.

Keep your imagination humming a bit longer. Consider what might be possible as enterprises and their network of partners morph into robust ecosystems that work together at scale on behalf of their shared or similar customers. What new combined customer value propositions might they bring to life? What market trends and opportunities might their combined insights uncover? How might they be able to quickly adapt to a rapidly changing customer-led marketplace? How might the network effects of this ecosystem enable it to distinguish itself from its competition, erect significant barriers to entry, and redefine the basis for competitive advantage for the entire marketplace?

As fantastic as this may sound, this isn't a pipe dream. It's already happening. Market-leading companies like Amazon, Alibaba, Salesforce, and Apple are already showing what's possible when partners come together as an ecosystem to engage their shared or similar customers and create interconnected products and services. This isn't just a possibility for the biggest companies in the world; it's a strategy being employed by well-funded start-ups all around the world.

Take the Sydney-based start-up Canva, for example. Canva is an online drag-and-drop design tool used in 190 countries to easily create and publish professional-looking layouts ranging from social media posts to presentations. Its diverse network of more than 12,000 partners includes brand ambassadors, YouTubers and bloggers, mass media publishers, and podcasters, as well as strategic integrations with companies like Hubspot, Wattpad, and Samsung. These new partners have added over one million new users and 150,000 new subscribers to Canva and are expected to contribute 5 percent of Canva's total revenue after just one year.[15]

Recent surveys of global consumer sentiment conducted by McKinsey & Company found that 71 percent of consumers are ready for integrated, ecosystem offerings.[16] According to the World Trade Organization, more than 75 percent of world trade is *already* flowing indirectly through third-party channels.[17] We have reached an inflection point: modern partnerships are how the world works. We have entered the partnership economy.

The Quick Summary

- Partnerships are today's growth strategy for business.
- Enterprises of all sizes, stages of growth, and business models, and in every industry and vertical, are forming partnerships. They are doing so because partnerships enable them to do what they need to do most: grow. The top enterprise benefits from partnerships programs include increased revenue, better brand awareness, higher market share, improved customer retention and customer lifetime value, increased conversion rates and customer advocacy, and improved product ratings. Partnerships also enable enterprises to make quick strategic pivots when facing market disruptions.
- In the referral partnership model, partners refer and recommend enterprise products, services, or experiences to their audiences, rather than purchasing them and reselling them to downstream partners or customers. These audiences are also target customers of the enterprise.
- There are multiple types of referral partners including coupon and deal, cashback, and loyalty sites and apps; influencers, podcasters, and brand ambassadors; mass media publishers; and strategic business partnerships between brands, community groups, associations, and nonprofits and online marketplaces.
- There are several reasons for referral partnership success. First, referral partnerships reflect today's customer preferences and customer journeys; indeed, they were derived from them. Second, referral partnerships enhance enterprise customer experience, today's primary source of competitive advantage, by increasing the effectiveness of enterprise customer engagement efforts and by continually enhancing enterprise value propositions. Third, referral partnerships build business competitiveness with each of today's business models.
- To succeed in partnerships, enterprises need a strong and broad organizational commitment to partnerships as a growth strategy; a vision for how partnerships can enable them to meet their critical business goals and a solid strategy for realizing the vision; and a robust partnerships growth engine, the latter being the right combination of, and alignment among, the necessary people, process, and technology to bring this strategy to life.
- It pays to get good at partnerships. Enterprises with the highest level of maturity significantly outperform companies that are in earlier stages of maturity on several key business metrics.
- We are in the early stages of modern partnering; however, we have reached an inflection point: forming partnerships at scale is how the world works. The future is exciting and includes powerful partnerships ecosystems that will change the game for everyone.

What's Up Next?

Why are today's partnerships able to drive significant and sustainable revenue, even as sales and marketing efforts and their reseller partnerships programs are struggling? Chapter 2 explores these ideas in depth.

Notes

[1] A Forrester Consulting Thought Leadership Paper Commissioned by Impact, "Invest in Partnerships to Drive Growth and Competitive Advantage," **impact.com**, June 2019, **http://bit.ly/forrester-impact-invest-in-partnerships**.

[2] Jay McBain, "Channel Data Is a Competitive Differentiator," Forrester, January 11, 2019, **http://bit.ly/Forrester-channel-data**.

[3] A Forrester Consulting Thought Leadership Paper Commissioned by Impact, "Smooth Your Partnership Journey by Learning from High Maturity Companies: How to Make Tactical Improvements to Your Partnership Program," **impact.com**, August 2020, **http://bit.ly/tactical-improvements-partner-program**.

[4] Jay McBain, "What I See Coming for the Channel in 2020," Forrester, January 7, 2020, **http://bit.ly/Forrester-channel-2020**.

[5] Jay McBain, "What We See Coming for Channels, Partnerships, and Ecosystems 2021," Forrester, March 10, 2021, **http://bit.ly/Forrester-channels-2021**.

[6] Ibid.

[7] "Global Meal Delivery Services Market Report," Grand View Research, May 2020, **http://bit.ly/grandviewresearch-industry-analysis**.

[8] Jonathon Tuska, **Rastellis.com**, interviewed by David A. Yovanno, **impact.com**, June 8, 2020, audio, 1:12, **http://bit.ly/Impact-Power-of-Partnerships**.

[9] *Rolling Stone*, "Readers' Poll: The Best Billy Joel Songs of All Time," September 2012, **http://bit.ly/rollingstone-poll**.

[10] "Ticketmaster +32% YoY Revenue Increase," Ticketmaster case study, radius by **impact.com**, accessed May 25, 2021, **http://bit.ly/Impact-ticketmaster-case-study**.

[11] "Invest in Partnerships," **impact.com**.

[12] "Smooth Your Partnership Journey," **impact.com**.

[13] "Invest in Partnerships," **impact.com**.

[14] Priest Willis, Sr., Senior Manager, Global Partnerships Marketing Strategist for Lenovo, interviewed by Lisa Leslie Henderson for **impact.com**, July 7, 2020, audio, 17:31.

[15] Simon Thomsen, "Canva's 2020 Went Globally Gangbusters as the Design Giant Signed Deals Around the World," *Startup Daily*, December 14, 2020, **http://bit.ly/startupdaily-canva**.

[16] Miklos Dietz, Hamza Khan, and Istvan Rab, "How Do Companies Create Value from Digital Ecosystems?," McKinsey Digital, August 7, 2020, **http://bit.ly/McKinseyDigital-ecosystems**.

[17] McBain, "What I See Coming for the Channel in 2020."

CHAPTER 2

Trust Is the New Black and Other Reasons Why Referral Partnerships Work

Booktopia is Australia's largest online bookstore. It sells an item every 4.8 seconds and has more than 5.8 million products available on its website. Partnerships have always been a cornerstone in the company's business model. The company leverages a wide range of partnerships that enables collaborative branding, marketing, and product innovation. As the company's chief marketing officer Steffen Daleng explains, "I consider partnerships one of the core pillars in everything we do around marketing."[1]

Two examples of Booktopia's strategic brand partnerships include a loyalty program with Qantas, Australia's flagship airline, where shoppers earn Qantas loyalty program points for every dollar they spend at Booktopia, and an integration with the ebook and audio platform Kobo, which provides its ebook customers with an extensive library of content. The bookseller also partners with First Nation communities to discover new voices, and with book clubs, co-branded store fronts, YouTube influencers, and other content creators.

When looking for new potential partnerships, Booktopia looks to companies that have the same or similar audiences. "A lot of women are buying books, so we want to work with companies focused on women," Daleng explains. "We have partnered with news magazines, such as *Mamamia*, to drive that audience engagement with that particular sector."[2]

Daleng encourages enterprises looking for fresh partnership opportunities to think of customers first. "Often, brand partnerships are driven by how to get the most eyeballs and accessing the largest database," Daleng explains. "My best advice would be: Don't do that. Sit down, understand your customer, and make it into a movie: What is the first thing they do in the morning when they open their eyes? What do they do? What coffee brand do they drink? Do they turn on the TV or an app? How could you work with that app, or get in front of them? Figure out who they are, and their patterns of behavior, then think about what your brand can do within that life cycle or journey that's relevant for them."[3]

These partner discovery strategies have been working well for Booktopia. In the past 18 months, the company's network of partners has grown by over 275 percent, translating to a year-over-year revenue increase of 219 percent.[4] "Measuring the value of our partnerships goes a lot further than looking at financial metrics and KPIs," Daleng cautions. "It's also looking at the brand value increase that we are getting by working very strategically with each of our partners. How do partners showcasing Booktopia on their own websites to their customers, and their ecosystems, benefit our brand?" Daleng's answer to this question: The future is bright!

Referral Partnerships Work

Booktopia is one of thousands of companies that are looking to partnerships to meet and exceed their growth targets. Many well-run organizations have already optimized their direct sales and marketing efforts and are looking for a boost from indirect sources. Continuing to battle their competitors by squeezing every bit more of optimization will be embracing diminishing returns. How is it that partnerships are able to drive significant revenue growth at a time when marketing, sales, and resellers are finding growth challenging?

Trust Is the New Black

There are several reasons for referral partnership success, and one of the most significant is trust. Partnerships are built on trust, inspire trust, and succeed because of trust.

What do I mean by trust? According to the Oxford Dictionary, trust is the "firm belief in the reliability, truth, ability, or strength of someone or something." Trust is so fundamental to human survival and success that the human brain has evolved to continually detect trust and distrust in the people, situations, and environments around us. The global communications firm Edelman has studied trust for more than 20 years and has found that trust "is the ultimate currency in the relationships that all institutions—companies and brands, governments, NGOs and media—build with their stakeholders. For a business, especially, lasting trust is the strongest insurance against competitive disruption, the antidote to consumer indifference, and the best path to continued growth. Without trust, credibility is lost and reputation can be threatened."[5]

We are currently operating in a highly distrustful climate. The 2021 Edelman Trust Barometer describes a "failing trust ecosystem," characterized by "misinformation and widespread mistrust of societal institutions and leaders around the world."[6] The pressure is on for business, which is seen as the only one of the four institutions studied that is both ethical and competent. This doesn't mean that people have faith in business advertising, however. Kantar's recent Dimension study found that advertising "is the least likely source people would use to garner information about a business."[7] Ninety-six percent of consumers don't trust advertising.[8] Roughly 25.8 percent of internet users block ads on their connected devices, and this number is growing.[9] Only 3 percent of people consider salespeople to be trustworthy.[10] Indeed, Accenture found that most businesses are 57 percent of the way through the buying process before their first meeting with a representative from the enterprise's marketing team.[11]

Consumers Look to Their Own Posse of Trusted Sources

If consumers don't look to businesses' own content or their advertising to learn about potential solutions for their needs and desires, who do they listen to? They build their own posse of trust sources to help them—friends, family, favorite influencers and publications, and communities that matter to them.[12] Each of us has a highly developed network of trusted sources that often differ depending on the area of life that we are making decisions about (Figure 2.1).

To drive this point home, think for a moment about recent nonroutine purchases you have made of large and small items for home or for work—a new type of deodorant, a car, or even an enterprise software platform (Figure 2.2). What major life area did this purchase address? What sources did you consult with before making a decision? Where did you go first, next, and last? Consider also the sources you didn't seek out. If you are like most consumers making personal or work-related purchases, you relied on many voices.

In an interview with *Adweek*, Magnus Jonsson, Clorox's vice president of brand engagement, explains why this posse of trusted sources is so important. "We still live in a world where people trust people. There's certain things we [companies]

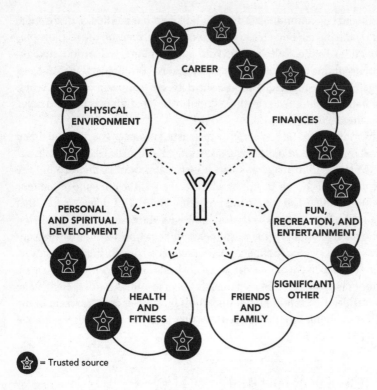

 = Trusted source

FIGURE 2.1   People have trusted sources for each of their major life areas.

Recent Purchase:
Which major life area did this purchase represent?

☐ Career   ☑ Health and fitness

☐ Finances   ☐ Personal and spiritual

☐ Family and friends   ☐ Fun, recreation, and entertainment

☐ Love life   ☐ Physical environment

Which sources did you consult? Where did you go first, next, and last?	
Which sources did you choose not to consult?	

FIGURE 2.2   Identify your trusted sources for a recent purchase.

can talk about and convey about ourselves, but there are other things that need to be validated by the people that consumers fundamentally trust."[13]

What does it take to become a trusted source? Relevance: Trusted sources have enough expertise in the realm in which they are being consulted to be listened to. Authenticity: Trusted sources must be real; they are not just mouthpieces for enterprises. Benevolence: Trusted sources act in the best interest of the person. Accessibility: People need to be able to find them.

Referral Partners Are Trusted Sources

Referral partners are trusted sources. They have established, authentic, and trusted relationships with their followers, readers, audiences, and/or customers. (The names of referral partners' audiences vary depending on the type of partner. To keep it simple, I'll just refer to referral partners as having audiences unless otherwise noted.) When referral partners talk, their people listen.

Audiences view these influencers, publishers, and consultants as trusted sources of information, not as referral partners. Whether they are category experts, taste-makers, or just brilliant entertainers, their audiences have sought them out and value their input. Importantly, these audiences do not perceive the referrals and recommendations made by their trusted sources as advertising. For example, when a Wirecutter devotee looks to the publisher to determine the best gas grill, mattress, multiroom wireless speaker system, or gifts for six-year-olds, they are looking for researched third-party recommendations, not corporate advertising speak. This is a key point of differentiation, and the fundamental reason why referral partners can get through to consumers when enterprises speaking on their own behalf cannot.

To maintain this valuable access, referral partners continually work on behalf of their audiences, staying on top of their emerging trends, needs, and desires and investigating and recommending products, services, and experiences that may be of interest to them. This curation is critical—it keeps referral partners relevant to their audiences.

Maintaining integrity when it comes to making referrals and recommendations is also key. Referral partners are first and foremost committed to their audiences. Their referrals are earned and verified through research and experience. They know that if their authenticity is sacrificed, trust will erode, and their audience will go elsewhere.

Enterprises' Target Customers Are Referral Partners' Audiences

Enterprises seek to establish referral partnerships with their target customers' trusted sources. Their target customers are their referral partners' existing followers, readers, audiences, or customers (Figure 2.3). They know that these bloggers,

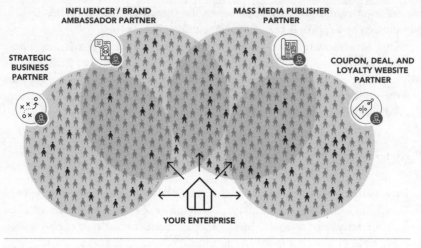

♠ ♠ ♠ Your target customers   ♠ ♠ ♠ Referral partners' audiences

FIGURE 2.3   Enterprises' target customers are referral partners' existing audiences.

editors, influencers, publications, brand ambassadors, and complementary brands have made it through their target customer's gates and are in conversation with them—this is where enterprises want to be! The cadence of these conversations may vary, but they are continually taking place. Forrester estimates that 35 million conversations about brands are taking place at this very moment.[14]

Referral Partners Generate Demand

Trusted sources are able to reach enterprise target customers, not in just any moment, but in the moment when they are aware of their need or desire and are searching for potential solutions. Partners are able to do this because they create the content and experiences that prompt their audiences to discover and understand their needs and desires, including what is important when it comes to selecting a solution, and they help them identify potential solutions.

Referral partners are able to do this for high-consideration purchases—most B2B purchases as well as consumer items such as credit cards and other financial products—and everyday routine purchases. The latter is because people do not necessarily default to their last purchase. A recent Google study of 1,800 consumer packaged goods shoppers in the United States found that shoppers often begin their shopping journeys quite undecided about what brand or product they want to purchase.[15] Similarly, according to Accenture's Global Consumer Pulse Research, 56 percent of consumers say that the number of brands they consider has increased significantly over the past decade, and 46 percent believe they are more likely to switch providers compared to 10 years ago.[16] What's going on here?

Google's research reveals that even with everyday purchases, people are looking to make the *right* purchase for them, not necessarily the familiar purchase. With no shortage of options available worldwide, and with ready access to information at their fingertips, consumers are looking for the product, service, or experience that may be "a little more perfect" than their last purchase.[17] They're happy to conduct a fair amount of research, turning to their trusted sources, to make the right purchase. Google's VP of marketing for the Americas, Lisa Gevelber, explains that this research "helps them get excited, lets them feel more confident and less anxious, and makes them feel like they're getting the most out of every moment. . . . In other words, the research process becomes part of the experience itself."[18]

When enterprises collaborate with referral partners, this world of conversations opens up to them. Partners bring enterprises into the conversation, literally by writing and talking about them (think Booktopia), or figuratively by cobranding or integrating their product offerings into their website or app (think Ticketmaster and Spotify). In doing so, partners are able to build trust in the enterprise and generate demand for its products, services, and experiences.

This is gold in today's business landscape, in which consumers turn a deaf ear to an enterprise's own content (at least initially) and advertising. Indeed, in the absence of these partner relationships, enterprises would not be part of many of these conversations. They would cede their position in the marketplace to their competitors who better understood this shift in consumer behavior and embraced the power of referral partnerships.

Referral Partners Capture Demand

Partners not only generate demand, but they are also able to capture this demand by creating an end-to-end experience. They are able to do so because they raise a subject, offer potential solutions, and provide referral links to an enterprise's own ecommerce platforms in their post, article, list, or mobile app that enable potential customers to learn more about the product—and make a purchase. Partners connect the needs and desires of their audience with solutions, content with commerce.

A quick word about referral links. These are unique URLs that are assigned to a specific partner. This link contains the partner's ID or username, which allows it to be credited with any associated consumer actions. When a potential customer makes a purchase through this referral link, the partner(s) is credited for that consumer action and receives a commission. This progression of events is illustrated in Figure 2.4. Mobile app deep links are a variation on this theme. They are used to send potential customers who are using a mobile device directly to relevant locations in an enterprise's mobile app, rather than a website or a store, which saves them time and effort.

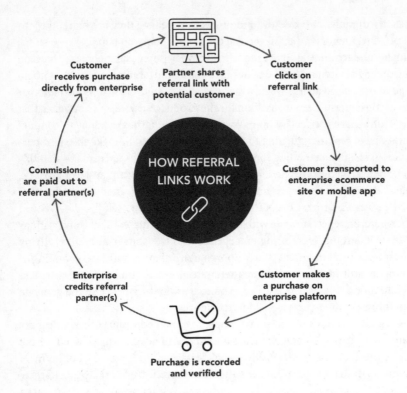

FIGURE 2.4   How referral links work.

This integrated path creates a seamless experience for consumers. Readers trust that the editors have done the research and that their recommendations have integrity, and they appreciate the convenience of everything in one place with link-based shopping. This arrangement works well for enterprises, too, because in addition to generating demand and fostering consideration for their brand and products, this commerce content helps them close deals. A streamlined process improves the chances that enterprises won't lose sales, which is a common occurrence when potential customers move unassisted between articles and ecommerce sites and stores. Commerce content works out well for partners, too, as they are able to provide their audiences with interesting content and opportunities, and they are able to monetize their efforts, as they receive a commission for every sale that their content prompts.

Partnership Referrals Are Not Advertising

Referral partners' ability to be present in consumers' moments of need and desire is quite a different experience for enterprises—and consumers—than most advertising in three important ways: context and timing, a warm versus cold invitation, and the use of personal identifying information.

Context and timing. Targeted ads, for example, are selected for people based on their previous behaviors—the sites they have visited and the links they have clicked on—and are displayed after the fact, often when consumers have moved on to a new context. For example, "Sarah" may have been interested in getting a fishing rod for her dad for Father's Day an hour ago and was searching the web for options, but now she is busy looking up recipes for dinner that will use the cauliflower that is sitting on the shelf in her fridge. The moment for selling that fishing rod has passed; Sarah's attention has shifted.

Referral partners can create an end-to-end experience. They write an article about "The Top 10 Father's Day Gifts" that prompts Sarah to think about her dad and the upcoming holiday—an article that highlights that fishing rod. And they combine their recommendations with compelling offers and an active referral link to enable Sarah and others to make the purchase right then and there.

Warm or cold invitation. Recommendations made by referral partners are warm invitations because they are positive endorsements from a trusted source. Display ads are cold invitations. They appear, uninvited and often unwanted, on people's screens, and people tend to tune them out, whereas people routinely choose to check in with their trusted sources to stay current and solve their challenges.

Use of personally identifying information. Referral partners are able to help enterprises acquire new customers without relying on cookie-based targeting or personally identifying information (PII). They operate with a pull rather than a push marketing strategy, attracting their audiences to them. This can be a huge advantage in today's business environment, where people are increasingly reluctant to share their personal data, legislation such as the European Union's General Data Protection Regulation (GDPR) and the California Consumer Privacy Act (CCPA) are giving consumers more control over their personal data, and the web browser policies of Google Chrome and Apple's Safari are blocking third-party cookies, making it harder for enterprises to track target customers across the web through advertising. This enables consumers to get to know a brand and its products before they need to share any PII, which can help build trust.

Just to be clear, once enterprises begin to interact directly with their target customers—after their target customers have clicked on a referral link that takes them to the enterprise's website or mobile app—they are able to collect first-party data, which is critical to being able to create smart, personalized, and satisfying future engagement. At this point, enterprises must go to great lengths to protect their target customers' PII, including avoiding unnecessary spamming, or face the possibility of eroding trust and losing customers, not to mention the expense of fines and lawsuits.

Trust Is Easily Eroded

Partnerships are built on trust and they inspire trust. Trust carries responsibility. It implies an implicit social contract—enterprises and their partners will stand up and be worthy of consumer trust, in big and small ways. Referral partners won't misrepresent enterprises and their product offerings in order to earn additional revenue. Enterprises will stand behind their products and create a seamless conversion process so that they are worthy of being recommended.

This trust is earned, not bought. It can't be mandated, turned on and off at will, or neglected. And this trust can be easily eroded. Human reaction to a breakdown in trust is swift and automatic and can have strong and long-term consequences. Sometimes the reaction is consumer disappointment, but sometimes it's disgust, even "seething brand hate."[19] The long-term consequences may be the loss of a customer, but quite often the impact is much greater as that former customer shares their disappointment, if not disgust, with their entire social network. In the age of cancel culture, former consumers may describe their experience even more broadly. The bottom line: if enterprises and their referral partners aren't willing or able to be truly trustworthy, they shouldn't be part of the partnership economy.

Referral Partners Enhance Enterprise Customer Experience

We've seen how trust contributes to the success of referral partnerships. A second reason for partnerships' success is their ability to positively impact enterprise customer experience (CX), a critical source of strategic advantage in today's customer-driven, if not obsessed, marketplace.

What do I mean by CX? CX is customers' holistic perception of their experience with an enterprise and/or its brand(s). Every interaction that a prospect or customer has with or about an enterprise and its brands(s) contributes to, or detracts from, an enterprise's overall CX. These interactions include customers' direct engagement with the enterprise's products and services. They also include their impression of the enterprise experience surrounding the product, including the enterprise's conversion pathway—how easy is it to make a purchase?—whether the products and services were delivered on time and where they were supposed to be, the usefulness of any conversations with bots and customer service, and their perception of the company's trustworthiness.

There is another important dimension to an enterprise's CX: the market's view of the company and its products. This includes reviews and recommendations generated by third parties such as friends, family, the enterprise's customers, influencers, bloggers, magazines, product review sites, podcasters, community groups, nonprofits and other purpose-driven organizations, consultants, and sometimes other trusted brands. As we have seen, in today's landscape of skepticism and misinformation, these indirect interactions have become quite powerful. They can often make or break an enterprise and its brands.

To deliver exceptional CX, enterprises have to identify what matters most to their customers, what *their customers* consider valuable, and embed that understanding into their products, services, and experiences. They need to be able to meet and/or exceed their customers' expectations, and do so in a way that distinguishes them from their competition. And they have to have positive supporting voices in the market that will go to the mat for them. Referral partners can help them accomplish all of this. And they can do so at scale.

Referral Partnerships Enhance Enterprise Customer Engagement

Partnerships can enhance enterprise CX by increasing the effectiveness of enterprise customer engagement efforts. As we have seen, the early stages of most customer and shopping journeys take place outside the reach of most enterprises. This means that enterprise early-stage CX is largely in the hands of others. This can be an extremely tenuous prospect for enterprises unless they have cultivated relationships with trustworthy referral partners that positively represent the enterprise to its target customers during the early stages of their customer and shopping journeys. When enterprises are represented by referral partners, their early-stage CX is likely to actually improve!

Here's why. Referral partners know their audiences well. This enables them to reach their audiences in the most effective ways and to curate the most promising products to bring to their attention. This means that their audiences are likely to feel seen, and attended to, and their recommendations are more likely to be successful. Their audiences would likely rate these trusted sources' CX as being excellent.

Partner CX excellence is a great thing for enterprises because partner CX effectively becomes enterprise CX—partners represent the enterprise in the marketplace. When partners prompt and nurture enterprise target customers through the early stages of their customer and shopping journeys well, when these journeys are characterized by connection, relevance, efficiency, and trust, these target customers are likely to continue, moving forward with confidence in the product, enterprise, and their purchase decision. This is likely to lead to an actual purchase, future purchases, and even customer advocacy for the enterprise.

Enterprises that recognize the relationship between their referral partners' CX and their own work carefully with their partners to enhance their success. As Aldo Bukit, associate director of marketing, affiliates, and APIs for Walmart eCommerce, said, "I believe our partners know their members and users better than we do because they are closer to them. Once that user comes to **walmart.com**, we have more insight [into them]. Our best strategy is to help our partners by equipping them with the right insights and data so they can interact with their members even better."[20]

Referral Partnerships Enable Innovation

The ability to continually enhance the value of their products, services, and experiences is essential for enterprises in *every* industry in today's customer-driven environment. Partnerships are able to help enterprises meet this need for constant innovation. Through their collaborations, enterprises are able to deepen their understanding of their target customers and expand the resources available to them to enhance the value of their own products, services, and experiences. Consider the positive impact of embedding Ticketmaster purchases into the Spotify app and of introducing Rastelli's to Sunbasket customers. These enhancements make new and unique product offerings possible for companies, offerings that would not be possible on their own.

Referral Partnerships Yield High ROI

A third reason that referral partnerships are able to drive significant enterprise growth is their high return on investment (ROI). This is a function of their ability to generate and capture demand combined with their efficiency and cost-effectiveness.

Partnerships are cost-effective. Partnerships offer a significant ROI with an impressive $15 for every $1 spent, according to Amnavigator.[21] The primary reason for this is the power of authentic referral. A second reason for this high ROI is that partner compensation is often performance-based; remuneration follows customer action, not simply impressions, as is often the case with traditional advertising. As a result, enterprises pay for results only after they have been achieved. Partnerships also generate additional benefits that serve as currency—positive brand associations and fresh and tested content that can be syndicated and repurposed—that can offset monetary exchange when determining commission rates.

Partners reduce the cost of marketing initiatives. First, they can reduce the length of buying journeys, which lessens the need for marketing spend. Second, high-performing content generated by an influencer, publisher, or media house can also be repurposed for use in an enterprise's social media or other campaigns, reducing the cost and effort associated with additional content creation. Third, partnerships can provide global enterprises with a local presence, even within their own countries, which enables them to tap into local marketing opportunities. This can increase the efficiency and reduce the cost of Google and Facebook ads, for example, as local businesses rank higher in search results and have more favorable pricing for keywords. Finally, partnerships are more predictable than many forms of advertising. They are long-term contracts, not coin-operated daily auctions. Partner payouts can and often should be dynamic, but they are bound.

Partnerships Improve Enterprise Competitiveness

The fourth reason that referral partnerships are able to drive significant enterprise growth is their impact on enterprise competitiveness. They work well with today's business models, they can build significant barriers to entry, they enable companies to quickly enact strategic pivots, and they allow enterprises to compete at a systems level.

Referral partnerships work with today's business models, not in spite of them. Ecommerce, marketplaces, and the movement from products as a one-time purchase to products as an ongoing subscription service and direct-to-consumer are hot business trends—and referral partners contribute to enterprise success in each of these arenas. Rather than trying to direct consumers to their own sites to make purchases, referral partners direct enterprise target customers to enterprise ecommerce sites and/or marketplaces. The benefits: enterprises are able to interact with their target customers directly, allowing for greater personalization in terms of messaging and pricing—an enhancement in overall customer experience—as well as access to first-hand customer data and analytics, which is critical in today's climate of increased consumer privacy protection. Partnerships can help businesses as they transition from offering products to services, by co-developing highly integrated solutions and extensions of services, and by continually engaging customers, driving retention.

Partnerships build barriers to entry. As enterprises scale their partnerships, they create another competitive advantage: barriers to entry. A barrier to entry is a cost that must be incurred by anyone entering the market, which incumbents have already incurred. Advertising channels like search or display ads are completely saturated. Bidding on keywords or ad impressions is hotly contested, and the massive competitive landscape drives costs up. The same goes for sales. Yes, you can continue to sell into the major retailers and big box stores, but your competitors are there as well. They are also competing for shelf space and end caps. In all likelihood, you've maxed out the possible number of relationships in the retail channel. Partnerships may represent one of the last places where enterprises can gain a competitive edge in this consumer landscape. Being early to the game enables enterprises to develop expertise, capabilities, and relationships that create sizable hurdles for later entrants.

Partnerships enable quick strategic pivots. Being able to compete at a systems level builds a vital antifragile capability within enterprises that enables them to turn market shocks into opportunities. I'm not only talking about resilience here, but the ability to thrive in the face of market disruption. When faced with a threat to one part of their business, enterprises are able to employ partnerships to move into less vulnerable parts of the market. Companies with strong partnerships and partnership capabilities can move forward when their competitors may be stunned. Think of how quickly Rastelli's was able to build a highly successful direct-to-consumer protein delivery effort with the help of its partner, Sunbasket.

Partnerships enable enterprises to compete at a systems level. In the past, partnership complexity limited the number and types of partnerships that any one company could realistically manage. Today's partnership automation technology provides enterprises with a single, intelligent platform that can automate much of the partnerships process for every type of partnership, wherever they are located around the world. In much the same way as cloud-based automation solutions revolutionized sales and marketing 20 years ago, partnership automation is revolutionizing partnerships.

Scalability enables companies to harness the knowledge, resources, and market presence of hundreds of partners, if not thousands, to create a customer-facing powerhouse. Borrowing features and capabilities from partners also enables everyday companies, with everyday-sized budgets, to be able to successfully compete against larger companies with deeper pockets and broader capabilities. They can compete at a systems level, rather than at a company level, enhancing their ability to rapidly understand, engage with, and adapt to today's customer-led marketplace.

The Quick Summary

- There are multiple reasons for referral partnership success in generating revenue, even as growth from marketing, sales, and reseller partnerships is slowing.

- One of the most significant reasons for success is trust. Partnerships are built on trust, inspire trust, and succeed because of trust. Referral partners are composed of consumers' trusted sources, which enables them to generate and capture demand, even in a highly distrustful operating climate.

- Partnerships enhance enterprise CX. As partners increasingly play an introductory and influential role in enterprise customer and shopping journeys, partner CX becomes an extension of enterprise CX. Partner CX tends to be quite positive as they are trusted sources that know enterprise target customers well and are therefore able to curate product recommendations that have high success rates. Moreover, partner referrals are warm invitations because they take place in context, and in moments characterized by high purchase intent, and they respect consumers' desire for privacy as they do not require the use of PII.

- Referral partnerships yield a high ROI because of their ability to generate and capture demand and because of their efficiency and cost-effectiveness.
- Enterprises look to referral partnerships to build their competitiveness. Referral partnerships work well with today's business strategies—D2C, ecommerce, marketplaces, and the transition from products to services. They build significant barriers to entry, they enable companies to quickly enact strategic pivots, and they allow enterprises to compete at a systems level.

What's Up Next?

How are enterprises employing referral partnerships to meet a broad range of business goals—acquiring new customers, entry into new markets, driving mobile app installs and usage, increasing customer lifetime value, and generating brand ambassadors? Keep reading.

Notes

[1] Nadia Cameron, "What Booktopia's CMO Is Doing to Ensure Brand Partnerships Flourish," CMO from IDG, February 3, 2021, **http://bit.ly/cmo-booktopia-brandpartnerships**.

[2] Ibid.

[3] Ibid.

[4] "Customer Testimonial: How Booktopia's Innovative Partnership Team Drove 219% Revenue Growth," **impact.com**, January 26, 2021, 3:07, **http://bit.ly/Impact-ct-Booktopia**.

[5] "2021 Edelman Trust Barometer," Edelman Report, 2021, **https://www.edelman.com/trust**.

[6] Ibid.

[7] Rebecca Stewart, "Advertising and Social Media Face Fresh Trust Issues Amid Global Crisis," *The Drum*, May 15, 2020, **http://bit.ly/TheDrum-advertising-trustissues**.

[8] Maureen Morrison, "No One Trusts Advertising or Media (Except Fox News)," *Ad Age*, 4A's Commissioned Survey, April 24, 2015, **http://bit.ly/AdAge-media-notrust**.

[9] "Share of Users Blocking Ads in the U.S.," Statistica Research Department, Statistica, January 14, 2021, **http://bit.ly/statista-adblocking**.

[10] Aja Frost, "Only 3% of People Think Salespeople Possess This Crucial Character Trait," Hubspot, April 29, 2016, updated July 28, 2017, **http://bit.ly/Hubspot-salepeople-trait**.

[11] Jason Angelos, Phil Davis, and Mark Gaylard, "Make Music, Not Noise: Achieve Connected Growth with Ecosystem Orchestration," Accenture Strategy, 2017, **https://accntu.re/3zf7N2G**.

[12] Note: Life coaches often think in terms of eight major life areas: career (what people do with their time to make money); finances (how they manage their money); friends and family (important platonic relationships); love life (significant other); health and fitness; personal and spiritual development; fun, recreation, and entertainment; and physical environment (home, physical location).

[13] Diana Pearl, "Clorox Is Leaning into Influencer Marketing and In-House Creative to Better Connect with Consumers," *Adweek*, June 28, 2018, **http://bit.ly/adweek-clorox-partnerships**.

[14] Jay McBain, **impact.com** growth event, New York, June 2019.

[15] Pedro Pina, "What's Perfect for Me? How CPG Shoppers Are Making the Best Choice," Think with Google, August 2018, **http://bit.ly/ThinkwithGoogle-CPG-Shoppers**.

[16] "Switching Economy," Accenture Newsroom, Research, January 21, 2015, **https://accntu.re/3gngvn1**.

[17] Pina, "What's Perfect for Me?"

[18] Lisa Gevelber, "No Regrets: The 3 Things Driving the Research-Obsessed Consumer," Think with Google, May 2018, **http://bit.ly/ThinkwithGoogle-research-consumer**.

[19] S. Umit Kucuk, "Consumer Brand Hate: Steam Rolling Whatever I See," Wiley Online Library, Psychology and Marketing Research Article, December 18, 2018, **https://onlinelibrary.wiley.com/doi/abs/10.1002/mar.21175**.

[20] Aldo Bukit, **Walmart.com**, "The Fast and the Reliable: How Walmart Leveraged Transparency and Data to Build Better Partner Relationships," interviewed by Mike Head, **impact.com**, video, 7:14, **http://bit.ly/Impact-interview-Aldo-Walmart**.

[21] Geno Prussakov, "20 Affiliate Marketing Stats That Will Blow Your Mind," *AM Navigator*, April 27, 2016, **https://bit.ly/amnavigator-affiliate-marketing-stats**.

CHAPTER 3

How Partnerships Can Help You Meet Critical Business Goals

"Partnerships are at the heart of our customer journeys," explains Siara Nazir, head of digital marketing for the technology company Autodesk. "Our software is enormously complex and our partners, who are experts in their domain, can readily address customers' needs from the top of the funnel all the way to the bottom—and they can keep them coming back. Our partners create tutorials and come up with hacks. They unlock deficiencies that enable us to build in more value and increase usability. They bring innovation into our company. Partnerships, in my opinion, provide the umbrella around the entire customer experience."

Partnerships Are Powerful and Flexible

Companies of all sizes, stages of growth, and business models, and in every vertical and region of the world, are employing partnerships to help them meet their most critical business objectives. In this chapter, I'll share some examples of how enterprises are employing partnerships to meet their critical business objectives. I'll also explore how these business objectives translate into specific partnership strategies. But first, let's start with a few more partnership stories.

Grow, Baby, Grow

Every company needs to attract new customers to stay in business; this is especially true for start-ups, which often have ambitious market share objectives and highly results-oriented investors. Partnerships can help companies quickly generate and capture demand for their products, and their pay-for-performance compensation model minimizes enterprise cost and risk.

Fintech innovator Revolut is one of these companies. A challenger brand, Revolut is out to disrupt the finance industry. Consumers love its product, which enables them to manage their entire financial lives from a single super app. From everyday spending and budgeting to foreign currency exchange, Revolut aims to create a better banking experience, giving its customers more control, more convenience, and more opportunity. The company's initial task was getting the word out to people so they could see the benefits of the app for themselves.

The company set an ambitious goal of increasing customer acquisition by 100 percent over an eight-month period and looked to partnerships to help it achieve this goal. Finance purchases are complex, however, and most consumers already have banking relationships that can create inertia for change. To be successful, Revolut knew that it needed partners that could both advocate for its brand and clearly and credibly articulate its value. As it considered its options, it became clear that some of the best partners to help it grow would be its existing customers, brand ambassadors who could speak from experience about Revolut in their own words and to their own worlds. Their words were likely to have an impact, as over 90 percent of consumers trust word-of-mouth recommendations.[1]

Revolut developed and launched a strategy to identify potential candidates. It would first nurture potential candidates into becoming customer advocates. Successful advocates would then be converted to official brand ambassadors, who would be measured and compensated for how many new customers they were able to bring in. By the end of the first week, Revolut had nearly 3,000 applications, 42 percent of which were eventually accepted into the program. At the end of the nine-month period, Revolut had experienced a growth rate of 700 percent, year over year, based on incremental customers acquired via partnerships—seven times its goal.

Today Revolut's partner program has more than 6,000 active members. Its website is populated with comments from happy customers: "If you haven't heard about Revolut yet, it's easy to split bills with friends, request money, and create virtual cards for online purchases" and "I recommend @RevolutApp to anyone. Use the debit card abroad, no charges, best exchange rate."[2] Mission accomplished.

Improve Your Conversions

Here's a question on every company's mind (and if it's not, it should be!): How do you compete against global giants like Amazon, Argos, eBay, and Alibaba? Richer Sounds, a British home entertainment retailer that operates online and through its 53 retail stores, found itself exactly in this position. The company has been on the UK's High Street for more than 40 years, but in the online market, it was less successful. Over 90 percent of UK shoppers are Amazon shoppers, which poses major challenges for Richer Sounds when it comes to maintaining market share, let alone growing it. The company needed to come up with a strategy that would enable it to grow sales online in a category dominated by retail giants. It knew it couldn't compete on the basis of price or speed of delivery, but it could win the day with product knowledge and exceptional customer experience, characteristics that made its physical stores popular with loyal audio and video enthusiasts.

To grow its sales online, Richer Sounds decided to create an elite partner network to take its expertise online. The partners in this small group, 17 in total, were selected because of their expert knowledge, passionate engagement, and alignment with Richer Sounds' philosophy. The company also collaborated with TopCashback and Quidco, the largest cashback sites in the UK, to reach a wide segment of savvy consumers. The focus here was on rewarding customers for their purchases and incentivizing them to increase their basket size.

Richer Sounds took a highly collaborative approach to setting and achieving partnership goals. It stayed in constant communication with its individual partners, keeping them up to date on all product developments in the technology sphere and supporting them to become passionate advocates. The company also offered competitive commission rates to its partners and designed their joint customer experience to be as seamless as possible. (The latter included deep linking that allowed interested consumers to easily move from a partner's site to individual product pages on Richer Sounds' ecommerce site and compelling, up-to-date creative.) In the end, Richer Sounds achieved 65 percent year-over-year revenue growth and a 30 percent improvement in its conversion rate.

Change Strategy—Quick!

In today's fast-paced, global, and customer-led marketplace, it takes a lot of effort to stay ahead of the game. If you have been in business long enough, you're all too familiar with pivots, moments when you fundamentally change the direction of your business because it becomes clear that what you have been doing is not going to work in the future. The goal of a pivot is to enable the company to improve revenue or to survive these changes in the market. While these times of change are challenging, partnerships can make them easier. Here's how partnerships enabled Uber to successfully make a strategic pivot during the recent COVID-19 pandemic.

The first laboratory-confirmed case of COVID-19 in the United States took place on January 20, 2020. Less than two months later, shelter-in-place and stay-at-home orders began to go into effect across the country, and nonessential businesses were shut down. The ride-sharing platform Uber Rides was deemed an essential business; however, the company immediately shut down its partnerships programs for its ride-sharing app to encourage people to stay home and help prevent the spread of the disease.

Not surprisingly, Uber's revenue from its flagship business declined considerably due to the pandemic; however, the company's food delivery service, Uber Eats, was well positioned to take off as people began to dine almost exclusively at home. Uber was able to quickly shift its focus to meet the food delivery market's skyrocketing opportunity. Members of partnerships teams began to work across business lines to recruit additional restaurant partners and delivery drivers. The company built partnerships with platforms like OpenTable and NextDoor, introduced the option of leaving food at customers' doors, and made it possible for people to make in-app donations to favorite restaurants. Uber's ability to quickly scale its partnerships to enable this pivot resulted in revenues growing 53 percent in the first quarter of 2020[3] and 52 percent over the course of the year, even as its core business suffered.[4]

What Kind of Growth Do You Want?

Enterprise business strategy sets the parameters for partnerships strategy. Getting specific about how an enterprise wants to achieve growth by identifying its critical business objectives is fundamental to a successful partnerships effort. It's important that the business objectives that any partnerships effort addresses are meaningful to the success of the company. If they aren't, the partnerships team will be playing in the wrong sandbox. Their wins will not be the wins their company needs. As a result, their partnerships effort will not likely have the organizational support that is necessary for it to come close to reaching its full potential.

A business objective finishes the sentence "We want to drive growth by . . ." As we have seen, some of the most common business objectives that partnerships are designed to address include acquiring new customers, expanding into new markets, creating positive brand associations, closing more sales, increasing customer retention and long-term value, driving mobile app installs and usage, and catalyzing innovation. In the past couple of years, we have also seen partnerships enable pivot strategies for companies facing market disruptions.

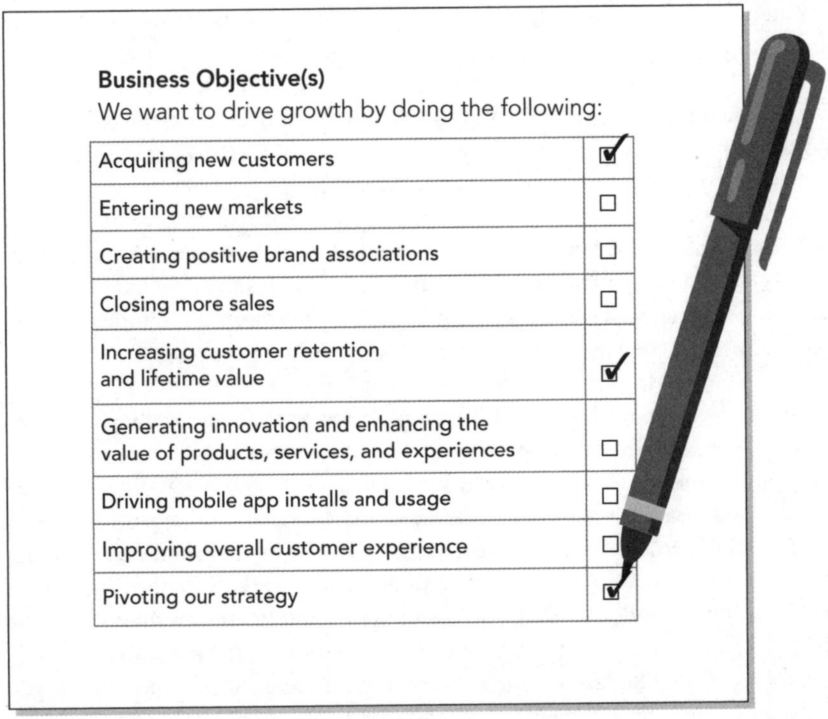

Business Objective(s)
We want to drive growth by doing the following:

Acquiring new customers	☑
Entering new markets	☐
Creating positive brand associations	☐
Closing more sales	☐
Increasing customer retention and lifetime value	☑
Generating innovation and enhancing the value of products, services, and experiences	☐
Driving mobile app installs and usage	☐
Improving overall customer experience	☐
Pivoting our strategy	☑

FIGURE 3.1   Common business goals behind today's partnerships.

How does your company want to grow? What are the tradeoffs you're looking to make between market share and profitability? For illustrative purposes, let's assume that we are a retailer that competes on the basis of price and convenience. Our company has ambitious growth goals. We want to drive this growth by expanding market share in our home market while also increasing the long-term value of our existing customers. And we are hoping that partnerships can help us achieve these objectives. These business objectives are captured in Figure 3.1.

Who Will Make This Growth Happen?

The next step involves getting specific about the enterprise's target customers. Who is actually going to make this growth possible? What target customers does the company want its potential partners to reach out to on its behalf? Simply stated, this step involves considering and completing this sentence: "We want this partnership(s) to target . . ."

The more familiar an enterprise is with its target customer segment(s), the more effectively it can determine where there is an audience fit with potential partners. Target customers can be defined by many variables. Some of the most common include demographics, psychographics, behaviors, previous purchases and shopping activity, and geography. Many partnerships teams work closely with their marketing departments to build out rich profiles.

A rich profile creates a picture of an enterprise's target customer; it makes meaning out of a collection of statistics. It should include basic demographics, personality characteristics, and behaviors. Where possible, it should include shopping habits and devices used while shopping. Critical for partnerships is understanding who and what influence these customers. Who are their go-to sources for understanding their world? What do they read? Which podcasts do they listen to? Who do they follow? Equally important is understanding who and what they don't consult with. From this information, an enterprise can infer its target customers' goals, needs, and fears—all of which should be verified.

It's a good idea to summarize everything you know about your target customer(s) in a central document. Be sure to name this customer segment and even add pictures and stories that capture their experience. Clearly acknowledge where there are holes in your understanding and assumptions and inferences that need to be verified. Over time, as you work with partners that have established trusted relationships with your target customers, your understanding will become even deeper. Update this working document as you glean relevant insights and be sure to share it with your marketing colleagues, as you care about the same customers and share the same overall goal: excellent customer experience.

Let's return to our fictitious retailer and explore its target customers for a moment. One of the company's most important target customers is what it calls Household Enthusiasts. This is actually a new and important market segment that was recently uncovered in research conducted by the coupon deal site RetailMeNot. According to RetailMeNot, "a Household Enthusiast is part of a unique audience that spans across millennial and Generation X demographics. They live in a household with at least one other person, often including children and spouses, and they are responsible for making the final decision on items purchased within the home for multiple people."[5] Savvy shoppers comprise this savings-minded customer segment, who generate 15 percent more income than the average consumer, 51 percent more than the millennial consumer, and 18 percent more than the general deal-seeker in a six-month period. This segment has strong purchasing power and is diligent about finding the best prices. And they are multichannel shoppers, making online purchases an average of 3.6 times per month and in-store purchases at least five times per month. Are you starting to get a picture of this customer segment?

Here's a bit more information to breathe more life into the Household Enthusiast profile. Generous discounts are compelling for Household Enthusiasts—76 percent of those surveyed say an offer or discount will be the deciding factor in a product purchase they are on the fence about. Discounts rated higher than free shipping (58 percent), positive online reviews (35 percent), and even items for which the customer had a dire need (33 percent). Mobile and email marketing can be effective with this target customer segment. Eighty-four percent of respondents were likely to do their shopping on mobile devices because they allow them to shop anywhere at any time (72 percent). Household Enthusiasts may also enjoy a personalized shopping experience (53 percent said it would make them more likely to be loyal to a brand or retailer), including personalized offers, email reminders of previously viewed products, and even recognition of special moments in their life such as their birthday.

Can you see this target customer? Do you know people who fit the profile? Has the description brought any of your friends, relatives, or colleagues to mind? I've taken a stab at summarizing what RetailMeNot described as the Household Enthusiast customer segment in Figure 3.2.

What Customer Behaviors Do You Want to Catalyze?

Once you know your target customer segment(s), it's important to get clear on what you want them to do. What do your target customers need to do for you to successfully achieve your business objective? Stated differently, what behaviors do you want your partner to catalyze for you?

BJ Fogg, founder and director of the Stanford Behavior Design Lab, developed the "Magic Wand" technique to assist in identifying the consumer behaviors you want to catalyze.[6] He recommends that you simply ask: If you could wave a magic wand to get target customer X to do anything, what would you have them do? The easy answer is of course: buy things! But for partnerships to be effective they need to be based on more specific behaviors. Fogg recommends "crispifying" these more general behaviors by asking: Who is doing what, when, where, with whom, with what outcome or result? With these answers in hand, enterprises and their partners can know what customer behaviors to catalyze, track, create success metrics, and design partner incentives around. Note that initially you may only be able to answer a few of these questions: Who is doing what, when, and with what outcome or result? Answers to the question Where do we want these actions to take place and with whom? will be filled in as you begin to better understand the range of partners, their capabilities, and where they have influence (i.e., social media, mass media publication, within their membership organization). Just keep the questions, and pursuit of their answers, upfront and center.

Who will make this growth happen?
A summary of our current understanding of our target customer segment(s):

	Target Customer Segment #1 Household Enthusiasts
Demographic Profile (Firmographic for B2B companies)	Span several generations Live in households with at least one other person Shop online and in-store
Psychographic Profile	Savings-minded and diligent about comparing prices
Geographic Profile	Assuming the United States, but don't know
Behavioral Profile	Responsible for making the final decision on items purchased within the home for multiple people
Key Sources of Influence (e.g., what they read, preferred podcasts, communities and associations with which they resonate) or other insights	Mobile and email marketing are likely to be effective Enjoy personalized shopping experiences

FIGURE 3.2 Summarize your understanding of your target customer segment(s).

To illustrate this concept, let's return to our fictitious retailer. It would like its target customers, Household Enthusiasts, to be aware of the special deals that it's constantly running, without them being inundated with messaging from the company itself. It would like its partners to help build this awareness in interesting ways that actually generate demand for these products, such as "best of" lists, product and price comparisons, or articles about "what's hot at Retailer X right now." In addition to building awareness, the company would like its partners to capture

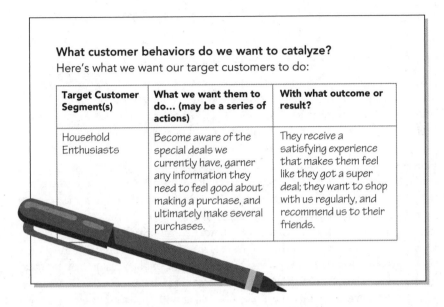

What customer behaviors do we want to catalyze?
Here's what we want our target customers to do:

Target Customer Segment(s)	What we want them to do... (may be a series of actions)	With what outcome or result?
Household Enthusiasts	Become aware of the special deals we currently have, garner any information they need to feel good about making a purchase, and ultimately make several purchases.	They receive a satisfying experience that makes them feel like they got a super deal; they want to shop with us regularly, and recommend us to their friends.

FIGURE 3.3   What customer behaviors do you want to catalyze?

that demand by directing interested customers from their blog, website, or YouTube channel to relevant product pages on the retailer's own website or mobile app, where they can garner any information they need to feel good about making a purchase, and ultimately make one or more purchases. The company would like its Household Enthusiasts to be highly satisfied with their purchases, to want to shop with them regularly, and to recommend the retailer to their friends. These desired customer behaviors are summarized in Figure 3.3.

In the partnerships world, we often think of these desired customer behaviors as micro and macro conversions. The macro conversion is the ultimate goal; it's the customer action that enables you to meet your business objectives. More often than not, this conversion is a purchase, but it could just as easily be a repurchase, an install of a mobile app, or movement from frequent purchaser to subscriber. Macro conversions can be whatever enables an enterprise to grow. Customer behaviors that lead up to that moment of conversion—conducting a related search, reading a blog post, visiting a coupon or cashback site for relevant deals—are considered micro conversions, important steps along the way to the ultimate conversion. Identifying the sequence of micro conversions that will likely lead to a conversion is critical to be able to design effective customer experiences and effective partnerships. When you know these critical behavior sequences, you know what actions you want your partners to catalyze.

Link Desired Customer Behaviors with Customer Journeys

The next step is linking these desired customer actions to the target customers' journey with the enterprise. This step is important, as it enables enterprises to identify the types of partners that will best help them achieve their objectives. Partnerships are nuanced. Each partner reaches a distinct audience and can catalyze consumer behaviors at different phases of their customer journeys.

One partner, for example, may connect well with price-sensitive women with young children living in western metropolitan areas, while another may engage small and medium-sized business owners who are planning to update their marketing communications stacks in the next 12 months. Similarly, some partners are great at introducing their audiences to enterprises and their products and helping them consider their options, but they might not be great at helping them get the most out of their purchase or understanding what other related purchases might make sense. Other partners may be great at finding discounts for customers once they know what they want, but they don't help them understand what they want or need. Still other partners may have great insights into the future of your business, but they don't know how to increase the perceived value of your offering today. Knowing who you are targeting and where along their customer journeys you want your partners to connect with them is key.

Customer Journeys Are Changing

Let's talk for a moment about customer journeys, because they are changing. As we know, customer journeys are narratives—they tell the story of the ongoing relationship between an enterprise and its customers: how they first met, when and where, and what has happened since then. When this relationship is working well, these stories often describe a series of positive customer experiences, marked by a growing emotional connection and trust between an organization and its customers. When this relationship is not working well, the story often ends, and sometimes it has a costly ripple effect beyond losing a customer.

Customer journeys are expanding. In the past, enterprises often saw their customer journeys as a multistage process beginning with a potential customer becoming aware of a need or desire and ending with a sale. In between these two endpoints, potential customers moved through consideration, when they explored and evaluated potential solutions, on to making a decision, and ultimately to a purchase. This was a natural reflection of the company's most critical business objective: customer acquisition.

In recent years, enterprises have been rethinking their customer journeys to include what takes place after a satisfied customer makes a purchase—and with good reason. According to the Gartner Group, 80 percent of a brand's future profits come from just 20 percent of its existing customers.[7] That's right, the majority of future profits come from a company's existing customers. Similarly, the consulting firm Bain & Company found that increasing customer retention rates by 5 percent ultimately increases enterprise revenue by between 25 and 95 percent.[8] This is true regardless of industry. There are many reasons for this, including the fact that existing customers don't have as high acquisition costs, they are more likely to repurchase from a company they know (assuming they had a positive experience), and they spend more than new customers do.[9]

Today's customer journeys reflect this broader view. Generally speaking, these journeys have three major phases that are centered around a customer making a purchase. This purchase is often referred to as a conversion (Figure 3.4). The first phase is the pre-purchase phase, where target customers become aware of their need or desire, consider their options, and explore and evaluate potential solutions before making a decision. The second phase is when they act on that decision, making a purchase. The third phase involves everything that happens post-purchase, including use of the product, service, or experience, subsequent purchases, and potential referrals to others. It's important to note that multiple shopping journeys are nested within this overall customer journey, as customers continue to engage with enterprises and make subsequent purchases. Rather than initiate new customer journeys, these subsequent shopping journeys expand the length of the post-purchase tail.

When enterprises understand the value of this after-sale activity, their vision expands from customer journeys that end with a sale to extended customer journeys that could potentially last for a lifetime. They begin to evaluate their customers in terms of their lifetime value (LTV)—the total revenue that a business can reasonably expect in the future from a given customer, rather than just the value of their initial sale.

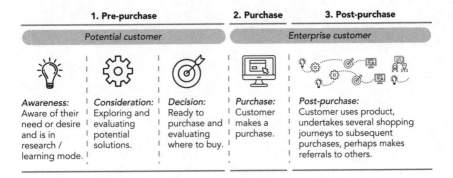

FIGURE 3.4   Three phases of today's customer journeys.

Where do our desired customer behaviors occur?
Here's where these behaviors occur on our customer journeys:

Target Customer Segment(s)	Awareness	Consideration	Decision	Purchase	Repurchase	Advocate for Our Brand
Household Enthusiasts	✓	✓	✓	✓	✓	✓

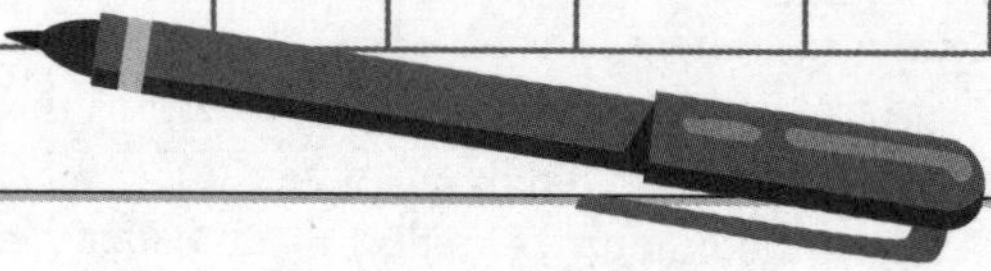

FIGURE 3.5   Link desired customer behaviors with their journeys.

When this shift happens, enterprises begin to look to both customer acquisition strategies and customer retention strategies to drive growth—and the good news is that partnerships can help them accomplish both. If partnerships bring in new customers, they are part of an enterprise's customer acquisition strategy. If they help reengage and build loyalty among existing customers, they are part of an enterprise's retention strategy. And more often than not, they can achieve both—often simultaneously.

Let's return to our retailer example one more time. Our desired customer behaviors included several micro and macro conversions that took place both before, during, and after a purchase. Flipping perspectives, we wanted our potential partners to generate and capture demand by building awareness, driving consideration, and closing sales. And we wanted them to do this over and over again and recommend us to their friends. These desired customer and partner behaviors are captured in Figure 3.5.

The Quick Summary

- Companies of all sizes, stages of growth, and business models, and in every vertical and region of the world, are employing partnerships to help them meet their most critical business objectives. These business objectives include acquiring new customers, entering new markets, converting more sales, increasing customer retention and lifetime value, generating innovation by enhancing the value of products, services, and experiences, driving mobile app installs and usage, improving overall customer experience, building customer advocacy, and enabling strategic pivots.

- An enterprise's business strategy sets the parameters for its partnerships strategy. What kind of growth do you want? Determining your business objectives for your partnerships program is the first step.
- Next, consider who is going to make this growth possible. Customers are at the center of today's partnerships. Know your target customer segments well so you can determine whether there is audience fit with potential partners.
- The third step is identifying the specific customer behaviors you want partners to catalyze. What micro and macro conversions need to take place in order for you to successfully achieve your business objectives?
- Finally, it's important to link these customer behaviors with customer journeys. This enables you to identify the types of partnerships you want to put in place.

What's Up Next?

When you know the customer behaviors that you want your partners to evoke, and where these behaviors take place along today's extended customer journeys, the question becomes: Which partners can help the company further develop and implement this plan? The following chapter tackles this question.

Notes

[1] Jonathan Carson, "Global Advertising Consumers Trust Real Friends and Virtual Strangers the Most," The Nielsen Company, July 8, 2009, **http://bit.ly/nielsen-global-advertising**.

[2] "Get More for Your Money: The UK's Fastest Growing Financial Super App Has Arrived in the US," Revolut, accessed May 12, 2021, **https://www.revolut.com/en-US**.

[3] "Uber Eats Revenues Soar Even as Company's Q1 Results Slide," PYMNTS, May 7, 2020, **http://bit.ly/Uber-eats-revenue-soars**.

[4] David Curry, "Uber Eats Revenue and Usage Statistics (2021)," revised April 30, 2021, **http://bit.ly/uber-eats-revenue-statistics**.

[5] "Household Enthusiasts, the Shopper Retailers Can't Afford to Ignore," RetailMeNot, accessed May 12, 2020, **http://bit.ly/Shoppers-retailers-cant-ignore**.

[6] BJ Fogg, Google, accessed May 12, 2021, **http://bit.ly/bj-fogg-google**.

[7] Stuart Leung, "12 Customer Service Tools That Will Make Your Customers' Lives Easier," **salesforce.com**, the 360 blog, January 20, 2015, **https://sforce.co/3xkN1x3**.

[8] Frederick F. Reichheld and Phil Schefter, "The Economics of E-Loyalty," Harvard Business School, July 10, 2000, **http://bit.ly/economics-eloyalty-harvard**.

[9] "Retention-Science-Infographic," Retention Science, accessed May 12, 2021, **http://bit.ly/customer-retention-science**.

CHAPTER 4

Engage Customers Wherever They Are on Their Customer Journeys

"Partnerships are key for us," explains Aldo Bukit, associate director of marketing, affiliates, and APIs at Walmart eCommerce. "We need them. We cannot fight this alone."

Walmart is the largest retailer, and the second-largest online seller, in the world. The company helps people around the world save money and live better. Each week, over 275 million customers and members visit their more than 11,300 stores in 27 countries and eCommerce websites.

This retailer is all about customer experience. "Our goal is to make it as easy as possible for customers to shop at Walmart, whether it's from the convenience of their couch using their laptop, or at the coffee shop on their phone, or on their way home from work, stopping by our stores to pick up groceries for dinner," Bukit explains. "We offer tens of millions of items online for customers to ship directly to their homes or to a nearby store where they can pick them up." Walmart+, the company membership plan, which provides customers with unlimited same-day delivery, expedited two-hour delivery, and discounts at Walmart gas stations, is further upping its game.

Walmart works with key partners to initiate and drive engagement across its myriad shopper journeys. "We recognize the value and the importance of our partners to our business," Bukit explains. "They have brought so much value to our customers—they are closer to our customers' daily lives—and to Walmart. They advocate for Walmart in their posts and articles. We want to work closely with key partners and help them be even more successful, creating more value for their customers."[1]

Like many retail businesses, Walmart employs a broad mix of partnerships to both attract prospects and to reengage its existing customers. When you consider how well the company has penetrated the market—95 percent of U.S. consumers shop at Walmart every year—and the nature of their purchases—everyday, low-cost purchases—you can see why customer acquisition and customer retention are both key objectives for its partnerships efforts. Walmart partners include network television, publishers and media houses, cashback and loyalty programs, coupon and deal sites, influencers, mobile app integrations, and strategic business partners. Here's a quick glance:

Network television and mass media publishers. Walmart works with partners like HGTV, BuzzFeed, and **CNN.com** to generate and capture demand from its current and existing customers.[2] Here's a taste of how they do it.

HGTV is the go-to network for people who love house design. Originally the Home, Lawn, and Garden Channel, the company's name was later shortened, but its programming continues to focus on home buying, renovation, and design. The network has broad reach and appeal: it's the fourth-most-watched cable network in the United States, according to recent Nielsen ratings, with more than 1.6 million viewers. In addition to producing television programming, HGTV is also an active publisher. It engages its viewers with how-to videos and other useful content on social media, through its websites, and in its newsletter.

A partnership between HGTV and Walmart, which sells a broad range of home products including furniture, rugs, appliances, and storage for every room in the house, is a match made in heaven. The power of this partnership was evident at the onset of the COVID-19 pandemic, when people were spending much more time in their homes than usual. Homebound, people began to think about how they might create a home office and enhance the look and feel of their homes. To address this desire, HGTV launched a new network series, *Design at Your Door*, which shared stories of how people were updating the look of their homes, and they were doing it exclusively with Walmart products.[3] This program was perfect pre-purchase content, generating demand for Walmart products among Walmart prospects and customers alike.

But it didn't stop there. To capture the demand it generated, HGTV also created the *Get the Design at Your Door Look* section on its website, **HGTV.com**. Articles in this section of **HGTV.com** highlighted items from the series—"11 Budget-Friendly Walmart Finds to Update Your Living Room" and "These Affordable Finds from

FIGURE 4.1   *Design at Your Door* content on **HGTV.com**—connected to TV series.

Walmart Will Inspire You to Change Up Your Space" (Figure 4.1). Each article contained exciting product descriptions and live links that would seamlessly transport interested readers to relevant product pages on **Walmart.com**. These product pages included customer ratings, pricing, and delivery and pickup options, along with "purchase now" buttons that made purchases possible right then and there. And depending on their choice, consumers could have the products they purchased on their doorstep, or be ready for pickup, a few hours later.

Similarly, Walmart works with mass media publishers like BuzzFeed and CNN Underscored to generate and capture demand for its products. Articles in these publications spur interest in Walmart products by helping shoppers think through what they will need for the moments they are in or soon will be, such as the supplies kids will need when heading back to school, and by highlighting Walmart's products that can help them meet that moment. These articles also capture demand by identifying who and what consumers should consider when making a purchase, and by providing a direct link to **Walmart.com** where that purchase can be easily made. Sometimes publishers' articles are more enterprise-focused. For example, an article may highlight the best deals currently available at Walmart.

What makes the relationship between Walmart and these publishers a modern partnership is the live link embedded in the publishers' content that takes interested readers directly to the right spot on **Walmart.com** for them to learn more about the product and to make a purchase. This convenience greatly enhances both the publishers' and Walmart's customer experience. This link also enables the tracking that allows publishers to share in a portion of the sales that their content generates for Walmart. It integrates content, customer experience, and commerce.

Social influencers. Walmart works with influencers, individuals who have a dedicated social following and are viewed as experts or influential in their area of interest, to generate and capture customer demand. Influencer Krista Hooper, for

FIGURE 4.2 Another great Walmart find!

example, searches high and low through Walmart's shelves to find the best products available at Walmart, which she then writes about on her website, Walmart Finds.[4] Hooper's product posts are embedded with links that take interested shoppers directly to the product page on Walmart's eCommerce site, where they can see the price and the inventory available at the Walmart store nearest them. The screenshot shown in Figure 4.2 captures one of Hooper's latest finds, the hand sanitizer bag charm.

Walmart also embeds influencer content into its own website to create a richer customer experience.[5] Located in the Ideas Section of its website, the Influencer Shop posts the latest content from myriad influencers. At last check, beauty enthusiast Elicia Aragon was sharing her secrets for creating a summer bronzed look with beauty products available at Walmart.[6] Daniela Duran, who writes about nourishing foods and other health practices on her blog *And a Pinch of Love*,[7] offered her thoughts on how to incorporate six superfoods into your diet. Live links make it easy for readers who are interested in the products they recommend to make a purchase.

Cashback and coupon sites. Everyday low prices are the cornerstone of Walmart's strategy, and several of the company's partnerships are designed to sweeten already good prices for its deal-loving prospects and customers. These coupon, deal, and loyalty sites offer its members great Walmart deals. Shoppers simply click on the deal(s) description, which unlocks a promo code that they can enter at checkout on **Walmart.com** to obtain a discount on, or cash back from, their purchase. Partners earn a commission for sales that result from their content.

Walmart is strategic in its use of these partnerships, employing them to catalyze different consumer behaviors. To encourage everyday sales across a variety of categories, Walmart customizes its cashback deal structures to reflect the product margins of each category rather than offering a single cashback percentage across the board. Products that have larger margins—home goods, for example—offer more room to discount than categories like electronics, where the margins are razor-thin. To quickly liquidate inventory—seasonal items, for example—Walmart may significantly increase the cash back on specific products. "Everybody wins," Bukit explains. "The customer gets more cash back and we can afford it."

Similarly, to encourage its prospects and customers to sign up for Walmart+, its membership program that offers subscribers benefits such as unlimited free delivery and fuel discounts at participating gas stations, the retailer provides special cashback and coupon deals on various coupon and cashback sites. On Giving Assistant, for example, Walmart offered shoppers a free 15-day trial, a discount on their first order, and an additional discount on Walmart grocery purchases. (See the screenshot from Giving Assistant's site in Figure 4.3.)

FIGURE 4.3   Cashback deals encourage Giving Assistant members to try Walmart.

FIGURE 4.4 Shoppable recipes app simplifies meal planning and creation.

Mobile app integration. Walmart's mobile app integration with Tasty, the network behind those food videos that make your mouth water and your stomach growl, enables the retailer to reach its prospects and customers while they are in the midst of perusing Tasty videos and recipes. Working together, Walmart and Tasty created Shoppable Recipes, a seamless grocery shopping experience. It's brilliant and simple. When Tasty app users find a recipe that speaks to them from a menu of more than 4,000 food videos, they can read through the recipe, note any ingredients they need, quickly generate a digital list of needed ingredients, and purchase all the ingredients from **Walmart.com**, right then and there in the app (Figure 4.4). Groceries can be picked up curbside at a Walmart store or delivered to the shopper's home the same day.[8]

Partnerships: Here, There, and Everywhere!

As this small sample of Walmart's collaborations illustrates, partnerships can be designed to achieve enterprise growth in many ways. They do so by prompting myriad consumer behaviors across today's customer journeys. These behaviors simultaneously achieve consumer, enterprise, and partner goals, creating the win-win-win outcome that is a characteristic of today's partnerships. This chapter will discuss the roles that partners can play across today's customer journeys.

**INTRODUCE
AND INFLUENCE**

CLOSE

**REENGAGE
AND RETAIN**

FIGURE 4.5   The three primary roles partners play.

Partnership Roles Across Customer Journeys

When considering how partnerships can influence customer journeys, it's helpful to think in terms of partner roles, rather than partner types, because any given partner can play many roles depending on what a given partnership is designed to achieve. The same partner may assume a different role at a different time or in another partnership. Even the roles of enterprise and the referral partner can be exchanged, a topic that will be discussed shortly.

There are three primary roles that partners can play and these three roles correspond with various stages of today's customer journeys: introduce and influence, close, or reengage and retain (Figure 4.5). Let's take a closer look at each of these partnership roles.

Introduce and Influence Partner Role

Introduce and influence roles are associated with the early and middle stages of customer journeys. Partners assuming this role generate demand by helping target customers become aware of a need or desire. The moment consumers become aware of their need or desire, demand that did not previously exist has been created. Next, these early-stage partners dive deeper into the need or desire with the consumer, helping them build out their decision-making criteria, evaluate various solutions, and ultimately determine which solution is their best option.

Partner content is critical to this introduce and influence role, as it's through content that partners meet target consumers in their exploration. Content creators at heart, partners create useful content that guides interested consumers through any and all of the stages of their journeys, from awareness to consideration and on to purchase. Sometimes this movement can take place all in one video, blog post, or article. Other times it takes place in a series. Take Krista Hooper's blog posts as an example of the all-in-one. Readers can peruse her blog, and if an item piques their interest, with one click—commerce content at work—they can find themselves on the associated product page on **Walmart.com**, where they can get any questions answered and make a purchase—a complete shopping journey. More complex purchases such as credit cards, health insurance, and B2B purchases often require more content paced across several interactions, as these decisions tend to require more consideration and involve multiple decision makers.

Traditionally the role of introducing and influencing in the B2C and D2C worlds has been the domain of social influencers, brand ambassadors, and mass media publishers, people who are in the business of creating informational content. This content may take the form of gift ideas, listicles, inspirational imagery, and comparison and review articles—think BuzzFeed, *Consumer Reports*, and Oprah. In the past few years, coupon, deal, and loyalty sites have become content creators in their own right, generating their own "10 best" lists and gift guides to stimulate demand among their members, as have communities such as Yelp and Tripadvisor.

Other brands can also be great early-stage partners. Consider how the online mattress and bedding start-up Casper has paired up with West Elm, a high-end furniture company, to enable shoppers to test-drive Casper mattresses before making a purchase. Casper gains physical storefronts without other overhead costs, which enables it to offer its customers an end-to-end experience. West Elm gets great mattresses to showcase its furniture and bedding. Both companies benefit from the brand association and the customer traffic each brand generates.[9]

B2B enterprises have similar types of partners. Like the B2C world, B2B companies have mass media publications, such as *Forbes*, *Fast Company*, and the *Wall Street Journal*, and trade publications specific to their industry, such as *Adweek*, *Marketing Land*, and *Ad Age*. They also have their own influencers and brand ambassadors, although they are likely to be called bloggers, consultants, agencies, analysts, and clients. B2B enterprises also have their own communities that often take the form of associations and conferences. And they partner with other brands, collaborations that are called product integrations or joint ventures, depending on the nature of the partnership.

Closing Partner Role

When partners are actively influencing the point of purchase, they are assuming a closing role. These partners can influence conversion by encouraging enterprise target customers to act—now. I am often asked why there is a need for specific partners to play a closing role when any of today's partners can theoretically accompany customers from awareness, through consideration, and on to purchase. The same partner can assume all three roles; however, the time between consideration and conversion can sometimes be swift and other times long. Often, especially with low-consideration items, one partner can play the role of introducer, influencer, and closer, and an entire shopping journey can be accomplished rather quickly. Other times, as we have seen with high-consideration purchases, there are many more steps involved and consumers may want multiple voices to weigh in on their decision.

Provide discounts or special offers. Still other times it takes a deal to close a sale. This is especially true when consumers are price conscious. Cashback, coupon, deal, and loyalty sites have traditionally played a closing partner role as price-sensitive shoppers have visited these sites to look for discounts, promotion codes, special deals, and/or points and other rewards before making a purchase. Consumers choose to become members of these communities in order to access great deals from a variety of enterprises and brands and to be rewarded for their purchases. And they are! As we have seen, Walmart regularly employs closing partners to reach out to its prospects and regular customers, many of whom are motivated by low prices. Enterprises also choose to work with closing partners to liquidate excess inventory, everything ranging from seasonal items like swim floats and shovels to high-purchase items such as diamond necklaces, knowing they have the attention of people who are looking for solid deals.

Retain and Reengage Partner Role

Retention strategies kick in after a purchase has taken place. The prospect is now a customer. Now the task is to retain these customers and to increase their lifetime value. The way to do that is by reengaging customers and continually increasing the value of the enterprise's product offering. Partners can help enterprises do so in several ways.

Realize additional value. Partners can showcase how customers can get more from their purchases. For example, influencers, publishers, and everyday people regularly create unboxing videos to show people how to get the most out of their Xbox, tablet, blender, or coffee maker.

Catalyze new shopping journeys. Partners can continuously catalyze new shopping journeys for an enterprise's existing customers. Technology partners like UpSellIt can create remarketing campaigns that let customers know when it's time to renew, refresh, or restock previous purchases. Another way partners can catalyze new shopping journeys is by continually generating demand and consideration for additional products, services, and experiences that the enterprise offers. Some partners like Krista Hooper may dedicate themselves to working with one enterprise and its offerings—in this case, Walmart. Other partners will feature an enterprise and its products when it makes the most sense for their audiences—when writing an article, say, or undertaking a product comparison. So it's important for enterprises to find ways to stay top of mind with their partners!

Increase the value of enterprise offerings. Partners can work with enterprises to increase the value of their products, services, and experiences in the eyes of their customers. Creating more holistic enterprise product offerings by integrating partners' features and capabilities into their products is one of the most exciting ways this is currently taking place. Shareable Recipes, the mobile app that integrates Tasty's recipes with Walmart's grocery store, is a perfect example. The combined value proposition embedded in the app increases its usefulness for many of its users by enabling app users to easily purchase any food items they may need to make their desired meal, right in the app, and have them delivered or ready for pickup a few hours later. Simplicity and convenience often increase value.

Link Partner Roles with Business Objectives

Enterprises can work with partners in each of these roles to meet their various business objectives. For example, when an enterprise is pursuing growth via customer acquisition, if all goes well, its target customers will journey from awareness to consideration, to making a decision, and ultimately a purchase. A partner, or group of partners, can guide enterprise target customers through each stage of these journeys by playing the role of introducer, influencer, or closer, or any combination of the three. Similarly, if an enterprise is looking to increase its customer lifetime value, it's likely to want to catalyze additional shopping journeys with its existing customers, with the help of retention partners who will introduce, influence, and close additional deals (Table 4.1).

Customer and Shopping Journeys Show What's Taking Place

When enterprises know their business's objectives, their target customers, the behaviors they want their partners to catalyze, where these behaviors occur along their customers' journeys, and the roles that different partners can play, they are ready to bring them all together. They can create a vision of a seamless customer experience, offered in conjunction with their partners, that enables their target customers to meet their goals while simultaneously allowing the partnership to meet its business objectives.

Toward this end, it's common for enterprises to map their existing customer and shopping journey to see who (e.g., partners) and what (e.g., retargeting ads,

TABLE 4.1   Business objectives determine partner roles.

Business Goals We want to drive growth by . . .	Partnership Focus We want our partnership(s) to address these phases of our customers' journeys . . .	Potential Partner Roles These are the roles we want partners to play . . .
Acquiring new customers	Awareness, consideration, decision, purchase	Introduce, influence, and close
Entering new markets	Awareness, consideration, decision, purchase	Introduce, influence, and close
Creating positive brand associations	Awareness, consideration, decision, purchase	Introduce and influence
Closing more sales and increasing average order value	Purchase	Close
Increasing customer retention and long-term value	Awareness, consideration, decision, purchase, and enhance value of products, services, and experiences	Retain and reengage
Generating innovation and enhancing the value of products, services, and experiences	Awareness, consideration, decision, purchase, and enhance value of products, services, and experiences	Retain and reengage
Driving mobile app installs and usage	Awareness, consideration, decision, purchase	Introduce, influence, close, and retain and reengage
Improving overall customer experience for new and existing customers	Awareness, consideration, decision, purchase, and enhance value of products, services, and experiences	Introduce, influence, close, and retain and reengage
Pivoting our strategy	Awareness, consideration, decision, purchase, and enhance value of products, services, and experiences	Introduce, influence, close, and retain and reengage

paid social) are currently interacting with their target customers and catalyzing the various micro conversions and macro conversions. With this information in hand, they can build a vision for how partnerships can enable a more seamless and effective customer experience. These maps, which are also referred to as conversion pathways, will look quite different depending on the nature of the purchase. In some cases partners will successfully lead target customers from awareness through to conversion entirely on their own. Other times there will be multiple partners, and an enterprise's own marketing efforts (e.g., retargeting ads), involved in a single customer's journey.

FIGURE 4.6   Illustration of a customer's shopping journey.

Figure 4.6 captures a fictitious example of one customer's shopping journey with an enterprise that includes multiple participants. This person's journey began seven days ago when they saw a post on an influencer's YouTube channel that featured one of the enterprise's products—let's say a cashmere scarf. The partner's introduction was successful. Over the course of the next six days, that same customer conducted several related searches—What should you look for when purchasing a cashmere scarf? What's the difference between a cashmere blend and 100 percent cashmere? What does cashmere mean?—which resulted in him receiving multiple retargeting ads. His final search led him to an article that compared different cashmere scarf brands, which enabled him to make his decision. An embedded link in the article allowed him to click through to the enterprise's ecommerce site to make a purchase. In this example, partners successfully introduced, influenced, and closed the sale.

When consolidated, these individual maps reveal useful patterns. At a minimum they reveal who and what are currently influencing enterprise customer journeys, how this varies by target customer segment and type of purchase, and how this may be changing over time. They also reveal an enterprise's most frequent paths to conversion and how many interactions it takes, on average, to convert a customer, an indication of the success of an enterprise's overall customer engagement efforts. At a more granular level, these maps reveal what happens before and after each touchpoint—who or what is driving subsequent micro conversions and macro conversions. They can reveal winning sequences, synergies among efforts—where a partner's blog may prompt a search or a search may lead to a partner blog—and how these combinations can accelerate conversions and reengagement.

Journey Maps Reveal Partnerships Opportunities

Consolidated journey maps also offer clues about gaps in coverage—places where partnerships may be able to provide meaningful interactions and successful

TABLE 4.2 Coverage maps identify partnership opportunities.

Customer Journey Stages	Pre-purchase Awareness	Consideration	Decision	Purchase	Post-purchase Reengage, Repurchase
Partners' Roles	Introduce	Influence	Decision	Close	Retain and Reengage
Partner #1	X	X			X
Partner #2				X	
Partner #3	X	X	X	X	X
Partner #4				X	

outcomes—and they can indicate where there may be redundancies or even negative customer experiences. To identify these opportunities, it can be helpful to summarize the findings in a coverage map, which identifies who and what are influencing the target customers at various stages of their customer journeys, like the simplified example in Table 4.2.

On this coverage map, potential sources of influence on a given target customer segment are listed on the vertical axis, and the various stages of this target segment's aggregated customer journey are located on the horizontal axis. As you can see, different partners play different combinations of roles even with the same customer segments. Partner 1 is active early in the customer journeys, whereas Partner 2 is in the role of closer, and Partner 4's strength is in retaining and reengaging. Partner 3 is able to do all of the above. Note that this does not mean that the company only needs to work with Partner 3, as each of these partners may help an enterprise reach its secondary business objectives. They may reach different audiences, promote different products at different price points, be more effective at leading target customers to install an enterprise's mobile app and to prompt enhanced usage, and contribute to the success of the other.

Design Your Ideal Customer Journeys

Journey maps provide a baseline against which you can experiment with various future partnerships and marketing strategies in service of creating more ideal customer and shopping journeys. What happens when you add the trusted voice of a partner into the mix? Does it shorten the number of interactions or enhance your conversion rates? What combination of enterprise marketing initiatives (i.e., paid advertising, search engine optimization (SEO), social media, email, content marketing, public relations) and partnerships will enable you to best reach your target customers and accompany them along their journeys, so they meet their goals and you meet yours? In doing so, they provide a context for your future partnerships efforts and a rationale for their specific partner recruitment efforts.

The Quick Summary

- Partnerships can prompt myriad customer behaviors across enterprise customer journeys.
- Partner roles are fluid. They can introduce, influence, close, or help enterprises reengage and retain their target customers, depending on where they impact enterprise customer journeys.
- Enterprises can map their customer journeys to reveal partnerships opportunities. Journey maps capture who (partners) and what (marketing initiatives) are currently impacting enterprise target customer journeys. This analysis can identify gaps and redundancies in customer coverage that can be proactively addressed. Journey maps can also reveal the impact that partnerships have on enterprise customer journeys—they often shorten them and reach customers outside the reach of traditional outreach methods.
- Current customer journey maps provide a baseline against which enterprises can experiment with various partnerships strategies. Enterprises can create future journey maps to proactively design their customer journeys to be more seamless and effective.

What's Up Next?

How do business objectives, target customers and desired customer behaviors, and partner roles become growth-catalyzing partnerships? The next chapter explores the five fundamental building blocks of today's partnerships. It also introduces the Partnership Design Canvas, a framework that facilitates the partnership design process.

Notes

[1] Aldo Bukit, **Walmart.com**, "The Fast and the Reliable: How Walmart Leveraged Transparency and Data to Build Better Partner Relationships," interviewed by Mike Head, **impact.com**, video, 7:14, **http://bit.ly/Impact-interview-Aldo-Walmart**.

2 "Design at Your Door with HGTVGO," Walmart Inc., accessed May 12, 2021, **http://bit .ly/walmart-hgtvgo-design**.

3 "11 Budget-Friendly Walmart Finds to Update Your Living Room," HGTV, June 12, 2020, **http://bit.ly/hgtv-update-living-room**.

4 "Design at Your Door with HGTVGO," Walmart Inc.

5 "A Taste of Summer," Walmart, Influencer Shop, accessed May 12, 2021, **www.walmart .com/cp/influencer-shop/6180583**.

6 "Go with the Glow," Walmart (@lishalovesmakeup), Influencer Shop, accessed May 12, 2021, **http://bit.ly/lisha-loves-makeup**.

7 *And a Pinch of Love*, Daniela Duran, April 13, 2019, **andapinchoflove.com**.

8 "Walmart and BuzzFeed's Tasty Stir Together Meal Planning, List Making and Grocery Shopping in One Easy Solution: Shoppable Recipes," Walmart, August 19, 2019, **http:// bit.ly/buzzfeed-tasty-recipes**.

9 Sara Ashley O'Brien, "West Elm Partners with Mattress Startup Casper," *CNN Business*, June 29, 2016, **http://bit.ly/westelm-partners-casper**.

CHAPTER 5

Six Building Blocks of Today's Partnerships

"**I** loved Harry's razors, everything about them. I loved their appearance, their shave quality, their shave comfort, their shave time, and their costs," writes Julie Strietelmeier, founder of *The Gadgeteer*.[1] Strietelmeier founded the blog to share with others her lifelong passion for gadgets.

Strietelmeier is not alone in her passion for the grooming company and its shaving, showering, skincare, and hair products—Harry's has received more than 20,000 five-star reviews. Its "brand moments" strategy, which focuses on improving the pain points associated with the traditional shaving experience, has created exceptional customer experiences that have endeared the company to many. Customers love the brightly colored razors, blades, and shave gel, and the clever shaving tips. And then there is the Mystery Surprise—a package that is designed to look like the timeless Bazooka Joe comics and that contains a Harry's product that may or may not yet be available for sale to the public.

Harry's exceptional customer service has enabled the company to effectively compete in an industry of giants like Gillette and Procter & Gamble (P&G). This exceptional customer experience and customer brand love caught the attention of several folks responsible for discovering and recruiting merchants for their company rewards and loyalty programs. In time, several strategic brand-to-brand partnerships were born.

Harry's rewards program partnerships follow a similar overall structure, which is illustrated with a representative company, ACME.[2] ACME is a financial services company with several popular credit card brands. The popularity of its brands is due in large part to the company's generous rewards programs, through which cardholders are rewarded for purchases made with their ACME card. ACME cardholders are able to see their accrued rewards and use them to "purchase" merchandise via ACME's rewards program platform. Harry's introductory gift package, which includes a brightly colored razor handle, a five-blade cartridge, foaming shaving gel, a travel blade cover, and a fun introductory note with helpful tips for getting the best shave, is one of hundreds of exciting options.

When a cardholder is interested in using their rewards to "purchase" the Harry's introductory gift package, they simply click on the image to unlock a more in-depth product description and to make the "purchase." Within a few days, the Harry's gift box arrives at their doorstep and the fun begins. In the future, when ACME cardholders need additional cartridges or shaving gel, they can "purchase" them in the same way.

This seamless shopping journey is beautifully simple to the cardholder; however, it's made possible by a fairly complex partnership. Here's what happens on the back end. A deep link connects the two partners' websites, which enables the cardholder to be instantaneously transported from the ACME rewards site to **Harry's.com** via a single click. (**Harry's.com** is where the cardholder is able to access more extensive product descriptions and to make a "purchase.") As soon as the "purchase" is made, ACME credits their card for the purchase amount and deducts that amount from the cardholder's rewards account. Separately it bills Harry's for the introductory gift package.

Why would ACME bill Harry's for the cost of the gift package? Shouldn't it be paying Harry's instead? To understand why this is the case, it's important to look at the overall structure of the partnership and the value it creates for each party.

The value to cardholders is straightforward: they are able to utilize their accumulated rewards to "purchase" the Harry's introductory gift package. Win number 1.

What's in it for ACME? The credit card company is able to bring a popular new merchant into its loyalty program. What's more, it's able to do so at no cost because Harry's underwrites the entire cost of the introductory gift package (hence, the bill). Win number 2.

Harry's is more than happy to pay for the gift package in exchange for being introduced to ACME cardholders. Here's why. When Harry's wins new customers, there are often substantial customer acquisition costs. Paid advertising, for example, is expensive, and prices are high for competitive keywords. In this partnership, Harry's customer acquisition costs are substantially lower because ACME has acted as a referral partner and made the introduction—there is no need for paid advertising! What's more, Harry's is a subscription business—if cardholders are pleased with the Harry's experience, they are likely to make subsequent purchases of cartridges, lotion, and more. The value of the ACME introduction could grow over time. Win number 3.

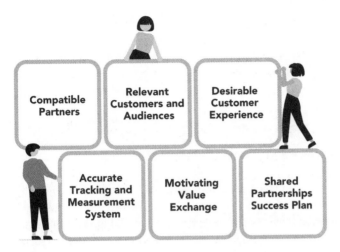

FIGURE 5.1   The six building blocks of partnerships.

Knowing that consumers quite like its products once they have tried them, in addition to covering the cost of the introductory gift package Harry's is willing to pay ACME a small referral commission for any new customers that it brings to Harry's—*and* an increasingly higher commission for any subsequent "purchases" those cardholders make. The more loyal the customer—as evidenced by the number of repurchases—the higher ACME's compensation. This "chained compensation structure" works well for Harry's, too, because rather than paying one large upfront commission that is based on an estimate of the average lifetime value of a new customer, Harry's pays a smaller commission based on the actual purchases made. It's a win-win-win all around.

Harry's, ACME, and the Six Building Blocks

The Harry's and ACME partnership is an example of a strategic B2B partnership. Like every modern partnership, the Harry's and ACME partnership has six building blocks (Figure 5.1):

1. Compatible partners
2. Relevant customers and audiences
3. Desirable customer experience
4. Accurate tracking and measurement system
5. Motivating value exchange
6. Shared partnerships success plan

This chapter explores each of these six building blocks and introduces the Partnership Design Canvas (PDC), a framework that enterprises can use to facilitate the upfront design of a potential collaboration. A downloadable version of the PDC is available at **thepartnershipbook.com/resources**.

Build Effective Collaborations with the Partnership Design Canvas

A well-designed partnership lays a solid foundation for a long-term, mutually rewarding working relationship. The Partnership Design Canvas (PDC) was created by **impact.com** to facilitate the upfront partnership design process. It can be helpful for the design of any collaboration and is especially useful as enterprises branch out into nontraditional and more complex types of partnerships where the partnerships process is less well defined.

The PDC lays out the six building blocks that comprise today's partnerships in one simple template (Figure 5.2). Enterprises are encouraged to customize this template to best serve their partnership design process. Undertaking the PDC process enables enterprises to ascertain what each party brings to the table, whether each party has the capabilities the other needs and wants what the other has, and whether potential partners are willing and able to build a modern partnership together now or in the future. It asks enterprises to define the collaboration's target customers, the behaviors the partner experience should catalyze, and preliminary ideas about the proposed customer experience. It captures the benefits that the partnership will create for both parties, the actions for which the potential partner will be compensated, and the metrics and key performance indicators (KPIs) that will determine the success of their partnerships efforts. Finally, it prompts enterprises and their potential partners to define key actions, milestones, roles, and responsibilities that are essential to their success and a timeline for their efforts. These details comprise a shared partnerships success plan that can also be used to determine if there is a fair value exchange between partners.

Compatible Partners

The universe of potential partners is huge. In theory, any entity that has something of value can be a potential partner; however, that doesn't mean it will be a compatible partner for every enterprise. To be compatible, potential partners must have five things: complementary business objectives; brand fit; competitor status; the ability to work together toward a shared outcome in a collaborative, transparent, and mutually rewarding way; and the desire to do so.

Partnership Design Canvas

Potential Partner: _____

Our goals for this partnership:

Compatible Partners

☐ **Complementary business objectives:**
What are our complementary objectives? Do we understand each other's goals? What does each of us bring to the table? What do they have that we need? What do we have that they need?

☐ **Brand fit:**
Does this partner meet our ideal partner criteria? Is there any brand risk? Would an endorsement from this partner about our product sound credible to our target customers? Why?

☐ **Competitor status:**
Does this partner already work with one of our competitors? What does that partnership look like, and can we be competitive against them?

☐ **Ability to collaborate:**
Does this partner have a history of collaboration? Are they prepared to contribute the necessary resources and effort for this partnership to succeed? What concerns do we need to address?

☐ **Desire to work together:**
Do we want to work with this partner? Is this a good use of our resources? Are we a priority for them?

Relevant Customers and Audiences

☐ Who will this partnership target? Are they one of our target audiences?

☐ Does this partner have access to, and a trustworthy relationship with, this audience?

☐ What is the size of the accessible target audience for this partnership?

Desirable Customer Experience

☐ What is our customer value proposition? What is the customer experience we will create? Who is doing what, when, where, and with whom, and with what outcome or result?

☐ Do we think this will be a desirable experience for our target customers? Is this experience what they are looking for? How do we know?

Accurate Tracking and Measurement System

☐ What set of customer behaviors do we want to catalyze? How will we track these actions?

☐ What consumer behaviors do we want to reward our partner for catalyzing?

☐ What metrics will we use to evaluate our success?

☐ What data and reports will be exchanged, and at what frequency?

Motivating Value Exchange

☐ How will we compensate this partner? Will it reward our partner for catalyzing our desired customer behaviors? Is the commission structure we are proposing fair and motivating?

☐ What are the benefits that this partnership will create for us and for our partner—financial and nonfinancial? What resources and effort are each partner contributing? What risks is each partner assuming? Are the benefits/effort/risk equivalent for each partner?

☐ Are there special terms we want in our contract?

Shared Partnerships Success Plan

☐ What are the key activities that need to take place for this partnership to get to productivity? Who is responsible for what and what is the time frame?

☐ What does our calendar contain for upcoming promotions, campaigns, and content around which our partner can plan?

☐ What are key milestones?

☐ How and when will we review our partnership's performance?

FIGURE 5.2 Build effective collaborations with the Partnership Design Canvas.

Complementary business objectives. In today's partnerships, two entities work together toward a shared outcome. Their goal is generative. Potential partners come together because they are convinced that the value they can create together exceeds what either could create on its own. The reasons for this are many, but at their core they are about each party having something that the other needs, values, and wants. Each is looking to a potential partner to supply it because they don't have it, they want it, and it may be impossible, too costly, or too time consuming for the party to achieve on its own. A partnership makes it possible.

Potential partners are looking for different things, but what they are looking for are related. Indeed, they are complementary; they fit hand in glove. Generally speaking, in referral partnerships the enterprise is looking for exposure to its target customers, something that the partner can provide, and the partner is looking for useful products and services to share with its audience, something the enterprise offers.

When designing a potential partnership, start with your business objectives. What are you looking to achieve with this potential partnership? What problem does this partnership solve for you and/or what opportunities does it create for you and your target customers? Then flip perspectives and consider each of these questions from your potential partner's vantage point. Get specific. What does each of you bring to the table? Finally, ask yourself: Would you and your partner want what the other has to offer? Why or why not?

Brand fit. Referral partners are customer-facing: they regularly interact with an enterprise's target customers. When enterprises and partners work together, they create powerful brand associations in the minds of their customers, audiences, and other stakeholders. These associations can turn people toward or away from a brand. As a result, it's important to be both strategic and mindful when selecting partners.

Assessing brand fit also involves examining a potential partner's user experience. In today's partnerships, the customer experiences that your partner creates with or for you become an extension of your brand experience. This is true even if the touchpoints you create together don't take place on your own branded properties. As a result, the quality and effectiveness of your partner-based customer experiences matter. They must be on par with the quality of your overall user experience, or the net effect will be negative. A poor customer experience, whether it takes place on the enterprise's own property or on that of its partners, is a poor customer experience. And when it comes to customer experience, one bad apple can spoil the whole bunch. A recent study by NewVoiceMedia found that 67 percent of customers are "serial switchers"; they are more than willing to switch brands because of a poor customer experience.[3]

When designing a potential partnership, consider whether a potential partner meets your ideal partner qualifications. Do you have similar brand purposes and values? Are your brands similar in quality and distinctiveness? Do you engage with your customers in similar ways? Does the connection between your two brands make sense to your shared prospects and customers? Are they a credible advocate for your company? Is there any brand risk that may result from working with this potential partner? Is your potential partner's user experience what it needs to be?

Competitor status. Explore their partnerships with other enterprises—especially those with which you compete. Partners do work with competitive brands, especially when they are creating product comparison guides and "10 best" lists. When you are a challenger brand, being showcased among top competitors can build your credibility. Nevertheless, it's a good idea to enter partnerships with your eyes wide open and ensure that you can be competitive against them.

Ability to collaborate. The ability to work together in a transparent and mutually rewarding way is critical to the success of innovative and productive long-term partnerships. Unfortunately, generative collaboration is not always the modus operandi of companies, even those that want to build successful partnerships programs. Many times the desire to collaborate is several steps ahead of the ability. Habit, brand ego, scarcity mindsets, and the desire for control often get in the way. For example, enterprises often operate as if partnerships are a finite undertaking rather than a long-term business relationship, and they negotiate as if it's a zero-sum game. They approach partners with a goal of getting as much as they can for as little money as possible. Similarly, partners often approach enterprises with the goal of getting paid as much as they can for as little effort as possible. Unfortunately, both parties are missing the boat. They are not acting as long-term partners that are working together toward a common goal and mutual success, and their results will suffer.

Compatible partners operate in a truly collaborative way. They recognize that relationships comprise today's partnerships, not algorithms, and that mutual trust is essential to building and maintaining these relationships. This mutual trust is earned in the trenches and over time. It requires that partners understand what is important to each other and that they be intentional about creating a partnership that is designed for their mutual success. This includes equivalent risk, reward, and level of effort and resources required.

When designing a potential partnership, inquire about your potential partner's partnership philosophy and try to assess its culture. What is most important to it? Does it see itself as a more traditional or experimental partner? Ask about past collaborations: What has worked and what hasn't? Is it potentially a high-maintenance partner? Are there any concerns that need to be addressed? Share your partnership philosophy and partner value proposition. (See Chapter 13, "How Does It Feel? Creating a Beneficial Partner Experience.")

Desire to work together. In the end, enterprises and their potential partners have to want to commit their time and resources to a potential partnership in order for it to work. This level of commitment will vary across partners and partner types, but increasingly, very few partnerships are of the "set it and forget it" variety. In our experience, success isn't about having as many partnerships in your portfolio as possible, it's having productive partnerships that bring mutual value to each partner and are worth the associated effort.

When designing a potential partnership, ask yourself and your team whether this partner is worth the effort. If it is difficult to work with at the onset of a partnership, chances are that it will not become any easier to work with over time. Then flip perspectives. Does this partner want to work with you? How much of a priority do you sense this partnership will be for it? How do you know?

Relevant Customers and Audiences

Similar or shared customers and audiences are at the center of today's partnerships. Placing the customer at the center of partnerships is not a nice-to-have, it's their primary purpose. These are the people who bring partners together and enable them to generate revenue and meet their business objectives. When partners lose track of this, it adversely impacts their results.

Being very clear about who your target customers are is critical for partnership success. With this understanding, you can readily assess whether a potential partner's audience is your target customer or not, or if they should be. Sometimes the link is clear—you both serve the same customer segments and there is a good brand fit. For example, an enterprise that sells bicycles may form a successful partnership with an influencer who writes extensively about active outdoor excursions around the globe. Other times a potential partner may serve a different audience than yours, but it enables you to tap into a new market for your existing products. This is the case when companies begin to expand globally. Still other times, partners can help enterprises develop markets around new use cases for their existing products by introducing them to new customers that may be interested in purchasing that product. This is often the case behind successful strategic pivots. Think of how restaurant partners enabled Uber to quickly build out its Uber Eats business during the COVID-19 pandemic.

When designing a potential partnership, identify your target customers for this partnership and explore the ins and outs of your potential partner's audience. Are they the same or similar? Does this partner have a trustworthy relationship with this audience? How large is this partner's total addressable market? Are you and your partner convinced that your products and brand will resonate with them?

Desirable Customer Experience

This is the moment of truth for partnerships. Remember back in Chapter 3, when I talked about waving a magic wand to have your target customers do what you wanted them to do? I then got more specific, answering the questions of who is doing what, where, when, with whom, and with what outcome or result. This is where all that visioning gets translated into actual customer interactions.

These customer interactions can take many forms: an Instagram post, a loyalty program reward, useful content, a more holistic product offering—even the opportunity to try out Harry's gift package. The goal is to create a desirable experience that your target customers will find useful—and even enjoy. David Bakey, former vice president of Harry's direct-to-consumer business, suggests that partners set the bar high, asking themselves: What can we do that will *delight* our shared customers?

Consider some of the customer experiences that Harry's has created with other brands. The company worked with British designer Tom Dixon to create "design-your-own razor handles" in conjunction with the London Design Festival. The partners co-designed aluminum shapes that attendees could assemble into their own custom designs, creating the feely part of Dixon's "TouchySmellyFeelyNoisyTasty" multisensory installation.[4] Razor handles were also part of the limited-edition shaving sets created by Harry's for Pride. Spanish artist José Antonio Roda illustrated and designed the bright boxes to house these limited-edition sets. All of the profits from this partnership were donated to The Trevor Project, the world's largest suicide prevention and crisis intervention organization for LGBTQ+ youth[5] (Figure 5.3).

When designing a potential partnership, explore your and your partner's respective visions for this customer experience. What is the unique and/or attractive value proposition that this partnership can create for your shared customers and audiences? What specific needs or desires are you hoping to address via your collaboration? How important is solving this need or satisfying this desire to your target customers and audience? How will this collaboration enable your targets to be successful? What customer behaviors do you want this experience to catalyze? How will this experience help you and your partner meet your respective business objectives?

What will be the actual experience you will offer to consumers? How will it translate into specific touchpoints? What will be the context of these touchpoints—the partner's website, mobile app, social media properties, email, newsletter, physical space, specially created virtual or offline venues such as a popup store or flash mob, or a promoted microsite? What testing might you need to do?

Accurate Tracking and Measurement System

Every partnership, whether it's designed to be performance-based or not, needs to have a tracking and measurement system in place to be able to ascertain the effectiveness of the partnerships effort. Did it achieve its agreed-upon outputs? Is it enabling its partners to meet their business objectives? This assessment can—and must—be based on actual partnership data rather than perceptions and opinion. Fortunately, partnership management platforms make this possible.

In the upfront design stage, partners work together to determine what success will look like and translate that vision into specific events they will track—clicks, downloads, installs, subscriptions, sales—and relevant metrics and KPIs. In the Harry's/ACME partnership, for example, the partners tracked initial and subsequent purchases of Harry's products made by ACME customers on the ACME loyalty site.

Once they have their tracking and measurement system in place, partners determine how they will share partnership performance data and how often they will come together to review progress toward their goals. Compatible partners understand that transparency is critical to optimizing their shared results and that information asymmetry creates an uneven playing field that erodes trust. Sharing partnership insights in real time, on the other hand, enables partners to understand what moves the needle for their specific collaboration, think proactively about how to best meet both partners' KPIs, forecast with greater accuracy, and make necessary adjustments on the fly. Over time these partnerships naturally optimize their shared results and become right-priced, enabling enterprises to pay for the value they actually receive and for partners to be compensated fairly and accurately for the influence they bring.

When designing a potential partnership, carefully define the customer behaviors that you want your partners to catalyze and ensure that you are able to accurately track those behaviors across devices and channels. Establish relevant metrics for your partnerships and know how they align with the metrics for your overall partnerships effort.

Motivating Value Exchange

Partnerships generate multiple benefits for enterprises and their partners (Figure 5.4). The most obvious benefit is meeting the need or want that initially brought both parties together. When you take a closer look, several more benefits often emerge.

For the enterprise, these benefits may include revenue, acquisition of new customers, expansion into new markets, ability to promote and liquidate specific inventory, increased customer loyalty and lifetime value, enhanced customer experience, growth in customer advocacy, increased installs and usage of its mobile app, fresh and successful content that can be repurposed for broader marketing purposes, deeper insights into its prospects and customers, the opportunity to express and act on its values and social commitments, the benefits that come from

HARRY'S
&
.Tom Dixon.

HARRY'S
&
José Antonio Roda

FIGURE 5.3 Harry's and its partners generate unique razor handles.

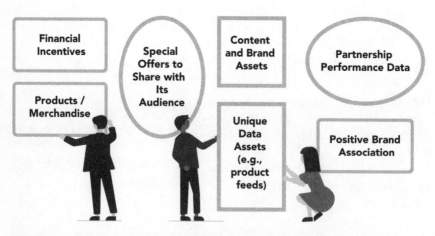

FIGURE 5.4 There are multiple sources of value in today's partnerships.

brand association, and more. Depending on the role that the enterprise's partner is playing, its benefits may include financial incentives, special offers to share with its audiences, content and brand assets, positive brand association, unique data assets to promote engagement and sales, products or merchandise, and partnership performance data with which partners can optimize their performance.

A Word About Partner Incentives

Thoughtful incentives can make a difference in how quickly a partner becomes productive and how engaged it's likely to be in the long run. If a partner receives significant benefits from the partnership, it's likely to be more responsive, more deliberate, more invested. Revenue is one of the several benefits of modern partnerships. I mention this not to downplay its significance, but to put it in context. The benefits, effort, resources contributed, and risk must be equivalent for both parties for a partnership to thrive and endure. The primary risk for enterprises is that partners defect to their competitors. Primary risks for partners include enterprises mistakenly trying to save money by turning off a program, significant changes to a commission structure in an attempt to test elasticity, terminating a partnership with little or no notice, or failure to adequately support the partnership with brand assets and product information. When the exchange of value and the effort and resources to generate the value are equitable, a quality partnership has been achieved. The collaboration has the opportunity to grow and reach its full potential. Where balance is lacking, it will need to be equalized with compensation.

As we have seen, monetary exchange in today's partnerships is based in whole or in part on performance. Compensation often takes the form of commissions that are derived from partners' ability to catalyze agreed-upon customer actions such as clicks, installs, purchases, subscriptions, or repurchases above a certain dollar amount. Under this cost-per-action (CPA) model, partners are remunerated when these macro and micro conversions take place. If a target customer doesn't undertake the agreed-upon action, the partner does not receive monetary compensation. This CPA model differs substantially from the traditional cost-per-impression (CPM) model that has heretofore dominated paid advertising, as it's based on customer action rather than on customer impressions. CPA compensation is made possible because today's partner automation technology can track and assess each partner's ability to catalyze customer behaviors along an enterprise's myriad customer journeys.

What type of incentive structure makes sense for your partnership? Common practices include offering a percentage of revenue that may be tied to catalyzing specific customer behaviors, a fixed fee per customer action, a participation bonus, direct placements, or, in some cases, a fixed fee. Fees and participation bonuses are often employed to bridge the gap between the revenue that partners assist in generating (often when they assume the role of introducer or influencer) and the revenue they are credited for generating when payouts are made on a last-click basis, as has historically been the case.

Chained Compensation Models Increase Customer Lifetime Value

As companies become committed to customer acquisition and retention, they are increasingly employing chained commission structures, which reward a given partner for catalyzing multiple micro conversions that lead to a major conversion for a target customer. This model is often seen under subscription business models, where a partner may be compensated for introducing a subscription business to a target customer, an additional fee if they sign up for a free trial, and another fee if they convert from the free trial to a subscription business. Or in the case of a travel company, a partner receives a commission for when a customer books a flight or hotel room and an additional fee once that customer has actually consumed the experience; in this case they have taken the flight or stayed in the room. This multiphased, linked compensation structure helps companies increase their customers' lifetime value better, as it matches commissions paid with increasingly valuable customer actions, and it provides an incentive for partners to keep promoting the enterprise and its products over time (Figure 5.5).

When designing a potential partnership, carefully map the value streams being generated by the partnership and who is receiving them. If there is an imbalance, or if you need to sweeten the deal to motivate a partner to work with you, carefully consider your commissions and your commission structure. Is the commission structure you are considering fair and motivating? Does it map well to the customer actions that lead to your desired business objectives? Does a chained compensation structure make sense?

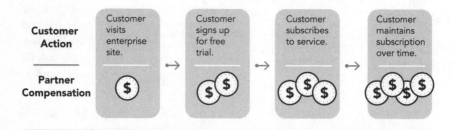

FIGURE 5.5 Chained compensation model increases customer lifetime value.
Source: https://monday.com/project-management.

Shared Partnerships Success Plan

Last but not least comes the shared partnerships success plan. Even the most compatible partners with the most well-designed partnership need a plan of action to bring the partnership to life. Partnership success—and trust—is made or broken in the details. Creating a shared partnerships success plan helps build a mutual understanding of what it will take for success to materialize. It clearly defines each task, milestone, and responsibility, assigns roles and responsibilities associated with each effort, and establishes an expected timeline. It also identifies dependencies and where coordination is needed. Finally, the shared partnerships success plan should also include expectations for how and when the partnership's performance will be evaluated.

Consider Using a RACI Matrix

Many partners use a RACI matrix as the basis for their shared success plan (RACI is an acronym that stands for responsible, accountable, consulted, and informed, which are the four key roles that team members generally play). The responsible party is the person (or people) who does the day-to-day work of the partnership. The accountable person is the project owner, the person who reviews the plan and with whom the buck stops. In the world of partnerships, the responsible party and the accountable one might be one and the same. At times, partnerships efforts require the input of the consulted party, a person or group of people who offer their expertise and/or are important stakeholders in partnerships effort. This may be someone in business development, or legal, or finance, depending on the partnership. Last but not least are the informed—team members who operate on a need-to-know basis, generally informed about the partnership, but not involved in the details. This may be a chief partnerships officer, a chief marketing officer, or a senior partnerships manager.

RACI matrices are customized for each partnership. As you can see from the RACI matrix shown in Figure 5.6, partnership actions are listed on one axis and the RACI roles (responsible, accountable, consulted, and informed) are listed on the other.[6] Names and sometimes photos of the people responsible for the task fill in the matrix and a status column enables everyone on the team to readily understand what is completed, what is in process, and where people are stuck and may need assistance. Continually monitor your RACI matrix to keep the partnership moving toward success and to ensure that the benefits and effort are equivalent for both partners. If they're not, how can you reallocate responsibilities to even the playing field?

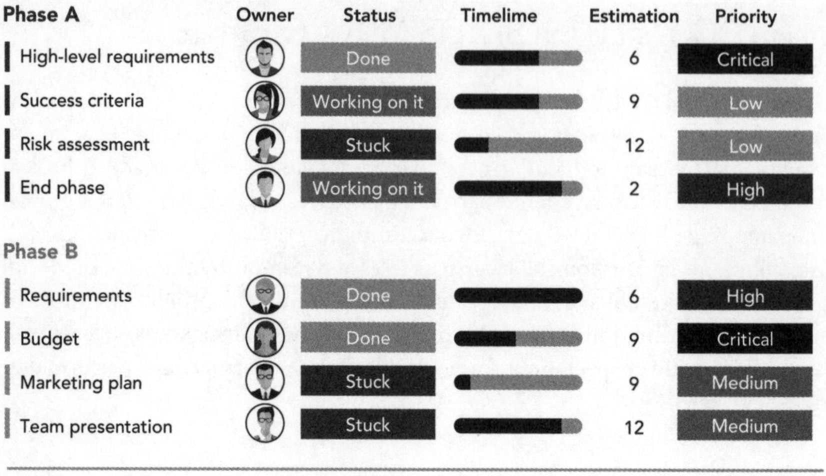

Phase A	Owner	Status	Timeline	Estimation	Priority
High-level requirements		Done		6	Critical
Success criteria		Working on it		9	Low
Risk assessment		Stuck		12	Low
End phase		Working on it		2	High

Phase B					
Requirements		Done		6	High
Budget		Done		9	Critical
Marketing plan		Stuck		9	Medium
Team presentation		Stuck		12	Medium

FIGURE 5.6 Here's a sample RACI matrix.

DJ Waldo, "What You Need to Know About the RACI Matrix (+ Examples)," mondayproject, monday.com, September 13, 2020, https://monday.com/blog/project-management/raci-matrix-with-examples/.

When designing a potential partnership, test and understand what makes your partnerships successful and then commit to doing your part. Carefully consider how you onboard and train your new partners and take care to create a relevant and robust flow of promotions, campaigns, and content to keep partners engaged and successful.

The Quick Summary

- Six building blocks comprise today's partnerships: compatible partners, relevant audiences, a desirable customer experience, a motivating value exchange, an accurate tracking and measurement system, and a shared partnerships success plan.

- Compatible partners have complementary business objectives; they enable each partner to tap into the qualities of the other. They also have a solid brand fit, endorsement credibility, a proven ability to collaborate, and the desire to work together.

- Similar or shared customers and audiences are at the center of today's partnerships. Partners need to have established and trusted relationships with an enterprise's target customers to work effectively as introductory or influence partners. It's important to evaluate the size of a partner's accessible audience to determine whether the partnership's potential impact is commensurate with the effort required to bring it to life.

- Partners come together to create a desirable customer experience for their similar or shared customers. When evaluating a potential partnership, consider the unique or attractive value proposition that this partnership will create for its shared customers and audiences—is it compelling? What specific customer behaviors will the experience be designed to catalyze and do these behaviors enable the enterprise to meet its business objective?

- Effective partnerships have motivating value exchanges. It's important that the benefit, effort, resources contributed, and risk are equivalent for both parties. Many of today's partnerships are designed on a performance basis—partners are paid when agreed-upon micro and macro conversions take place.

- Tracking and measurement systems enable an enterprise and its partners to evaluate the effectiveness of their partnerships. Tracking often takes place through live links and promotion codes. Sharing partnership performance data enables partnerships to naturally become right priced, enabling the enterprise to pay for the value it receives and for its partners to be compensated fairly and accurately for the influence they have.

- A shared partnerships success plan recognizes that both parties need to commit to making a partnership successful. This plan clearly defines each task, milestone, and responsibility; assigns roles and responsibilities associated with each effort; and establishes an expected timeline. It identifies dependencies and where coordination is necessary, and establishes clear expectations for how and when the partnership's performance will be reviewed.

What's Up Next?

That's it for the first part of this book—welcome to the partner economy! The next part, "What Are Modern Partners?," describes six major types of modern partners more fully.

Notes

[1] Dennis Moore, "Harry's Razors Review," The Gadgeteer, December 4, 2016, **http://bit.ly/ harrys-razors-review**.

[2] "Harry's Razor Blades for Men," TechSmith screencast, accessed May 12, 2021, **http://bit .ly/harrys-razors-screencast**.

[3] Shep Hyken, "Businesses Lose $75 Billion Due to Poor Customer Service," *Forbes*, May 12, 2018, **http://bit.ly/poor-service-billions-lost**.

[4] "Tom Dixon's Touchy Feely Razor Bar ft. Harry's Razors," Tom Dixon, accessed May 12, 2021, **http://bit.ly/tom-dixon-harrys-razors**.

[5] "Shave with Pride Set," Harry's, accessed May 12, 2021, **http://bit.ly/harrys-pride-set**.

[6] "What You Need to Know About the RACI Matrix (+ examples)," DJ Waldow, *Monday Blog*, September 13, 2020, **http://bit.ly/know-raci-matrix**.

PART II

What Are Modern Partners?

CHAPTER 6

Coupon, Cashback, and Loyalty Partners: Reach New Audiences, Drive More Sales

botta is a mobile app and browser extension that promises to give its users one big thing: cash back on their purchases. It's free and easy to use. Before users shop, they set up a personal Ibotta account through which cashback offers will flow. Next, they open the Ibotta app and select "find offers." This action activates relevant offers from participating merchants that can be used for online or in-store purchases. Sometimes users are asked to watch a video or complete a survey before the offer is extended. Then the shopping begins! Whenever users make a future purchase they're rewarded for their purchase with cash back into their account. The cash can add up quickly. The average active Ibotta user earns between $10 and $20 a month, but some earn as much as $100 to $300 a month.[1]

Ibotta began with the vision of helping consumers earn cash back on groceries and everyday purchases. Today, the company's mission has evolved to "make every purchase rewarding." Ibotta works with more than 1,500 enterprises and brands, giving its users the opportunity to earn cash back on purchases ranging from

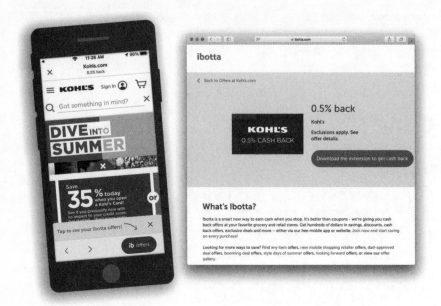

FIGURE 6.1 The Ibotta app generates sales for Kohl's.

groceries to clothing to electronics. The company says it has paid more than $860 million in cash rewards to more than 35 million users since it was founded in 2012.[2]

With so many active, engaged users turning to the app to make everyday purchases, Ibotta is a great partner for enterprises looking to reach new audiences, drive more sales, and generate additional revenue from existing customers. When the retailer Kohl's was looking to engage with budget-friendly, fashionable consumers, Ibotta was a natural choice because it has so many price-conscious customers.

When Ibotta users log into the app they are served relevant offers. If they ultimately choose and redeem a Kohl's offer, Kohl's pays a commission to Ibotta for that lead or sale. A portion of this commission is paid to users in the form of cash back on their purchase (Figure 6.1). The partnership helps Kohl's find new budget-conscious customers, rewards Ibotta through commissions, and is ultimately beneficial to Kohl's shoppers looking to save.

Tried and True: Partnerships That Drive Revenue

Coupon, cashback, rewards, and loyalty sites and apps are some of the oldest, most well-established forms of performance-based partnerships. Quite often, they're referred to as "affiliate" partnerships because many of them have been around since the early days of affiliate marketing, the original term for performance-based structured partnerships. Many of these sites often fit into two or all three categories—they offer their users coupons, deals, and loyalty points—which is why I've often considered them together here. However, the following definitions can be used.

> **Coupon and Deals.** The partner promotes a brand by offering discount codes or highlighting promotional deals on its websites or apps. These partners often require people to create accounts and log in to access special offers, and brands can work directly with the sites to provide customized offers and codes. Examples include **coupons.com**, **couponcause.com**, Frugga, Groupon, Living Social, Hip2Save, RetailMeNot, Krazy Coupon Lady, Smart Source, and **Savings.com**. Note that many publishers and media houses are also in the coupon business; some, like **CNN.com**, have their own coupon sections on their websites.

> **Cashback and Rewards.** These partners offer consumers cash back or rewards for purchases made through their interfaces. In some cases, consumers are able to apply their cash to a savings account for college (e.g., Upromise) or the nonprofit of their choice (e.g., Giving Assistant). Examples include Rakuten, Ibotta, TopCashback, BeFrugal, MyPoints, Extrabux, Lemoney, Mr. Rebates, Capital One Shopping, RebatesMe, and Honey.

> **Loyalty.** Customer loyalty programs reward customers who repeatedly interact with a partner's brand. These rewards can include credit card points, which banks give out for purchases made with some of their cards, such as the Chase Sapphire Rewards card. This category also includes frequent flyer miles, which are common with airlines; hotel points; and even branded rewards programs, like My Coke Rewards and Pepsi Stuff. Customers earn points or other benefits that can be redeemed for discounts, products, or other insider perks. Loyalty programs are customer retention strategies that encourage customers to keep coming back rather than go to competitors.

Popular Then and Now

Coupons have been around for more than a century, and they've been effective for just as long. Coca-Cola invented the coupon in 1887, offering a free sample of the one-year-old soft drink.[3] In 1895—eight years later—executives bragged that Coke was a nationwide hit. Its popularity has remained strong. In 2020, 88 percent of survey respondents in the United States stated that they had used coupons for shopping.[4] Coupons are popular around the world, as evidenced by the fact that approximately 31 billion digital coupons were redeemed worldwide in 2019.[5] The top reason cited for using coupons was "because it lets them buy the items they always use at a better price."[6]

Although there are still coupon sections in the Sunday newspaper, people increasingly employ digital coupons to receive discounts. In the United States, 52 percent of internet users use digital coupons.[7] Mobile apps like Ibotta are the top source for people looking for coupons in the United States[8]—30 percent of U.S. consumers have installed an app to receive and manage coupons and searched for coupons using a browser.[9] By the end of 2021, the number of digital coupon users in the United States will top 145.3 million.[10]

Who doesn't love a little extra cash? This is precisely what cashback partners offer consumers. An evolution from mail-in rebates, cashback sites and apps provide consumers with the ability to know ahead of time how much they will receive back on a purchase with a given brand. Cashback can take the form of free shipping, a free membership, a percentage of the total purchase price, or a flat sum. Some cashback sites offer rewards for taking surveys, watching videos, or other desired actions. The cashback site or app receives a commission from the brand that, after a purchase is confirmed, is shared with the customer who made the purchase. Research shows that cashback payments increase the likelihood that consumers will return to the cashback site or app for additional purchases, and it also increases the size of their purchases.[11]

Loyalty programs also have a history going back decades and are now ubiquitous in consumers' lives. The *New York Times Magazine* estimated that a customer "might encounter half a dozen opportunities to accrue loyalty points" each day, "from morning coffee (Starbucks Rewards) to daily commute (Exxon Mobil Rewards+) to lunch break (Chipotle Rewards) to after-work errands (CVS Extra-Care points) to date night (Regal Cinema's Crown Club)."[12] Less than 8 percent of consumers say rewards are not at all important to their purchasing decisions, according to the Wirecard 2019 Consumer Incentives report.[13] And according to Accenture, there are 3.3 billion loyalty memberships in the United States alone.[14] What's the attraction? Fifty percent of loyalty program users say their primary reason for joining is to earn rewards for everyday purchases.[15]

The Value Proposition: Incentivizing Engagement

As we have seen, coupon, cashback, and loyalty partnerships attract customers through the opportunity to save money or be rewarded for their purchase. The value-add of coupon and deal sites is the ability to source great deals and aggregate them for their users in a way that is simple to use. Interested shoppers become members of a site by signing up for an account, which allows them to make purchases either online or in store. Shoppers can peruse offers in several ways—by retailer, category, or product—depending on how granular their search. When they shop by retailer, customers can often see all of the deals that are currently available from that retailer. If users shop by product, they can review several brands' offerings for a type of product. If their interest is piqued and they want to make a purchase, they can do so in several ways: direct in-app purchases, downloading coupons, and scanning or uploading receipts.

Whenever customers make purchases through these sites, the partners themselves are rewarded for their influence with a commission from the enterprise making the offer. These sites in turn split some portion of their commission with the consumer, generating the cash reward or, in some cases, a proprietary point system (such as Swagbucks' points system). These "cash" rewards can take many forms, including gift cards, corporate scrip (promotion points, etc.), a bank check, or a payment via a platform like PayPal. Rewards generally take a few days to weeks or months to complete, as both the affiliate site and the brand must verify the sale.

Enterprises, Affiliates, and the Customer Journey

Enterprises employ affiliate partners to reach their target customers and to provide them with a call to action, giving potential purchasers a reason to purchase—now. Coupon and loyalty sites have traditionally been viewed as closing partners (the consumer has already decided to make a purchase and is now looking for the best deal). The customer journey map shown in Figure 6.2 illustrates this often-told story. This shopper had 10 interactions over the course of 23 hours, which commenced with an introduction by a social influencer that built awareness; led to interactions with bloggers, publishers, and a comparison site that helped drive

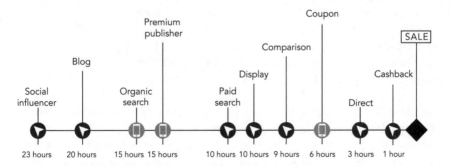

FIGURE 6.2   Coupon and cashback sites traditionally have been closing partners.

consideration; and, finally, prompted visits to a coupon site and a cashback site before a sale was ultimately completed.

This last-click positioning has raised questions of incrementality: Would these sales have taken place without a coupon, cashback, and loyalty program in place? Proving incrementality is a common practice with search and display channels, and has more recently been implemented as a key performance metric across partnerships programs. The rationale: enterprises don't want to pay a commission on sales that were already in the door.

In recent years, these partners have expanded their remit, expanding their impact from the point of sale to across the customer journey, from awareness, through conversion, and on to repurchase and loyalty. They can do this because they are brands in their own right, with loyal followers—in fact, their users are often referred to as members. These members check in with the sites regularly to see what deals are on, especially before making a purchase. Many of these sites have also become publishers, creating content for their members in much the same way mass media partners do for their audiences.

Expanding their remit has increased their value to their members and to the enterprises with whom they work. The fresher and more robust the content and the offers these partners make available, the more often their members check in and are likely to find a reason to buy.

What's more, coupon, cashback, and loyalty rewards have proven to be quite good at motivating customers to try new brands, making them powerful customer acquisition strategies for enterprises and powerful retention strategies for partners. More than 70 percent of Gen Z and Gen X respondents to a 2018 CrowsTwist survey said that they could be persuaded to choose one brand over another due to the presence of a loyalty program.[16] About one-third of consumers said they would be willing to shop at a new store if presented with a cashback offer,[17] and nearly 20 percent of consumers surveyed said they had made a purchase or spent more than planned because of a cashback offer in the previous 12 months. Clearly the savings matter, as 47 percent of consumers surveyed said they would be willing to make a purchase with the ability to combine a coupon with a cashback offer.[18]

In addition to better serving their members, having a broader impact on enterprise customer journeys benefits enterprises. The reach of these partners is considerable, and their ability to use their own data to personalize product recommendations to their members makes their influence strong on purchase decisions early in the journey. They are also strong digital wallets for members, which is making them a starting point for shopping. This means that in addition to serving as closing partners, they are also acting in the capacity of introductory partners and retention partners. They are often able to shorten enterprise customer journeys because of their all-in-one nature—they can go from tapping into a consumer's interest to a sale in one shopping experience. Broader influence enables these partners to enjoy larger commissions, as they are able to earn commissions for introducing, influencing, and closing.

But We Are Not a Discount Brand!

In the past, brands may have considered partnering with coupon, cashback, and loyalty sites to be risky—out of fear of being perceived as a discount brand. However, not partnering with these brands actually carries greater risk. First and foremost, brands may miss out on opportunities that are greatly benefiting their competition. Second, these sites can still feature a brand and promote its sales or products, but without a partnership in place they have no obligation to adhere to brand guidelines. It's far better to develop a working relationship that gives enterprises both access to this audience and control over the message.

Importantly, brands do not have to discount their products to successfully participate on these sites or apps as long as they make their offer compelling in some other way. One option is to offer free shipping, or free shipping on orders that reach a certain dollar threshold, or free shipping when complementary purchases are made (think computer, printer, and flash drives). By doing so, instead of discounting their products, enterprises are actually increasing their average order values.

Brands that choose not to partner with discount-based affiliates often feel comfortable partnering with rewards-/loyalty-based brands. This is because rather than giving a discount, an enterprise can reward shoppers with points or other forms of digital currency that have value for them. The enterprise sees itself as providing additional value to consumers, not discounting its products. There is strong evidence that this strategy works. According to a survey conducted by Wirecard, 75 percent of consumers report that they are more likely to make another purchase after receiving a loyalty reward.[19] What's more, according to Bond's 2019 Loyalty Report, members of top-performing loyalty programs are 77 percent more likely to choose that brand over the competition.[20]

There Is More Than Meets the Eye

Coupon, cashback, and loyalty sites and apps are data machines, which provide them with powerful targeting capabilities as well as the ability to generate valuable consumer insights. Take Prodege, for example. The company's family of consumer loyalty websites, including Swagbucks, My Points, Shoply, Couponcause, Upromise, and others, enables it to reach more than 100,000 active engaged users across multiple channels (Figure 6.3). This combination of sites makes it possible for Prodege to drive enterprise sales online, offline, or a combination of both through a variety of methods, wherever customers prefer to shop. Brands or specific products can be featured in newsletters, emails, and social media, on its blog, and via direct placements on its sites, which gives it an advantage over its competition. Another fun and engaging option for brands is to participate in Swagbucks Live, the live trivia game show where consumers can earn cash for answering questions.

FIGURE 6.3 Prodege offers a full suite of products.

Questions range from "What is your favorite Disney musical?"—which gave winners a subscription to the Disney+ channel—to "What is the perfect cocktail for Labor Day weekend?"—which was sponsored by premium sparkling winemaker Chandon. Incentives can be designed to prompt any number of shopping behaviors, and awards can be made in digital currencies or cash.

Prodege's member-based model offers enterprises sophisticated targeting capabilities. Want to reach new customers who fit a certain profile? No problem. Prodege has lookalike and propensity modeling capabilities that can identify potential customers who meet your success criteria and who are also likely to respond to a given offer. Want to target customers with a particular shopping history? That can be accomplished, too. Prefer to customize outreach to your own customer base, perhaps to activate lapsed customers who previously spent over a certain dollar threshold? Simple.

Tips for Getting the Most Out of Coupon, Deal, and Loyalty Sites

Here's what I recommend for successful relationships within this type of partnership:

> **Track every touchpoint.** Knowledge is power, and it's only through tracking that you can truly assess a partner's performance. Make sure you're tracking everything from clicks to site to intermediate success events so you can understand the full impact your affiliate partners are having and compensate them accordingly.

Use metrics that determine incrementality. With tracking in place, it's much easier to monitor the important metrics. First and foremost, most enterprises measure return on ad spend (ROAS). But don't stop there. It's important to determine the incrementality of each partner to determine which ones are the most important contributors to your program. Tracking incrementality means going deeper, looking at more granular measures such as new customers acquired; partner's uniqueness factor (their ability to take consumers through the entire buyer journey without assistance from other partners or marketing tools); how much revenue partners assist in closing, even if they are not the last click; profit margin; and other metrics that are critical to achieving your business goals. For more information, see *Always Be Growing: Optimize Your Partnerships and Partnerships Program* at **www.thepartnershipsbook. com/resources**.

Manage deduplication. It's important to give partners the credit they deserve for a sale or conversion, but you don't want to inadvertently pay two partners or two channels because you're using two different partner tracking systems. Avoid a conversion conundrum by using a system that looks across all channels and deduplicates your touchpoints.

Lock down promo codes. One of the biggest issues with coupon and cashback sites is the misuse of promo codes. Public codes are designed for everyone. Private codes, on the other hand, are designed to target a specific partner or consumer. Restricted codes are reserved for a targeted single user and can only be used once. They are generally used as a thank-you or an apology from a brand—"you just made your tenth purchase" or "sorry your shipment was delayed." Misuse of promo codes happens when they are used by people other than those for whom they were intended. Consistent promo code policies lead to more accurate data and make managing programs much easier. Set custom rules and parameters so you can ensure that only the original owner of the promo code will receive credit for sales made with the code. Then make sure that you are monitoring coupon code usage by comparing the unique coupon code with the actual referring domain to make sure the latter is the partner for whom it was intended.

Tips for Coupon, Cashback, and Loyalty Partners

Stay up to date. As a partner, success (and resulting payouts) often comes down to demonstrating ROI. Just as enterprises need to monitor and control their promo codes, partners need to make sure that they are sharing the most up-to-date offers, sales, and promo codes. Sharing an inaccurate or out-of-date offer isn't helpful for the enterprise; therefore, it isn't good for the partner, either. Partners should work closely with the enterprise to ensure that all of the promotions are as up to date as possible.

Communicate and engage. Enterprises are using partnerships because they want to grow their business. They want these programs to succeed and deliver a high ROI. If partners have ideas or strategies about how to help enterprises perform better on their site, they should feel free to share them! Partners should keep an eye on their performance, so that if they are exceeding their goals, they can command more enterprise focus or negotiate better payout terms. Remember, these are partnerships, so the more united they are, the better the experience for all.

The Quick Summary

- The concept of coupons is just as effective now as it was in the late 1800s—maybe even more so.

- Customers have infinite choices for rewards and loyalty point programs, ranging from credit cards to fast casual dining to their pharmacy. When crafting a new loyalty-based partnership, think about how it will fit into your target audience's life, and how it will add value.

- Identify ways that you can use coupon, discount, and loyalty partners across the customer journey, rather than simply at the point of purchase. Many of these partners have grown their own brands, and, as a result, can play a critical role in engaging with consumers throughout the sales process.

- Affiliate partners are data machines. Work closely with them to learn even more about your target audience, and use those insights to power your overall partnership strategy.

- The idea of the "discount brand" is a thing of the past. Odds are that your competitor is using a modern coupon, deal, and loyalty program to reach new customers. At the same time, partnering directly with these entities lets you control the interactions and messaging.

What's Up Next?

This chapter covered the modern iteration of a well-established, tried-and-true partnership type. The next chapter takes a look at a newer partnership type: creators, influencers, and brand ambassadors who are eager to work with enterprises through a powerful new word-of-mouth play.

Notes

[1] Alexandria White, "Ibotta Has Paid Out Over $860 Million in Cash Rewards to Date— Here's How to Start Saving," CNBC, revised January 29, 2021, **https://www.cnbc.com/ select/ibotta-review/**.

[2] "About Ibotta," **ibotta.com**, accessed May 12, 2021, **https://home.ibotta.com/about/**.

[3] Kim Gittleson, "The First Coupon," *The Lodown by The Leonard Lopate Show*, June 17, 2011, **https://www.wnyc.org/story/141353-first-coupon/**.

[4] "Consumers Who Ever Use Coupons for Shopping in the United States from 2017 to 2020," Statista Research Department, December 18, 2020, **http://bit.ly/coupon-use-us**.

[5] Evangelina Chapkanovska, "Coupon Statistics: Is Couponing Growing or Slowing?," SpendMeNot, revised May 4, 2021, **https://spendmenot.com/blog/coupon-statistics/**.

[6] Alexander Kunst, "Reasons U.S. Consumers Used Coupons in 2016," Statista, September 3, 2019, **http://bit.ly/why-coupons**.

[7] Tugba Sabanoglu, "Percentage of Adult Internet Users in the United States Who Use Digital Coupons from 2015 to 2021," Statista, November 30, 2020, **http://bit.ly/users-digital-coupons**.

[8] "Where Do You Typically Look for Coupons?," Statista Research Department, February 26, 2016, **http://bit.ly/places-consumers-look-coupons**.

[9] Alexander Kunst, "Mobile Device Usage for Couponing According to Users in the United States as of August 2016," Statista, September 3, 2019, **http://bit.ly/mobile-coupon-access**.

[10] Tugba Sabanoglu, "Number of Adult Digital Coupon Users in the United States from 2015 to 2021," Statista, November 30, 2020, **http://bit.ly/adult-coupon-users**.

[11] Kirk Kardashian, "Does Cashback Make Consumers Come Back?," Tuck School of Business at Dartmouth, accessed June 9, 2021, **http://bit.ly/Dartmouth-Tuck-Cashback**.

[12] Jamie Lauren Keiles, "The Man Who Turned Credit-Card Points into an Empire," *New York Times*, January 5, 2021, **http://bit.ly/credit-card-point-empire**.

[13] "Consumer Incentives 2019: The Digital Transformation of Rewards, Rebates, and Loyalty," Wirecard North America, Inc., accessed May 12, 2021, **http://bit.ly/digital-transformation-rewards**.

[14] Robert Wollan, Phil Davis, Fabio De Angelis, and Kevin Quiring, "Seeing Beyond the Loyalty Illusion: It's Time You Invest More Wisely," Accenture Strategy, accessed May 12, 2021, **https://accntu.re/3gd32zl**.

[15] "2019 Road to Rewards Report: Mapping the Path to Loyalty Success," PDI Software, accessed May 12, 2021, **http://go.pdisoftware.com/roadtorewards**.

[16] "CrowdTwist Consumer Loyalty Study Shows 87% of Gen Z Consumers Want Omnichannel Loyalty Programs," CrowdTwist via *PR Newswire*, October 11, 2018, **http://bit.ly/customer-loyalty-study**.

[17] "New Survey Finds Nearly One-Third of Consumers Would Be Willing to Shop at a New Store with a Cash Back Offer," RetailMeNot, April 6, 2017, **http://bit.ly/consumer-survey-finds**.

[18] Ibid.

[19] "Consumer Incentives 2019," Wirecard.

[20] Bond Brand Loyalty, Inc., "The Loyalty Report 2019," accessed May 12, 2021, **https://info.bondbrandloyalty.com/loyalty-report-2019**.

CHAPTER 7

Creators, Influencers, and Brand Ambassadors: The Powerful New Word-of-Mouth Play

Marla Catherine is a Utah teenager who has a unique thing going for her: she has more than 1.6 million YouTube subscribers, and her weekly videos are frequently viewed a quarter of a million times or more. Marla's videos frequently delve into the joys, anxieties, and mundanity of being a suburban Gen Z girl. Video titles include "senior year homecoming 2020: get ready with me!," "casual summer outfits for 2020!," and "talking about my insecurities + more (Q&A)." Her videos often lean heavily into shopping, style, and beauty tips, and she regularly shares clothing "hauls" after shopping trips. Her video for her back-to-school shopping haul in 2019 has more than 1 million views.

The popularity of Marla Catherine's videos makes her an influencer, meaning that her viewers turn to her for recommendations that feel authentic and real. Marla Catherine is just one of many influencers who are successfully partnering with brands that are looking to distance themselves from "traditional"-looking ad messages as they seek to drive growth.

TechStyle, an up-and-coming collection of women's fashion brands, is one of the enterprises that has partnered with Marla Catherine. Through the partnership,

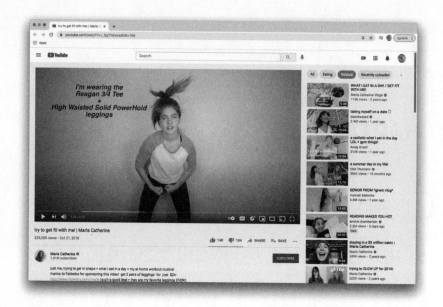

FIGURE 7.1 Marla Catherine recommends Fabletics to her followers.

TechStyle's Fabletics brand, which focuses on activewear and fitness clothes, is featured in Marla's videos in a way that looks and feels organic.

At the start of one video about her fitness routine and eating habits, titled "try to get fit with me!," Marla talks about the brand and how much she loves their leggings, all while wearing different pieces of apparel. Within the YouTube description, there is a vanity URL link that sends Marla's viewers to the Fabletics shopping experience to buy those leggings and other products (Figure 7.1).

This kind of relationship rewards influencers like Marla Catherine for the audience she has built on her own and also brings a level of authenticity that is absent from staid traditional advertising, with its professional photo shoots and tightly controlled messaging. Marla Catherine and other influencers have built avid, engaged followings by letting their fans see their real lives. As a result, promotions and partnerships with brands feel more natural, and don't turn off viewers in quite the same way traditional ads do.

A Rapidly Growing Domain of Authenticity

Creators and influencers are writers, editors, photographers, bloggers, publishers, community managers, experts, and people just like us. They have something to say—an editorial position—and connect with others to talk about their shared interests. People engage with influencers for real talk about things that are of interest to them. They are looking for information that is important to them for whatever need they are trying to fill—they are not looking to be sold to. That doesn't mean that they don't enjoy product, service, or experience recommendations, however. Influencers build and maintain their followers by continually creating high-quality, useful, authentic, and relevant content for them.

Influencers are active on social media (the most active are Instagram, Facebook, YouTube, Twitter, TikTok, Pinterest, Twitch, and Snapchat), blogs, and may even have their own podcasts. Because consumer behavior is always changing, new platforms emerge and fall away, giving rise to new generations of influencers.

Influencers are a popular form of referral partnerships for enterprises because they tend to be trendsetters or authorities on subjects, and as a result, they are able to generate demand for enterprises' products, services, and experiences. This makes them particularly successful in building brand awareness and reengagement.

The connection influencers have with their followers also feels quite personal, infusing authenticity into brand messaging, allowing enterprises to reach buyers through the content creators they relate to most. Their recommendations and endorsements, even if paid, carry the weight of a word-of-mouth recommendation from a friend or trusted confidant. Whereas 84 percent of millennials don't like advertising or trust it,[1] and 25 percent of consumers don't believe advertising anymore,[2] they *do* trust influencers: 49 percent of people admit to relying on recommendations from influencers when making purchasing decisions.[3] These don't need to be big celebrities, either; 82 percent of consumers are highly likely to follow a recommendation from a micro-influencer[4]—that is, someone with between 10,000 and 1 million followers.

More than two-thirds of marketers employ influencers and this number is expected to increase. eMarketer forecasts that 72.5 percent of U.S. brands with 100 or more employees will use influencers for paid or unpaid brand partnerships by 2022.[5] This means that influencer marketing will grow to a market size of $13.8 billion.[6]

Influencer partnerships generate opportunities for influencers as well. They often provide influencers with the chance to try out new products and services that they may enjoy at no cost and can choose to recommend to their audiences. Referral partnerships also enable influencers to generate income from their work without having to deviate from their core output. They don't have to become an ad sales expert—they can simply be themselves and speak to products and services that they know and use, in the same voice their followers have come to trust. As influencer Mike Perry, Broad City Designer, explains, "As long as I get to do my thing and someone wants to write me a check for it, I'm all about it."[7]

Three Ways to Use Influencer Partnerships

Influencer partnerships may be used by a majority of enterprises, but that doesn't mean that each enterprise uses its partnerships for the same reasons. The way that enterprises use influencers often depends on what they want to accomplish. What works in one situation will not necessarily work in another, so enterprises must be adaptable if they want to produce results. Here are some of the key ways to utilize influencers:

- **Brand awareness.** Quality content can drive traffic and engagement early in enterprise customer journeys. Micro-influencers are often able to reach highly targeted customer segments that often escape other methods.

- **Customer reengagement.** Influencer content can also prompt reengagement by keeping brands top-of-mind with enterprise target customers. This may take the form of articles and photos of new products as well as videos of how to assemble or get more out of purchases.

- **Repurposed content.** Enterprises can repurpose successful influencer content in their own content or on their websites and mobile apps. This content provides third-party authentication, social proof, and useful tips surrounding potential purchases that can enhance an enterprise's customer experience and conversion rates.

Many enterprises eventually develop long-term relationships with influencers, employing them on an evergreen basis or intermittently throughout the year, depending on current trends, seasonality, and the products they are promoting, effectively turning their campaign-based relationship into a true influencer partnership.[8]

LightInTheBox Taps Micro-Influencers for Content

LightInTheBox is a global online retail company that delivers products directly to consumers around the world. Founded in 2007, LightInTheBox offers customers a convenient way to shop for a wide selection of lifestyle products at attractive prices (Figure 7.2).

The brand saw the value of influencers, but could only execute 10–20 placements a month given how time-consuming it was to find, recruit, negotiate, track, and aggregate them. It wanted to grow its program globally, but needed to do so in a scalable fashion.

Light in thebox.com

FIGURE 7.2   LightInTheBox taps micro-influencers to promote its brand.

By using automation technology, LightInTheBox automated its recruiting, negotiation, tracking, and aggregation. That helped the brand build a program that generated more than 200 placements a month and leveraged influencer-generated assets across social media, email, and the website's product pages. As a result, LightInTheBox saw better content, lower costs, and higher engagement. Conversion rates were up 15 percent on product pages enriched with influencers' content compared to the same product pages without enrichment.[9]

Nurture Influencer Partnerships for Better Results

The first step is to identify your audience and find influencer partners that reach them. Many brands make the mistake of going for the biggest influencers with the highest volume of followers, when actually what they need is a more targeted approach. For example, travel brands targeting students would want to include a broad range of influencers who speak to different kinds of students. Macro-influencers have big followings, but that scale means that there are plenty of followers who fall well outside a brand's target. Smaller micro-influencers may be a better fit, because they speak directly to the audience you're after.

Next, stay in touch with your influencers to build long-term relationships. Keep an ongoing flow of information about company news, programs, and upcoming campaigns so they can be knowledgeable about your organization. Offer them exclusive content and encourage them to create their own that, if successful, can be repurposed in other channels. And always be honest and responsive with influencers.

Give influencers time and space to succeed. Influencer relationships can also take time to mature. Don't have big expectations straight away. Instead, give them time to do their thing. Influencers know their audience and know how to reach them authentically, which is why you're turning to them in the first place. Toward this end, encourage influencers to talk about *your* brand and products with *their* voice. It's important to let influencers shape their own content to be able to "preserve the authenticity of what is being communicated."[10] This is a key point of differentiation from traditional marketing, where brands have full control over the narrative.

If things aren't necessarily going well, consider a number of different approaches for engaging with the influencer. Here's a spin on Dr. Gary Chapman's five love languages:

1. **Words of affirmation.** Positive feedback and encouragement go a long way.
2. **Gifts.** Deploy a payment model and rewards based on good performance.
3. **Acts of service.** Show you care and offer support along the way.
4. **Quality time.** Make your influencers feel special and check in throughout the campaign.
5. **Physical touch.** Set up regular communication channels so that you're in touch and able to help if problems arise.[11]

Track influencer performance. Be sure to track influencer performance so you know how influencers are impacting your target customers and so that you can work with them to optimize their efforts. Remember, the value of influencer partnerships is not in scale or follower count, it's in *return*. Comments, likes, shares—these are vanity metrics. They're the same as earned media, which can be valuable but may be perceived as arbitrary. Instead, measure your key performance metrics, treating influencers as true partners.

There is ample room here for opportunity, as the majority of influencers have not yet been incentivized to be focused on ROI. A recent study revealed that only 7.5 percent of influencers prioritize ROI for their brand partners.[12] Two short stories follow on how two apparel companies, Ivory Ella and Savage X Fenty, employ tracking and performance-based compensation to grow their influencer partnerships programs.

Ivory Ella Grows Brand Awareness

Ivory Ella offers high-quality apparel and gear and makes people feel good—in other words, good clothes for a good cause. All in the name of elephants (Figure 7.3). Ivory Ella wanted to reach new audiences through its partnership program and leverage

FIGURE 7.3   Ivory Ella rapidly scales its influencer program.

influencers more efficiently. The brand brought its existing micro-influencers onto a single platform, and then went to work finding new partners.

By using robust promo code tracking, Ivory Ella was able to scale its program rapidly, with better tracking that helped attribute sales to each influencer partner even if those partners weren't using tracking links. It also grouped its influencer partners and managed each segment differently to take advantage of the different ways each segment added value to its program. The results were 11 percent of revenue coming through partnerships and a 19x ROAS.[13]

Savage X Fenty Succeeds with an Influencer-First Model

TechStyle, the company behind Fabletics, which I talked about earlier in the context of YouTube influencer Marla Catherine, knew of the value of influencers, but it wanted to shift its strategy. It had succeeded with a strategy of using celebrity influencers for big campaigns and using micro-influencers, who were given products in exchange for posts. What the company didn't have covered was a middle ground where influencers were paid to post and promote products. Jennine Matthias was tasked with leading this expansion for TechStyle's Savage X Fenty brand, for which she is director of influencer marketing.

Savage X Fenty used a performance-based model in this expansion to ensure that the money spent on influencers was going toward hitting sales targets. "Brands have realized it's more than a brand awareness play," says Matthias. She sees smart brands understanding that influencer partnerships can be a performance channel as much as a branding channel. "People are getting more weary of spending on influencers and having it not be measurable, so I think that's the direction it's headed in," she says.[14]

Savage X Fenty's influencers are also an incredibly important part of the company's content strategy. "They're the best content creators," Matthias says of her influencer partners, whose content regularly appears in paid media campaigns on channels like Instagram. The brand will regularly use influencers who have relatively small follower counts, and finds that the creative still resonates because it feels more authentic.

With such a heavy focus on influencers, it's critical that the channel is recognized for the sales it drives. Savage X Fenty has a multitouch attribution model it can use to determine the sales that its influencers have a hand in, but a big part of that understanding actually comes from customers themselves. At checkout, Savage X Fenty asks customers how they heard of the brand; people frequently answer that it was from an influencer. Often, they'll even include the influencer's name, making it much easier to determine which partners are driving value.

Matthias's advice for getting started with influencers is to have the program run in-house. "It's so valuable to have someone who works for the brand and really understands the brand be the advocate and look for those influencers, rather than hiring an agency who might not have the same exact understanding or interests." She also recommends starting slow, and spending time on social platforms to find the best possible partners. "The key is starting out slowly and building gradually, rather than going out and signing a million people." Armed with this advice and a performance-driven approach, enterprises can emulate the Savage X Fenty model for success.

If You Are an Influencer

If you're an influencer looking to build more partnerships with brands, think about the products that you already use and love on a regular basis. What do you love about these brands, and what will your audience love about them? The best kinds of partnerships occur when an influencer truly believes in the companies they are recommending. Your audience can detect authenticity, and they'll trust you more when it's clear you're telling the truth.

It's important for brands and influencers to have constant two-way communication. If your brand partner isn't making its goals clear to you, ask for a more precise direction. The best way to grow a relationship and succeed as an influencer partner is to help carry out the brand's vision and help it with its business goals.

For influencers looking to grow their partner base, partnership platforms offer a great point of entry. Influencers can list themselves on these platforms and share some details about their content, audience, and expertise, and brands that are searching for new influencer partners can find them more easily. This also helps ensure that the brands that find you as an influencer are more in line with your interests.

Customers Are Brand Ambassadors

Customers who are already passionate about your brand or cause, who are willing to share your brand story or message, can be highly effective brand ambassadors. Testimonials by happy customers are a clear source of social proof and can be incorporated into enterprise customer acquisition efforts. Customers can also be critical partners in helping enterprises innovate. Who can better provide an "in the field" proof of concept and also create momentum and support for new products before launch? A company's customers can also be a great source of competitive information. Important insights can be gleaned from asking: What is it that you really like about our brand? What are we doing well? Where could we improve?

Over 90 outdoor enthusiasts are part of Patagonia's ambassador program. These are actual users of Patagonia's products, not just well-known names. These athletes' interests and outdoor activities overlap with Patagonia's main areas of focus: climbing, fly fishing, snowboarding, trail running, kite surfing, and more. Patagonia's ambassadors are part of the company's new product development and customer engagement efforts. Ambassadors test, refine, and validate products in the field. They also produce content for Patagonia's blog and social media accounts, capturing moments when they are doing their thing.

Enterprises have to nurture satisfied customers into becoming brand ambassadors because these referrals and insights don't organically happen at scale. A recent study conducted by Advisor Impact, Charles Schwab Advisor Services, and Texas Tech University of satisfied customers utilizing the services of financial advisors found that while 93 percent of people surveyed said they were likely to continue to work with their financial advisor, only 29 percent gave a referral in the previous 12 months.[15]

In support of this goal, get clear about your goals and objectives: What are you trying to accomplish with brand ambassadors? How will your brand benefit from a brand ambassador program and how will potential ambassadors benefit from an association with you? Understand who comprises your ideal ambassadors. Be clear on the value you place on their involvement and on their commitment. What do you want them to do and not do? As with all referral partnerships, stay in touch with brand ambassadors, keeping them abreast of company developments and repurposing successful content in your other channels.

The Quick Summary

- Influencers are writers, editors, photographers, bloggers, publishers, community managers, experts, and, most importantly, people just like us. Their power comes from the authentic way they communicate their viewpoint, which helps them connect with their followers.

- Don't think about influencers strictly in terms of reach. Micro-influencers, with as few as 10,000 followers, are still highly trusted and can serve as strong brand advocates to their loyal followers.

- The important thing about influencer relationships is tapping into trust. They've built a following through being true to themselves, so the partnerships that will work best are those that align with their passions.

- Take a more personalized approach to influencer relationships from the outset, nurturing connections with these partners so that the relationships are more likely to grow and stay stable in the future.

- Influencer relationships can also take time to mature. Don't have big expectations straight away. Instead, give the influencer time and editorial space to do their thing.

- Don't overlook your satisfied customers who can serve as powerful brand ambassadors. Ambassadors generate social proof and can also be key partners in innovation.

What's Up Next?

Now that you have your head around the fast-growing and ever-evolving world of creators, influencers, and brand ambassadors, it's time to kick it old school. The next chapter looks at mass media publishers, which you're likely familiar with from paid advertising and PR efforts, and explores how these companies have adapted to challenging times to grow *their* revenue through partnerships—and how they can help you do the same.

Notes

[1] Andrew Arnold, "Millennials Hate Ads but 58% of Them Wouldn't Mind if It's from Their Favorite Digital Stars," *Forbes*, January 21, 2018, **http://bit.ly/millenials-add-preference**.

[2] Ramona Sukhraj, "7 Must-Have Word-of-Mouth Marketing Strategies [Infographic]," **IMPACT**, April 18, 2021, **http://bit.ly/seven-marketing-strategies**.

[3] Eric Burgess, "Recommendations from Influencers Rival That of Friends," ion.co, accessed May 13, 2021, **https://www.ion.co/twitter-has-released-a-report-showing-consumers-seek-product-recommendations-from-influencers-almost-as-much-as-they-do-from-friends**.

[4] Helen Langan, "Research Shows Micro-influencers Drive Consumer Buying Behavior at Much Higher Rates Than Previously Thought," *Expert Voice*, October 29, 2019, **http://bit.ly/value-of-micro-influencers**.

[5] Debra Aho Williamson, "More Than Two-Thirds of U.S. Marketers Will Use Influencer Marketing," *eMarketer*, January 12, 2021, **http://bit.ly/marketers-use-influencer-marketing**.

[6] "100 Influencer Marketing Statistics for 2021," Influencer Marketing Hub, accessed May 17, 2021, **http://bit.ly/one-hundred-influencer-statistics**.

[7] "5 Quotes to Remember from MRY's Influencer Marketing Panel," Tidal Labs, July 7, 2015, **http://bit.ly/five-quotes-influencer-markteting**.

[8] "100 Influencer Marketing Statistics for 2021," Influencer Marketing Hub.

[9] LightInTheBox, case study, Mediarails, December 2018.

[10] Forrest Cardamenis, "Influencer Marketing Needs to Prioritize Content over Commerce," *Luxury Daily*, January 27, 2016, **http://bit.ly/content-over-commerce**.

[11] Dr. Gary Chapman, *The Five Love Languages* (Chicago: Northfield Publishing, 1992).

[12] Deborah Aho Williamson, "Why Disclosure Is a Must—and How Branded Content Tools Fit In," *eMarketer*, February 18, 2018. **https://www.emarketer.com/report/influencer-marketing-2018-why-disclosure-Mmstand-how-branded-content-tools-fit/2002202**.

[13] Ivory Ella, case study, **impact.com**, accessed May 17, 2021, **http://bit.ly/impact-case-study-ivory-ella**.

[14] "Influencers by Savage X Fenty: The Channel, the Myth, the Legend," **impact.com**, accessed May 17, 2021, **http://bit.ly/influncers-savage-fenty**.

[15] IE Staff, "'Engaged' Clients Are a Great Source of Referrals for Advisors: Report," *Investment Executive*, December 8, 2010, **http://bit.ly/client-satisfaction-loyalty**.

CHAPTER 8

Mass Media Publishers: When Old-School Advertising Doesn't Work Anymore

Ziff Media Group (ZMG) is one of the largest names in online publishing, with more than 100 million readers visiting its digital properties around the world each month. The digital media company produces and distributes content related to three core verticals: technology, gaming, and shopping. Its publications include *PCMag*, *Mashable*, IGN, and TechBargains. ZMG's large publishing portfolio enables the publisher to facilitate consumer touchpoints across multiple verticals, at every stage of the shopping journey, and across multiple devices.

In 2011, ZMG had an "aha" moment when it recognized that a single referral link embedded in one of its articles could drive $1 million worth of sales for an enterprise. That realization kicked off a successful partnerships program for ZMG, where it would serve as the referral partner to any number of enterprises. Under this scenario, ZMG shares in a portion of the revenue that enterprises derive from its publications, a collaboration that has become known as "commerce content." Over the past decade, ZMG readers have purchased more than $1 billion of the products and services that the company's publications have recommended.

Here's an example of commerce content at work. During the 2019 FIFA Women's World Cup, ZMG worked with fuboTV to drive new subscribers to the streaming service through its digital publication, *Mashable. Mashable* readers were able to easily locate the World Cup schedule on the site, along with information on how to livestream the matches through fuboTV (Figure 8.1). At the end of the day, *Mashable* readers were able to watch the games, fuboTV gained visibility and added new subscribers, and ZMG received compensation for the subscriptions it helped to generate. A win-win-win partnership.

"It's important to understand that our customer is our first audience," explains Jessica Spira, vice president, partner growth and management at ZMG. "This is not a case of 'here is some money, now write a review.' We don't do that. Editorial and business are separated like church and state. . . . Our editors and writers don't know anything about the commission we generate."[1]

PC Mag's product reviews, for example, are lab-tested and undertaken completely independent of any monetization strategy. After reviews are published, Spira's team then gets to work on monetizing content, primarily through referral links. For brands that are not getting organic coverage but whose brand and products resonate with ZMG's consumers, Spira's team can work with them to create more branded content experiences, such as deal posts for publications like *Mashable*—"Best 8K TV deal—Upgrade to a 65-inch Samsung 8K for less than $2,700"—or push marketing email campaigns across its portfolio of publications. In this way, ZMG combines editorial expertise and service journalism with shopping insight to meet its audiences' and its partners' needs—in that order.

FIGURE 8.1 *Mashable* encourages readers to try out fuboTV.

Assuming that there is a brand and audience fit, ZMG will work closely with enterprises to develop optimal content strategies across its portfolio of publications. ZMG brands operate differently around user intent. To guide its efforts, ZMG uses what it calls the "primed consumer" framework. At one end of the journey are "enthusiasts," folks who are in discovery mode and open to seeing products and services. Further along the journey are "in-market consumers," people who have expressed purchase intent by conducting searches such as "best laptop computer." "We can take an upper down to lower-level funnel approach to drive performance and value for our partners," explains Spira, "which is one of the benefits of working with a mass media publisher."

Beyond PR and Advertising: A New Way to Work with Mass Media Publishers

Enterprises' public relations and paid advertising teams have been working with mass media publishers like *Sports Illustrated*, *PC Mag*, CNN, and the *New York Times* to reach their stakeholders for as far back as most of us can remember. Aware of potentially newsworthy moments, enterprises, or their PR agencies, would send out press releases and pitch story ideas to selected publishers with relevant audiences. If the editors agreed and ran a story, the resulting earned media would give the enterprise a third-party endorsement, enhancing its position in the marketplace. Just down the hall, the advertising team might also be working with the same publisher, although their goals, methods, and point of contact would differ. Looking to ignite consumer awareness and demand, these teams would purchase ads in the publisher's physical and digital properties in the hope of driving conversions.

These ways of collaborating worked well for a long time—and there is a place for them today as well. However, both PR and advertising face a credibility challenge that is rooted in who the message comes from. Ultimately, PR and advertising are ways that brands talk about themselves, and people today are skeptical about the claims brands make about themselves. More credible brand messaging can be delivered by partnerships. This is where commerce content comes in.

How Does Commerce Content Work?

Commerce content starts with audiences and editors. Editors from digital publishers—Meredith, Condé Nast, *BuzzFeed*, the *New York Times*' Wirecutter, CNN's *Underscored*, *Business Insider*, *Forbes*, ZMG, Vox Media—create content that they believe will resonate with the current needs and interests of their audiences.

Topics are often prompted by insights derived from ongoing analysis of the publishers' audiences, along with search engine and marketplace trends. Sometimes ideas come from the commerce team.

Content may take the form of listicles, how-tos, gift guides, editor's picks, buyer's guides, product reviews, comparison articles, new product launches, and seasonal content, which feature different enterprises' products, services, or experiences. Embedded within this content are referral links or exclusive promotion codes that enable audiences to click through to an enterprise's website or mobile app to conduct additional research, check out prices and other terms, sign up for a trial or subscription, make a purchase, or undertake any number of other agreed-upon behaviors.

When these customer behaviors take place, either immediately or in the future, the publisher that acted as the referral partner—introducing, influencing, and perhaps closing the deal—is recognized and compensated for its influence. Figure 8.2 is an example of how a publisher embedded a referral link—"$60 at fuboTV"—directly into its review of the streaming service.

Commerce content may also take the form of a shopping experience directly on the publisher's site. In this case, a site like *Better Homes & Gardens* has a designated "SHOP" section where preselected Editors' Choice products are available for purchase. Products are listed, along with the store that would actually fulfill the order should a prospective customer click through (Figure 8.3).

FIGURE 8.2 Favorable product reviews drive subscriptions.

FIGURE 8.3   *Better Homes & Gardens* Editors' Choice products.

Why Does Commerce Content Work?

Commerce content is a win-win-win for enterprises' target customers (publishers' audiences), enterprises, and publishers. Readers and viewers enjoy useful, educational content that meets their needs, whether that is in discovery of new brands and products or in evaluating potential options.

Enterprises are able to reach qualified buyers—new and existing customers who are open to exploring new options. What's more, customers discover brands and products from a trusted, third-party source rather than an ad or PR placement. The information provided may help them differentiate one product from another, or share what makes a product truly unique. This, in turn, will drive some customers to click through and take further actions. And because publishers' content contains referral links, it shortens the time and simplifies the steps between when target customers become aware of a need and when they act on that need.

Mass media publishers also have extensive omniplatform distribution and they can craft content distribution strategies to meet consumers wherever they are. Some publications may be better suited for enthusiasts, while others are designed for in-market customers. Knowing their enterprise partners' larger KPIs empowers publishers to work across their portfolios to best meet their audiences' and their partners' needs. When content performs particularly well, mass media publishers are able to quickly repackage it for alternative distribution channels. This extends the life of the content, maximizing potential sales value, and enlarges enterprises' digital footprints. Enterprises can further magnify the impact of this content by resharing on their own websites and email newsletters and bulletins, or by publishing it in other venues such as Facebook instant articles.

Another enterprise benefit of commerce content is the linking of publisher compensation to results. Instead of paying for impressions, enterprises pay for outcomes. Often enterprise KPIs are broader than sales and may include new users or clicks to store websites. Sometimes corporate budgets have restrictions—they are meant to be used for branding, not sales, for example. As a result, commerce content compensation may be constructed purely on a performance basis, on cost per click, or on a hybrid of flat fee plus performance.

What's in it for publishers? Publishers have large followings on their digital and nondigital properties that they need to continually engage with compelling content. Commerce content does this effectively. Creating relevant and actionable content for their audiences has always been their strength; generating demand for products and facilitating the consumer's transaction by conveniently directing them to where they can purchase a recommended or reviewed product, and sometimes with an exclusive deal, provides even more value to their readers and viewers—it's one-stop shopping!

The integration of content and commerce also provides a new, and needed, revenue source for publishers. Traditionally, subscriptions and advertising have funded publisher operations. Although most publishers are experiencing an increase in viewership, their ad revenue is down. There are several reasons for this, including the challenges of targeting, tracking, and measuring the effectiveness of advertising as cookies and other identifiers are disappearing, as well as the rise of ad tech such as programmatic buying, which have cut into their margins. Being compensated for the customer behaviors their content generates provides publishers with a new source of revenue. Importantly, this revenue is derived from their traditional wheelhouse—how well *their own* content performs, rather than from any fundamentally new business.

Is There a Conflict of Interest?

What about editorial bias? As seen with ZMG, editorial integrity is vital to commerce content. Although publishers are compensated for sales generated via commerce content, editorial and business teams know that the secret to their success—and very existence—is maintaining their audience's trust. While ideas may come from anywhere, including the partnerships team, to avoid any conflict of interest, writers and editors conduct their research and make their recommendations without regard to established partnership relationships. "There is transparency without influence," explains Breton Fischetti, VP of commerce at *Business Insider*.[2]

Wirecutter, a product review content site owned by the *New York Times*, explains how it handles any potential conflict of interest on its website:

> *Wirecutter is reader supported. When you buy through links on our site, we may earn an affiliate commission.*
> *The choices we've made here with our team took weeks or months of research and years of experience with a wide variety of gear. In addition to*

our own expertise, we include interviews and data from the best editorial sources around. We also employ the help of engineers, scientists, and other subject-matter experts. And we pore over customer reviews to find out what matters to regular people. Most gear we choose here isn't top-of-the-line models that are overpriced and loaded with junk features; we aim to recommend items that are of high enough quality to warrant the price, but not items that cost more for extra features you'll rarely use. These are the same gadgets we'd recommend to our friends and family, and these are the same things we'd choose for ourselves.[3]

What Matters to Content Publishers

The number-one challenge of working with commerce content, according to a recent survey conducted among **impact.com** customers, is getting the attention of publishers they want to work with for their commerce content initiatives.[4] The **impact.com** survey asked several content partners what they look for when contemplating working with brand partners. Establishing a positive working relationship is at the top of the list. Publishers often talk about brand ego—enterprises' asymmetrical approach to partnerships where they are convinced that they should call the shots and that they know their target customers better than anyone else—as a major disincentive.

Get to know each other. Publishers know their audiences in and out. They have nuanced insights into their audiences' ways of thinking, doing, and being, and about how they like to engage. They also are deeply connected to other writers and editors across different publications and platforms and are able to offer great suggestions for placement both inside and beyond their own properties. Publishers have a lot to offer brands that are willing to listen. It's best to approach publishers humbly—"let me know if this is a good fit"—and ready to learn. Don't try to force a content publisher into your program. Instead, work to create a mutually rewarding partnership. Ask: How can we support you? How can we grow together? What can we do to enable your creativity?

Humility doesn't negate advocating for your brand. Indeed, another important criterion for publishers is for enterprises to take the time to bring their editorial board up to speed about their brand. It's hard to consider a brand for a given content piece if editors are not familiar with it. Publishers recommend that enterprises create an introductory package for the editorial board so that they can get to know you. The package should show the value and value proposition of your brand—samples are helpful. It's also important to provide your perspective on why a content site should recommend you over another brand. This is especially important for young brands without a strong data history.

Once you are approved for a commerce content program by the business side of a publisher organization, the collaboration doesn't stop. Develop a relationship with the editorial team so that they know about your company, its products, and the latest developments. Do all of this under the auspices of sharing information. After all, these journalists earn consumer trust because they are experts who are always up to date. What's new with your brand? What is your brand doing that really matters to people? Can you offer a sneak peek into what is coming next for your brand and/or early access to a promotion exclusively for its audiences? Keep in mind that there can be long lead times for article publication when developing and evaluating commerce content partnerships. By helping publishers (rather than pitching them), you can help influence the content that writers and editors create.

Perfect your conversion experience. To be featured in a "10 best" guide, your product has to be one of the best in a test. This includes the product itself and the experience surrounding it. The effectiveness of an enterprise's ecommerce user experience—its path to purchase—is important when it comes to commerce content. How smooth is your customer buying experience? Amazon Prime sets the benchmark for conversion experience. Do you have free shipping? Will packages arrive within two days? Is it one- or two-click shopping? How are returns handled? Is the site safe and reliable? No matter how good the potential narrative, if your click rate is low because of poor user experience, there is no money to be made for either partner. Invest in your user experience.

Know what matters. Know your KPIs and prioritize them, knowing that you cannot grow them all simultaneously. Understand your content partner's KPIs as well, the most important of which is generally earnings per click (EPC).

Be transparent with your data. Most of the time, tracking takes place on enterprises' technology platforms; publishers do not have visibility into what their audiences are purchasing so they cannot see the impact of their work. Platforms have always provided offerings that work directly with publishers. What's changed lately is enterprises' willingness to tear down the walls that created information asymmetry. Brands are now treating their publisher partners as true partners, providing the data transparency needed to better optimize the partnership. Sharing data about the impact of content enables enterprises and publishers to have honest and productive conversations about the contribution publishers are making, what brands are paying for, and at what price. Transparency enables optimization and enables enterprises and publishers to work together toward mutual outcomes. They become partners in the true sense of the word.

Compensate your content partners fairly. Reward your content partners with reasonable commissions. They know that partnerships have high profit margins and expect that they should receive similar payouts when their content leads to sales. Commerce content compensation usually comes after a publication has written about a brand and/or products independently. A brand will negotiate contracts with publishers, whereby it pays for traffic that comes to it via a referral link. This incentivizes the publisher to promote the content through other channels, such as social, SEO, email, or paid search. More traffic to the article leads to more sales via the referral link, which leads to more compensation for the publisher. The most common content monetization strategy is percentage of revenue from referred sales (41 percent); however, brands also utilize revenue from view-through attribution (34 percent), and a fixed amount generated by a campaign (34 percent), among others.[5] Seasonal or temporary commission increases can be highly motivating, as are tiered commissions that offer a higher commission rate for when specific milestones are met in a given time period.

Who to Approach at a Publisher?

It's important to get to the commerce content team when approaching a mass media publisher. This might take a bit of doing, as brands are often first directed to advertising departments. When brands make contact with commerce content teams, they are likely to be connecting with the monetization folks, who are charged both with explaining how commerce content works for their publications and with determining whether a particular enterprise and its product offerings are a good fit for the publisher and its audiences.

If a potential publisher determines that there is not a brand and audience fit, it's best for the company to move on and develop relationships with other publishers that make more sense. If a publisher gives a brand the green light, it doesn't mean that it will be featured in content right away, as the editors have editorial calendars that are planned well in advance—although there is always room for important emerging trends! In this case it pays to be patient and to stay in touch with publishers, continually sharing news of new product launches and other reasons for the publication to write about the brand.

Once the content is completed, the writer or editor turns it over to the producers, who work with developers to create the tracking links. Analytics teams then follow the pieces to understand how they are performing.

It's always a good idea for partnerships teams to coordinate their commerce content efforts with their own PR team, who may also be working with the same publishers. Coordinating editorial and promotional calendars makes a lot of sense—more bang for the buck—and it just might be time to transition some of those working relationships to performance partners.

An Authentic Path Toward Growth

Commerce content enables enterprises and mass media publishers to work together in a mutually rewarding way. It enables enterprises to reach new and existing customers during their point of need with a trusted, third-party recommended solution.

TABLE 8.1	What marketing tactics will U.S. marketers rely on more in 2020 and beyond? (% of respondents, March 2020 and May 2020).	

	Pre-coronavirus pandemic (March 2020)	Post-coronavirus pandemic (May 2020)
Social media marketing	50%	65%
Video marketing	63%	61%
Content created with partners	24%	32%
Influencer marketing	31%	29%
Loyalty marketing	34%	28%
Reviews/customer testimonials	26%	24%
Events	19%	18%
Podcasts	15%	18%
Articles/blog posts	16%	15%
Research reports	12%	15%
Newsletters	6%	12%

Source: "COVID-19 Marketing Outlook," Chief Marketer, July 21, 2020.

It also dramatically shortens the time, and simplifies the steps, between influence and conversion. These are some of the reasons that marketers are increasing their commitment to content created with partners from 24 to 32 percent in the future, according to *Chief Marketer*[6] (Table 8.1).

Research from **impact.com**'s current customers reveals even higher rates of commerce content adoption and commitment. According to a recent survey, 72 percent of customers say that commerce content is already a part of their partnership program—34 percent of surveyed customers work with 20 or more commerce content publishers.[7] Forty percent of surveyed customers say that commerce content is receiving an increased budget this year.[8] Executives and professionals in the digital publishing industry agree. In a recent study that **impact.com** conducted with FORTUNE Brand Studio, a solid majority (57 percent) of respondents anticipate more than 50 percent annual growth in commerce content revenue.[9]

The Quick Summary

- Enterprises are no strangers to working with mass media publishers on paid advertising and PR opportunities, but partnerships represent a new path that is mutually beneficial to both parties.
- Publishers know the nuances of their audiences' interests and behaviors. Work closely with them when crafting partnerships so that you engage with prospects in a way that feels natural.

- Prioritize the organic feeling of mass media partnerships. Journalistic integrity is important to both the publisher and the potential customer, and these publishers must maintain trust at all times.

- Commerce content is a win-win-win because the originating partner, publisher, and the customer all get something of value. Work with your partners to make sure that value chain stays intact.

What's Up Next?

Mass media partnerships represent new ways to think about old media. But there's a reason it's called "old" media—consumers have infinite opportunities for interacting with brands and content, and that's why enterprises need help cutting through the noise. The next chapter looks at the mobile world, which has transformed consumer interactions, and represents a great way to capture engagement. There's a huge opportunity for enterprises willing to explore something new.

Notes

[1] "Perspectives on Performance Partnerships: Mass Media Publishers," Acceleration Partners, accessed May 25, 2021, video, 59:15, **http://bit.ly/accelerationpartners-massmedia**.

[2] "Monetize Not Just What's Around Your Content, but within Your Content," **impact.com**, PX 2021, video, 44:15, **http://bit.ly/Impact-monetize-content**.

[3] Wirecutter, "About Us," *New York Times* Wirecutter, accessed May 25, 2021, **https://www.nytimes.com/wirecutter/about/**.

[4] "Customer Testimonial," **impact.com** study, April 20, 2021.

[5] FORTUNE and **impact.com**, "Commerce Content Providers Need to Scale Up to Meet the Surge in Online Sales," proprietary research and white paper, July 2021.

[6] Audrey Schomer, "Content Publishers Drive Evolution in the Affiliate Channel," *eMarketer*, Publishers and Commerce 2021 Report, April 9, 2021, **http://bit.ly/emarketer-report-2021**.

[7] "Customer Testimonial," **impact.com**.

[8] Ibid.

[9] FORTUNE and **impact.com**, "Commerce Content Providers."

CHAPTER 9

Mobile Partnerships: Be Where Your Customers Are All the Time

Sanjit is headed to a meeting in an area of San Francisco that he doesn't know well and is in dire need of a coffee (and perhaps a pastry . . .). His go-to local guide app, let's call it ACME Local Guide, suggests Blue Bottle Coffee, which it describes as a trendy cafe offering upscale coffee drinks. The cafe enjoys great consumer reviews and is located right where he is headed—1.5 miles away.

A quick time check reveals that Sanjit doesn't have enough time to walk to the cafe and enjoy a coffee before his meeting. Just as a sense of disappointment is settling in, Sanjit sees a new feature in the ACME Local Guide app: a "get a ride" button (Figure 9.1). The button not only will arrange a ride for him, but it gives him a time estimate of how long it will take for an UberX car to get to him and an estimate of how much the ride will cost. Seeing that a car is a mere three minutes away, Sanjit opts to take a car so that he can refuel with a red eye before his meeting. All is right in the world.

The "get a ride" feature that made things all right in the world for Sanjit is a simple mobile app integration between Uber and any number of partners that

FIGURE 9.1   Find a coffee shop and secure a ride all in one place via mobile integration.

have transit, restaurant, city guides, or local business apps. The button, which Uber engineers say can be installed in 10 minutes with just a few lines of code, makes it super easy for partner customers to secure a reliable ride when their intent to travel is high.[1]

The benefit to consumers is clear: they can easily get where they want to go. The benefit to Uber is more riders enjoying its car service. The benefits to partners are many. Partners are able to offer a global transportation option to their users right in their app, which enhances overall customer experience—no need to open the Uber app to get a car. Incorporation of the Uber button also drives increased user engagement, according to studies conducted by Button, the mobile monetization company. Button found that integration of Uber buttons yields an 11 percent increase in time spent by users in partner apps or websites. Finally, these integrations yield a new revenue stream for partners, as they can monetize their integration through Uber's partnership program, generating a bonus for every new, U.S.-based rider who signs up and takes a ride. It's a win-win-win.

Welcome to a Mobile World

We are living in a mobile world. Let me paint a picture of where we are with a few recent statistics:

- 5.9 billion people now use mobile phones.[2] Smartphone adoption is growing around the world. There are approximately 3.5 billion smartphone users worldwide—just five years ago, there were 1 billion fewer smartphone users.[3]
- The average global user spent 4.2 hours a day on their mobile device in 2020, a 30 percent increase in just two years.[4] To put this in context, consider that the average internet user now spends six hours and 43 minutes online each day.[5]
- Mobile phones account for more than half the time we spend online.[6] We can expect this number to increase given the emergence of 5G technology, which will increase internet speed and connectivity.

What's up with mobile? What are people doing and how are they using their mobile devices?

Mobile devices are now the central command center for simplifying and managing the day-to-day for many. A 2017 Google study found that 75 percent of people said their smartphones "help them to be more productive."[7] Beyond simply getting things done, there's an emotional uplift that comes with phone-based productivity. The same Google study found that 54 percent of people say their phones reduce stress and anxiety.[8] Because they are always close at hand, mobile devices are often the most convenient way to accomplish a task and have a bit of fun and connection.

Mobile Is Changing Customer and Shopping Journeys

As mobile devices change consumer behaviors, they're also changing customer and shopping journeys. Consider the early stages of the journey, when people are often in query mode. Over 80 percent of mobile device users initiate online searches through their phones. These queries can be impactful, as many inquiries begin with questions such as "best place to buy . . ." or "alternatives to . . ." and return search results that answer those questions.[9]

"Near me" searches are also common on mobile devices as people look to their devices' GPS capabilities to provide information that is distinct to the area from which they are searching—perhaps the closest gas station or coffee shop.[10] Consumers are also making use of two other distinctly mobile capabilities: voice search and image recognition. As many as 60 percent of smartphone users say they have made use of voice search and image recognition. In the past 12 months, 20 percent of adults have used mobile voice search at least once daily.[11] Image recognition services such as Pinterest Lens and Google Lens are also becoming more important for internet users, especially among younger audiences.

People are also actively using mobile during the consideration phase of their shopping journeys. Forty-six percent of people read reviews of all potential purchases on their mobile phones and 62 percent use mobile to compare pricing.[12] Shoppers often create a blended shopping experience, using their mobile phones as companions before and during excursions to physical stores. They read product reviews, compare products and prices, and locate alternative store locations.[13] How many of us have also shared photos of products with family and friends while in-store to solicit their feedback?[14] Once again, these trusted sources trump enterprise voices. Nearly 70 percent of internet users in the United States say that they will often skip approaching retail associates in stores, preferring to go directly to their smartphones to look for customer reviews. Just over half of users search for deals on their phones first before speaking with employees.[15]

People use their phones and tablets to make purchases—more than half (51 percent) of internet users purchase products online.[16] The dollar amounts of these purchases are significant; they comprise almost three-quarters (72.9 percent) of ecommerce sales.[17] In 2021, mobile ecommerce is forecasted to reach $3.5 trillion; then there are mobile-influenced in-store purchases to consider, which are estimated to be more than $1 trillion.[18]

What does this mean for enterprises and partnerships? It means that enterprises need to have a strong mobile presence in order to attract customers and grow their businesses. In fact, almost 60 percent of shoppers say that being able to shop on mobile devices is a key factor when it comes to choosing a brand or retailer to buy from.[19] It also means that partners that show up in mobile searches or are go-to trusted sources for people can generate and capture demand for enterprises in mobile environments.

Apps and the Mobile Web: A Tale of Two Environments

What type of mobile presence is important for enterprises—mobile web, mobile app, or both?

Mobile-friendly websites and apps both offer unique advantages, and they can work well together. Traditionally, websites have been a great way to start relationships with customers, and apps have helped enterprises deepen existing relationships.

One of the reasons websites have been seen as a great way to start relationships with customers is because they are easier for people to find when searching online. Potential customers don't have to find an enterprise's app at the app store and then download it onto their phones; they just have to surf the web. Apps take up space on phones and people are often reluctant to download apps they don't really want to use. Tricking people into downloading apps often backfires: 78 percent of U.S. smartphone users don't complete a transaction if an enterprise requires them to download an app.[20]

Apps are often seen as a great way to deepen existing relationships with customers because they enable enterprises to capitalize on features that are native to phones and tablets that make for unique and contextualized customer experiences. For example, apps can deliver customized local recommendations via geolocation and can invite users to special events and alert them to deals. Note that this advantage is decreasing. Website design capabilities have come a long way in recent years and can now deliver a pretty exceptional ongoing experience themselves. Some companies, like the outdoor retailer Patagonia, have chosen to disable mobile apps, opting instead to drive all traffic to their mobile website. In a note to consumers, the company described its rationale (Figure 9.2).

FIGURE 9.2   Patagonia says goodbye to its app.

Other enterprises have chosen to commit themselves to offering a mobile app experience, or a combination of a mobile-friendly website and an app. General usage statistics certainly support this decision. Mobile apps now account for 10 out of every 11 minutes people spend on their mobile devices.[21] The popularity of apps is driving downloads: 218 billion apps were downloaded globally in 2020, according to App Annie's State of Mobile 2020.[22] A more granular look at the data reveals the exact opposite trend in the United States, however. In one quarter during 2019, two-thirds of smartphone users did not download a single app.[23]

Having your app downloaded is just the beginning. Apps have to be used to have impact and nearly 90 percent of apps are churned within 30 days of download.[24] A download by itself doesn't offer a great deal of value aside from, perhaps, bumping up its ranking in the app stores. App makers need to think about ongoing use, and develop strategies to stay relevant and reduce these high churn rates. Basic app analytics can reveal the percentage of users who are downloading but not taking action after that initial download.

What apps do consumers use most often? The most frequently downloaded apps are social (39 percent), followed by gaming (10 percent), communication (10 percent), and retail-related (7 percent).[25] When it comes to retail-related apps, people are most likely to use large retailers' apps such as Target, Walmart, Costo, or Amazon.[26] In terms of total time spent, social apps come in first, capturing 50 percent of users' total usage time. Video and entertainment apps, like Netflix, come in second, with 21 percent of total usage time.

The bottom line is, it's increasingly a mobile world—and it's highly competitive. Enterprises need all the help they can get when it comes to acquiring and retaining customers.

What Do Consumers Prefer?

As it turns out, consumers are not binary in their approach to mobile environments. They don't think: mobile web or mobile app. Rather, they often toggle between apps and the mobile web and then back again. And they may even shift to a desktop web browser during their exploration as well—remember, mobile accounts for 50 percent of people's time on the internet while desktop accounts for the other half. What's the rhyme or reason? Why do people move across so many channels?

People do what works best for them at a particular moment—technology serves them rather than the other way around. If they are looking up a quick fact on the fly, the mobile web is likely to be the best bet. If they are making a one-time purchase, desktop or the mobile web works well. If they are shopping in-store and want to check reviews or compare prices, the mobile web often works well. If they are deal seekers and are consistently looking for ways to save money, a coupon or deal app might be just what they need. There are other variables that are related to people's preference for desktop, mobile, and mobile apps—gender, vertical, income, geography, time of day (are people at work?), and income—but these variables are quite nuanced. Situational factors and use cases tend to be the primary differentiator.

What does this mean for enterprises? It pays to know your customer journeys well. Study how your target customers are using their desktop and mobile devices initially and over time. Identify and explore your mobile touchpoints—when, where, and why your customers interact with you on their mobile devices. What difference does it make? What role are partners playing in these mobile interactions? Then ensure that you have optimized the customer experience among those interactions to create the most seamless and enjoyable experience possible, a topic I'll get to shortly.

Samsung and Target

Samsung is a trusted mobile device manufacturer, known for its Galaxy line of smartphones. Whenever Samsung users open up the web browser on their smartphones, they see a search/URL box, and, underneath it, a series of icons that provide quick access to various web properties.

In a creative partnership construct, Samsung has turned these icons into partnership inventory, making this valuable real estate available to brands. By partnering with Samsung, enterprises across several industries get a premier placement whenever users open the browser. Samsung combines this prominent linking with the ability to share collaborative offers with Samsung device users, as well as target users by device, browsing history, geography, and demographic. Target is one of these brands. A quick-access link encourages easy redirection to Target's website (Figure 9.3).

As a result of this partnership, Target's brand gets promoted across 50 million eligible devices. The quick icon within the browser is viewed 580 million times a month, and users click through 1 million times per month. That's 1 million visits to Target's website that are made quickly and easily via a partnership, along with more than half a billion monthly brand exposures. It's clear that something as simple as a partnership that displays a quick link on a mobile browser can be a major revenue driver, especially for brands that have serious mobile commerce operations.

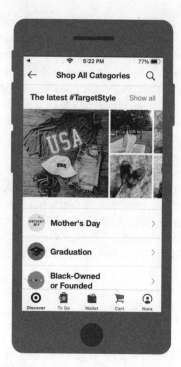

FIGURE 9.3 The Target app enjoys premiere placement on Samsung phones.

Consider the Mobile Partnership Opportunity

This increasingly mobile world creates new partnerships opportunities for enterprises. Partners' content that shows up in mobile searches can generate demand and catalyze new customer and buyer journeys. Partner reviews and product comparisons can enable consideration. And through referral links, partners can also capture that demand, directing an enterprise's target customers to the most relevant enterprise mobile environment, website, or app, to close the deal. As we saw with Samsung and Target, partnerships can also encourage people to use an enterprise's mobile app for the first time—then over and over again. Partnerships link streaming music apps to concert ticket sales apps. They connect branded retail apps with deal apps. And they can even connect things like ordering takeout with branded rewards.

When considering the mobile partnership opportunity, it's helpful to start with a look at existing customer journeys and where mobile already comes into play.

When enterprises know their omnichannel customer journeys, they can then stand back and proactively think: What are the key customer behaviors that we want to catalyze and what are the micro conversions that surround them? How are partners currently being helpful? How else might partners be useful?

Don't be afraid to think outside the box when it comes to mobile web and app partnerships. Look for relevant apps in adjacent or complementary verticals (such as restaurant review apps, if you are a hospitality company) or affinity-based apps (wine rating apps may appeal to a specific target audience, such as high-net-worth individuals). You may also want to consider audience reach. There are apps with massive reach, and then there are apps that have smaller, dedicated user bases that may align well with your desired audience.

Another key factor to look at is traffic. Mobile has its own unique version of traffic networks called cost-per-install (CPI) networks. CPI networks are an easy way to find qualified partners that will help drive app installs. Even when using these networks, remember the importance of maintaining a direct relationship with your most important partners and their apps. This ensures that all of the data and results from consumer activity are shared transparently, ensuring clean measurement and value assessment of the partnership.

It's Gotta Be Seamless

Ease of movement between enterprises and their partners across mobile web and app environments is critical in creating a winning partnership. As we have seen, there are seemingly infinite ways for users to interact with their devices, and equally infinite opportunities for them to engage with businesses. But along with those opportunities come challenges, because the customer experience can quickly become fragmented between web and apps. This isn't good for the customer, nor is it good for the enterprise and its partners. There is a cost to these misses: people who have a negative experience on mobile are 62 percent less likely to purchase from that brand in the future than if they have a positive experience.[27]

The following example illustrates this miss, examining the step-by-step experience of a young woman—let's call her Dafina—wanting to purchase a denim jacket:

> Step 1: While riding the subway, Dafina completes a quick search for a denim jacket on her mobile phone (Figure 9.4). A number of options surface, and she clicks through to a *retailer's app* from the search results.
>
> Step 2: Dafina finds exactly what she is looking for—the perfect fade and size—and adds it to her shopping bag (Figure 9.4).
>
> Step 3: Before checking out, being the deal-savvy shopper that she is, Dafina decides to open up her go-to cashback app to see if there's a discount available

Step 1

Step 2

FIGURE 9.4   Steps 1 and 2 of Dafina's jean jacket purchase.

for that retailer. There is one—and it's 10 percent off (Figure 9.5)! Excited, Dafina clicks on the discount link that takes her to the *retailer's website*.

Step 4: Here's the miss: the jacket that Dafina placed in her shopping bag moments earlier isn't there (Figure 9.5).

Step 5: Frustrated by the thought of having to go through the whole search process again, Dafina cuts her losses and checks her texts instead (Figure 9.5).

What happened here? A linking problem between different mobile environments. Dafina started her search on the *mobile web*. When she clicked on one of the search engine options, it took her to the *retailer's app*—a different web environment altogether. Dafina's go-to *cashback app* provided her with a great discount; however, it routed her back to the *retailer's mobile site*, rather than to the retailer's app where she started. The retailer's website didn't have any knowledge of Dafina's previous activity so her shopping bag came up empty. As a result, everyone loses. Dafina didn't get her jacket. The retailer missed a sale. And the cashback app missed a commission. Here's the rub: if the cashback site had redirected her to the retailer's app, Dafina would have found her jacket waiting in her shopping bag, with a discount code applied, ready for checkout. Everyone wins. Happiness flows.

Step 3   **Step 4**   **Step 5**

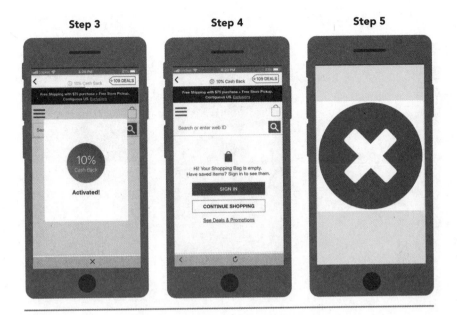

FIGURE 9.5   Steps 3, 4, and 5 of Dafina's jean jacket purchase.
Source: impact.com, "What Darwin Can Teach Mobile Marketers: Why customer experience is key to partner-ship success," impact.com, accessed May 28, 2021, http://bit.ly/Impact-cx-partnership-success.

There Is a Better Way

Websites and apps are built on different technologies. Links and tracking setups don't translate easily from web to app or from app to web. Platforms and tracking providers typically focus just on web or just on apps (not both). This is a core reason that the user experience broke down in the earlier retailer example. The traditional way brands work with partners and measure their contribution just won't work in the app world. But all of that has been changing.

Deep linking technologies make it possible for partners to link from anywhere directly into an app, mobile website, or the app store. It allows for the ultimate control to create the best user experience possible. Target customers can toggle back and forth between mobile web and apps in whatever way works best for them. The result: everyone wins. Deep linking leads to conversion rates that are three times greater, double purchase frequency, and increase average order value by 140 percent. No partner would want to miss out on those metrics.

What does the user experience look like when deep linking technology is applied? Check out the journey pictured in Figure 9.6—this time Dafina is looking to purchase concert tickets to hear the band Real Estate. (She loves the song *Darling*, but that's another story. . . .)

Step 1   Step 2   Step 3

FIGURE 9.6   Steps 1, 2, and 3 of Dafina's concert ticket purchase.

Step 1: Dafina is listening to Real Estate in her favorite music app, Spotify.

Step 2: In the Spotify app she is able to find out where Real Estate will be in concert—Port City Music Hall in Portland.

Step 3: Dafina prepares to purchase tickets and gets routed to the Ticketmaster app, where she chooses the number of tickets, selects her seats, and makes a purchase. Seconds later, she's all set.

Measuring Performance: KPIs for Mobile Partnerships

The mobile customer journey is different from the desktop customer journey, and measuring success ultimately depends on the goal of the partnership. Enterprises looking to simply drive installs of their apps will measure success differently from those that are looking to drive revenue through their app or are looking to find new high-lifetime-value customers through mobile. Still, there are several basic KPIs that enterprises can use to measure the success of their mobile partnerships. Understand the following metrics, then use what is appropriate to accurately assess mobile partnership success:

- **Cost per acquisition (CPA)** measures the price of acquiring a new customer on your app.
- **Cost per install (CPI)** is a measure of the price you pay for every install within a partnership.
- **Cost per install+ (CPI+)** refers to the price you pay for every install that is confirmed by a subsequent success event after the user finishes downloading and opens the app. It could be anything from registering a new account on a retail app, to funding a brokerage account for a stock trading app, to taking the first ride through a ridesharing app.
- **Conversion rate** is the percentage of users who complete a desired action. This is usually tied to a post-app install action within the app itself. It could be a sales event within an ecommerce app, an intermediate event such as account creation, or funding a newly created account for a stock trading app.
- **Active users** is a measure of the total number of people who are returning to your app and using it within a designated time period.

Another set of critical metrics measures potential losses—that is, consumers who download an app but don't stay fully engaged.

- **Retention rate** is the portion of people who continue using an app a certain number of days after install.
- **Churn rate** is a measure of how many users stop returning to an app after downloading it.
- **Uninstall tracking** goes one step beyond churn rate, illustrating the number of users who completely remove an app from their device along with when that happens (such as how long after initial download). Note that most churned users simply stop using an app without taking the additional step of uninstalling it from their mobile device.
- **Reengagement rate** is a way to measure success in inspiring inactive users to open an app again. Comparing it to churn and uninstalls is a critical way to assess partnerships focused on reengaging users.

Fraud: A Unique Mobile Consideration

The partnership landscape described throughout this book is one where companies work together, and partners that contribute to a sale in some way are typically rewarded by the enterprise with a commission. There are undoubtedly unscrupulous players in every type of partnership, and solid partnership management can spot inconsistencies and weed out partners that are taking commissions without actually contributing.

This process is more complicated in the mobile landscape, so partner managers need to be vigilant about spotting fraud in all of its forms. The issue in part is because the outcomes—be they installs or completed purchases—take place on apps themselves. Knowing whether both the referral and the event are genuine is a complicated business.

There are two persistent forms of mobile fraud in the partnership universe to look out for:

1. **Install fraud** is when a bad actor downloads an app with the intent of being paid for the install, even when there really is no intent to use the app. Partnerships programs that pay on CPI then run the risk of sending their budget to bad actors generating low-value installs that aren't contributing in any meaningful way—although sadly, some app owners may turn a blind eye to this type of fraud because they believe it helps them elevate their app's ranking in the app stores.[28]

2. **Attribution fraud** occurs when bad actors "bomb" clicks into a target app. It can result in two outcomes: the bad actor injects one last click before a real, payable event and takes credit, or it takes credit for the fake in-app events that its clicks generate.

Whether paying for installs or actions taken within an app, it's important to be vigilant and ensure the integrity of a crediting system for mobile partnerships.

Future-Facing Connections for an Evolving Customer Journey

The mobile environment has reshaped the entire customer experience. Research, interaction, and purchase decisions are increasingly happening on mobile, and customers are switching back and forth between desktop and mobile environments throughout the day. While this has undoubtedly intimidated many organizations focused on growth, partnerships represent a powerful way to tame the mobile environment. New channels present myriad opportunities and mobile partnerships can take many different forms. There is a rich opportunity across both apps and the mobile internet, provided that enterprises align their priorities and work closely with the right partners.

The Quick Summary

- Mobile devices have transformed people's lives. They are now the central command center for simplifying and managing the day-to-day, becoming productivity tools that help people get things done.
- Mobile has altered the customer journey. Customer experience on mobile devices is guided by where the research takes them, and that often includes jumping from apps to the mobile web and then back again.
- Ease of movement, from the mobile web to app, and from app to app, is critical in creating a winning partnership. Partnerships need to link up in the ways that consumers want them to; otherwise, the customer can feel left out.
- Downloads are important, but they are not the end of the mobile experience. Partnerships are helpful for finding users who will continue to use apps after the initial install, as well as reengaging users who have installed but stopped using an app.
- Fraud remains an unfortunate complication in the mobile landscape, so partner managers need to be vigilant about spotting fraud in all of its forms.

What's Up Next?

Mobile partnerships can often require deep integrations, and that concept sets the stage for what comes next: strategic business partnerships. The next chapter discusses how enterprises are leaving the idea of "turnkey" behind and combining their offerings with their partners to create new value for their customers and deliver an experience that exceeds what either company can do individually.

Notes

[1] John Park, "Have a Map in Your App? Add the Uber Button!," Uber Engineering, August 2, 2016, **https://ubr.to/3xgZFxm**.
[2] Simon Kemp, "Digital 2020: 3.8 Billion People Use Social Media," We Are Social special report, January 30, 2020, **http://bit.ly/billions-use-social-media**.
[3] Ying Lin, "10 Mobile Usage Statistics Every Marketer Should Know in 2021 [Infographic]," Oberlo, April 22, 2020, **http://bit.ly/ten-mobile-usage-stats-to-know**.
[4] Sarah Perez, "Consumers Now Average 4.2 Hours per Day in Apps, Up 30% from 2019," *TechCrunch*, April 8, 2021, **http://bit.ly/coronavirus-increased-screen-time**.
[5] Simon Kemp, "Digital 2020."

[6] J. Clement, "Percentage of Mobile Device Website Traffic Worldwide from 1st Quarter 2015 to 1st Quarter 2021," Statista, April 28, 2021, **http://bit.ly/mobile-percentage-website-traffic-statista.**

[7] Sara Kleinberg, "How Mobile Became a Power Tool in Idle Moments," Think with Google, March 2018, **http://bit.ly/mobile-productivity-boosting-tool.**

[8] Ibid.

[9] "Mobile Searches for 'Best Place to Buy' Have Grown by Over 70% in the Past Two Years," Google Data, U.S., Oct. 2015–Sept. 2016 vs. Oct. 2017–Sept. 2018, accessed May 25, 2021, **http://bit.ly/mobile-search-data-best-place-to-buy.**

[10] Joseph Johnson, "Mobile Search—Statistics & Facts," Statista, April 29, 2021, **http://bit.ly/mobile-search-stats-facts.**

[11] Quoracreative, "101 Mobile Marketing Statistics and Trends for 2020," updated January 7, 2021, **https://quoracreative.com/article/mobile-marketing-statistics.**

[12] Ibid.

[13] Ibid.

[14] Lucy Koch, "Two-Thirds of Shoppers Check Phones In-Store for Product Information, Skipping Store Associates," *eMarketer*, May 8, 2019, **http://bit.ly/how-consumers-use-smartphones.**

[15] Dave Chaffey, "Mobile Marketing Statistics Compilation 2021," March 30, 2021, **http://bit.ly/mobile-marketing-statistics-compilation.**

[16] Simon Kemp, "Digital 2020: April Global Statshot," DataReportal, April 23, 2020, **https://datareportal.com/reports/digital-2020-april-global-statshot.**

[17] Dyfed Loesche, "Mobile E-commerce Is Up and Poised for Further Growth," Statista, March 6, 2018, **http://bit.ly/mobile-ecommerce-poised-growth.**

[18] Quoracreative, "101 Mobile Marketing Statistics and Trends for 2020."

[19] "59% of Shoppers Surveyed Say That Being Able to Shop on Mobile Is Important When Deciding Which Brand or Retailer to Buy From," Google, accessed May 28, 2021, **http://bit.ly/mobile-shopping-brand-statistics.**

[20] Anne Freer, "78% of Consumers Will Abandon Transaction if App Installation Is Required," Business of Apps, February 8, 2021, **http://bit.ly/BusinessofApps-installation.**

[21] "The State of Mobile 2020," App Annie report, accessed May 28, 2021, **http://bit.ly/appannie-2020-mobile-report.**

[22] Ibid.

[23] Kelly Lewis, "Global State of Mobile," Comscore, December 4, 2019, **http://bit.ly/comscore-global-state-of-mobile.**

[24] Blake Morgan, "When It Comes to Customer Engagement, Loyalty Matters at Citi," *Forbes*, May 2, 2019, **http://bit.ly/Citi-loyalty-customer-engagement.**

[25] "30 Truly Fascinating App Usage Statistics to Know in 2021," WebsiteBuilder, updated March 20, 2021, **https://websitebuilder.org/blog/app-usage-statistics/.**

[26] "Nearly 80% of People Use Shopping Apps While at Home, and Most Use Them Frequently—at Least 2–5 Times a Week," *PRNewswire*, April 10, 2019, **http://bit.ly/prnewswire-80percent-used-shopping-apps-at-home.**

[27] "People Who Have a Negative Experience on Mobile Are 62% Less Likely to Purchase from That Brand in the Future Than if They Have a Positive Experience," Think with Google, April 2017, **http://bit.ly/thinkwithgoogle-brand-experience.**

[28] For more information see: **https://impact.com/protect-monitor/performance-fraud/install-attribution-fraud.**

CHAPTER 10

Strategic Business Partnerships: When Two Work as One

Planning a vacation takes work. It often involves several steps: booking accommodations and transportation, exploring the range of events and activities available during a trip, securing necessary travel inoculations and documents, and taking care of important details like finding a babysitter or house sitter and boarding a pet. Although these tasks are all related in the context of planning a vacation, people often have to undertake them separately each time they travel, because the services are often provided by different companies or people.

Qantas and Airbnb looked to ease some of the friction in the vacation planning process by bringing together two of these services. By embedding Airbnb's vacation rental reservation capability into Qantas's website, the two formed a partnership that combined booking flights and finding a place to stay (Figure 10.1). They also adopted a great slogan: Fly there, live there. The rental reservation integration means that Qantas customers can book their accommodations at the same time they book their airfare.

To further encourage customers to take advantage of the partnership, Qantas offers one mile in its frequent flyer program for every dollar that customers spend on qualifying Airbnb reservations. So a customer spending $500 for their Airbnb rental will now have a flight, a place to stay, and 500 miles toward their next flight.

FIGURE 10.1 Qantas and Airbnb create a more holistic customer experience.

There's an obvious benefit to customers who choose to use both of the partners, and the integrated nature looks a little different from some of the other types of partnerships that have been examined. Still, the roles are largely the same. Qantas fills the role of the introducing partner, while Airbnb serves as the acquiring enterprise—that is, the partner looking to add or retain customers. Qantas customers use the brand's site to book flights, and they often need a place to stay; Airbnb has rental properties across the globe that it would like to rent out to these Qantas customers. Clearly, there's an audience overlap.

By joining forces in this way, the two brands have created a stronger customer experience than either could offer on its own. Qantas has a way to retain customers through the added value of seamless accommodation booking and more miles incentives. Airbnb taps into an overlapping customer base, reaching people at the moment they are most likely to turn their attention toward accommodations. It's a win-win-win for the two companies and their customers.

Committing for the Long Haul: Strategic Brand-to-Brand Partnerships

Strategic brand-to-brand (SB2B) partnerships, such as the one between Qantas and Airbnb, are some of the most powerful forms of partnerships. What's different is that the parties to SB2B partnerships are both enterprise brands—they are not influencers, brand ambassadors, mass media publishers, or traditional affiliates. They are like-minded businesses choosing to work together to create compelling customer experiences that are greater than the sum of their parts.

Often these brands work together as referral partners with complementary goals. One brand is pursuing a customer acquisition strategy while the other is looking to retain its existing customers. Sometimes this is accomplished via a joint promotion; other times it's accomplished by a more extensive product integration that creates new-to-the-world joint value propositions. This chapter will cover the range of options.

Entry-Level SB2B Partnerships: Based on a Promotion

SB2B partnerships are perhaps best viewed along a spectrum of complexity. The entry-level version is a joint promotion.

Disney+ and Lyft

The Disney+ and Lyft partnership is an example of an SB2B partnership designed around a promotion. The impetus for the partnership was twofold. Disney wanted to expand its streaming service subscription base beyond its traditional stronghold of families with children. Lyft wanted to reward its existing customers with additional value. By working together the brands could both make strides toward accomplishing their goals.

Here's how they did it. Lyft app users were offered a free seven-day Disney+ trial as a perk for using the ride-sharing service. If at the end of the trial period Lyft riders decided to become full-time subscribers to Disney+—whose offerings include entertainment produced by Disney, Pixar, Star Wars, and *National Geographic*—they received a $15 Lyft credit. Through the partnership, Disney+ reached a new audience that was tech-savvy and diverse and Lyft was able to reward its existing customers with useful perks, while also generating referral income. Customer acquisition meets customer retention. And their shared customers win.

HyreCar and DoorDash

HyreCar and DoorDash is an example of the types of partnerships that HyreCar builds and grows to continually enhance its customers' experience and generate an additional revenue stream for the company. HyreCar is a car-sharing platform for gig economy workers. The company rents cars to Lyft, Uber, and food and package delivery drivers to enable them to deliver their goods, whether those goods are people or food. (A two sided-marketplace, HyreCar also makes it possible for people with vehicles to carshare, monetizing their cars by renting them to Hyre-Car drivers.) HyreCar is committed to helping its ride-share and delivery drivers maximize their success in the gig economy. Toward this end, it has entered into partnerships with several companies—DoorDash, for example—that employ gig drivers to build working relationships that help HyreCar drivers maximize their opportunities to earn income.

Here's how it works. When drivers apply to rent a car via HyreCar, they are asked to indicate the types of partners they might like to work with: Lyft, Uber, DoorDash, Uber Eats, Postmates, or Instacart, for example. HyreCar then introduces its drivers to these companies. If a HyreCar driver ends up delivering for one or more of those companies, everyone wins. People get their food or rides. Partners find great drivers. And HyreCar creates a highly valuable resource for its drivers while also generating additional revenue. HyreCar continually shares new opportunities to earn additional income via its partnerships with its drivers, based on each driver's preferences.

"Partnerships add a lot of value to our customer experience," explains Reese Moulton, HyreCar's director of marketing, "which is why we're continuing to invest our time and resources into growing partnerships."[1]

Complex SB2B Partnerships: Based on a Product Integration

At the complex end of the spectrum are deep product integrations where two brands work together to create an entirely new customer value proposition. When done well, both brands fit natively within the enhanced customer experience. The Qantas and Airbnb partnership is an example of a successful integration. In this case, Qantas is acting as the referral partner, directing its customers to Airbnb, which is gladly receiving those referrals. The airline can do so not because of a stand-alone promotion, but because of the more holistic product offering—the ability to book air travel and secure accommodations all in one place—it's able to make available to its customer base because of this SB2B partnership. The end result: Quantas creates a more useful, and therefore stickier, customer experience while earning referral revenue. Airbnb benefits as well, from the brand association and by gaining exposure to new customers at a moment when purchase intent is heightened. And, once again, their shared customers win as well.

This product integration model shows up quite often in the partnerships world. Recall the Spotify and Ticketmaster partnership. Spotify enhances its value proposition by making it super fast and easy for its customers to discover and purchase tickets to upcoming events from Ticketmaster while also earning referral income. Meanwhile, Ticketmaster benefits from the brand association and the referral traffic that this integration brings. Ticketmaster also enjoys similar integrations with other platforms including Facebook, Pandora, and YouTube.

This same structure fuels the Tasty and Walmart partnership. Tasty, the world's largest food network, is able to enhance its customer experience with the inclusion of the Shoppable Recipes feature in its app. This feature enables Tasty users to order ingredients they may need to prepare any of its more than 4,000 recipes available directly in its app. The food items come from Walmart, whose extensive distribution and rapid delivery options further enhance the partnership's overall customer experience. Walmart, of course, benefits from all of those orders.

What makes these product integrations complex is perhaps obvious—they require some type of code development to develop the integration. In the case of Spotify and Ticketmaster, to effectively determine whether there are relevant events in the future for a given listener, Spotify needs to be able to integrate with the Ticketmaster API, the application programming interface that allows the two software applications to communicate with each other, to query whether the band that the listener is enjoying has upcoming events in a relevant geography. Ticketmaster, on the other hand, has to ensure that all the event, venue, and seat availability data that it collects is accurate and available in real time via its APIs. (This is why there are product integration folks within partnerships organizations.) Also, because these product integrations are permanent, the approval process within both organizations can often take more time. Close working relationships between partnership and product organizations smooth the process and set up enterprises well for additional growth of this kind in the future.

Financial Services SB2B Partnerships

Financial services (finservs) are no strangers to SB2B partnerships. For example, Robinhood, a stock trading and investment app, and TurboTax, the tax preparation software, enjoy a partnership that allows Robinhood users to automatically import their trade history and 1099s into the TurboTax software (Figure 10.2), greatly simplifying tax preparation. Robinhood customers also receive a $20 discount if they sign up for TurboTax. In this partnership, Robinhood is acting as the referral partner, bringing new customers to TurboTax. Robinhood benefits from the enhanced value proposition that the partnership enables, which makes it easier for its customers to complete their taxes and make the most of their investment deductions.

Loyalty programs are another example of finserv SB2B partnerships. Examples of these partnerships include bank credit card rewards programs, which offer cardholders cash back or reward points for using their cards. Chase, for example,

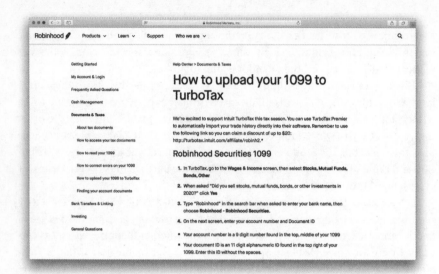

FIGURE 10.2 Robinhood and TurboTax create new value for Robinhood app users.

FIGURE 10.3 Chase's Sapphire Ultimate Rewards program is full of SB2B partnerships.

deploys these kinds of partnerships with its Sapphire Ultimate Rewards program, and customers can redeem points for gift cards from brands as varied as Gap, Whole Foods, ULTA Beauty, and Bath & Body Works (Figure 10.3). Banks and card issuers also generally work with travel providers to provide perks to shared customers and allow loyalty point transfers between bank points and airline miles or hotel points. In these cases, the bank is acting as a partner, promoting other brands' goods and services.

Is Your Company Ready for SB2B Partnerships?

The SB2B partnership opportunity is real; however, it's a more complex form of partnership than the partnerships that have been discussed so far. It involves working with another brand to create a shared and permanent customer experience that may include integration of your products, services, and experiences. This type of commitment is substantial. It requires a high level of sophistication, commitment, and engagement from all parties.

Creating these partnerships requires a strategy and skill set that skews closer to business development and strategic sales than it does to affiliate or influencer management. It also involves identifying and connecting with the right people within potential partner organizations—sometimes that is marketing, product development, product integration, or the business development team. Once you've found the right people, it's important to speak the right language. If you start talking about affiliates with someone who is very steeped in these strategic partnerships, they may come away with the impression that *you* have no idea what they're talking about.

Finding Potential SB2B Partnerships

Identifying potential partners can be quite fun and rewarding because SB2B partnerships are creative by design and there is an abundance of potential partners. Let's work with a relatively straightforward example: complementary customers.

A great SB2B partnership can be built from two brands that have the same target audiences but minimal overlap in customer base. That way, both brands can introduce each other to their desired, but not yet acquired, target customers. Can you find a way to align with the partner in a way that feels natural? To answer that question, simply start with the customer experience and closely study the user journey to understand the path of purchase that your customers take for a group of products, not just yours. When you understand how these customers think when they're not interacting with your brand, you can find ways to reach the target audience through partnerships at high-intent stages on the path to purchase. When you start thinking about ways to tap into new audiences and build brand associations, unique pairings can often come together.

In one unexpected example, Hollister, the California-style teen and young adult clothing brand, teamed up with Xbox, the video game console. These companies have completely different products but share an overlapping target audience—millennials—and saw a way they could mutually benefit from associating their brands with each other. In the partnership, when members of Hollister's "Club Cali" loyalty program made a purchase for more than $25, they received a free one-month subscription to Xbox Game Pass Ultimate, thereby granting them unlimited access to hundreds of games on the Xbox platform.

The outcome? Hollister customers enjoyed a free perk for being part of the clothing company's loyalty program, a perk that many were likely to value and enjoy. Hollister itself was able to catalyze additional sales by prompting members of its loyalty program to make an additional purchase in order to qualify for the one-month Xbox subscription. It also benefited from the brand association with Xbox and the opportunity to build deeper loyalty with its customers, who were likely to stay on the lookout for future offers. Xbox gained access to new target customers who, after enjoying a month-long trial, might quite possibly convert into long-term subscribers.

Partnerships agencies can be good sources for potential partnership identification and introductions. Juststuf is a UK-based boutique agency that specializes in building partnerships. Its small team is focused on one thing: connecting brands that would benefit from each other's audience base. This has led it to connect hotel brands with luxury auto manufacturers in order to build relationships that produce something meaningful to the end customer.

Construct a Successful SB2B Partnership

As in any partnership, constructing a mutually beneficial brand-to-brand partnership relies heavily on strategic alignment. Often SB2B partnerships require more upfront relationship building to ensure aligned vision. Working through all aspects of the Partnership Design Canvas can be highly useful in determining whether strategic alignment exists. (See Chapter 5, "Six Building Blocks of Today's Partnerships.") Think through your overall business goals for the partnership, what you are looking to give and get, your target customers, and the desired customer behaviors you are looking for your partnership to address. Be thorough in your investigation of whether a potential partner fits your ideal partnership qualifications. Some technology integrations may be necessary, which means there will be sharing of proprietary data. This sharing of data is what creates an exceptional customer experience. When you are considering permanently integrating your products into a combined customer experience, and sharing proprietary data, there cannot be any question about whether partners can and should work together—for a long time to come.

You will also want to creatively and carefully consider your SB2B partnership contract (likely to be bespoke), payment structure, metrics, and tracking ability. When brands invest the time to cultivate a relationship and the resources to develop a technological integration, it's critical that both parties understand the value they are creating in as much detail as possible. Build in this kind of measurement up front, tie the resulting performance to the payment structure, and both parties will have transparency into just how much mutual benefit they are truly providing.

The Quick Summary

- SB2B partnerships are not just joint marketing strategies, but relationships built upon detailed business strategies and immense levels of trust. This is where two brand strategies align to create a customer experience that is greater than the sum of its parts.
- These partnerships are closer to business development and strategic sales deals than they are to affiliate relationships, so approach them appropriately. Make sure you are talking to the right folks and speaking the appropriate language.
- Strategic alignment is critical in SB2B partnerships. Consider using the Partnership Design Canvas found in Chapter 5, "Six Building Blocks of Today's Partnerships," which was developed for this express purpose.
- When thinking about your ideal partner, consider shared prospects and customers, reputations, transparency, a willingness to collaborate, and the prospective partner's customer and user experiences.
- A great SB2B partnership is one in which you have the same target audiences but minimal overlap in customer base. Closely study the user journey and understand the path of purchase that your customers take for a group of products, not just yours. When you understand how these consumers think when they're not interacting with your brand, you can find ways to reach the target audience through partnerships at high-intent stages on the path to purchase.
- Even though SB2B partnerships look different, they require measurement and performance assessment, as is the case with all successful partnerships.

What's Up Next?

If SB2B partnerships are about two enterprises united around creating more value for their shared or similar target customers, then the next form of partnership is about creating impact for society and the world. Community groups, associations, and cause-based partnerships are all about building something better alongside customers. They're about uniting behind a higher good and helping your business in the process. These are also the final examples of modern partnerships that the next chapter touches on.

Note

[1] Reese Moulton, director of marketing at HyreCar, Inc., "HyreCar/Impact Sync," interviewed by Jaime Singson, **impact.com**, accessed June 1, 2021, audio.

CHAPTER 11

Community Groups, Associations, and Cause-Based Partnerships: When the Higher Good Is Good Business

Giving Assistant's goal is simple: enable consumers to make a positive social impact every time they make a purchase. The company does so by combining a loyalty platform and charitable giving in one.

Here's how it works: customers join the Giving Assistant Community, a loyalty rewards platform that enables them to earn cash back on purchases from thousands of favorite brands including Nike, eBay, Walmart, Home Depot, Glossier, and H&M. Shoppers access these offers through Giving Assistant's website or via The Button, its browser extension that automatically searches the web and alerts shoppers at checkout when cashback offers are available on their purchases. Shoppers can choose to keep the cash and receive payment or donate some or all of their savings to one or more nonprofits of their choice (Figure 11.1). It's one-click, effortless giving that makes people quite happy.

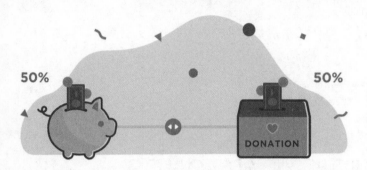

Shop for good.

50%   50%

Keep or donate your cash back.

FIGURE 11.1 Giving Assistant members can readily donate their savings to their favorite nonprofit organization.

When companies' values align with those of their customers, a powerful sense of solidarity and belonging is created. Seventy-seven percent of consumers say they feel more emotionally connected to organizations driven by a purpose and values.[1] This emotional connection translates into sales, loyalty, and advocacy. It works in the other direction too: nearly 60 percent of consumers are likely to stop shopping at a company that doesn't support an issue they find important.[2]

Companies welcome the opportunity to facilitate "shopping for good," as it's a noncontroversial expression of their commitment to corporate social responsibility. It also catalyzes meaningful engagement with their prospects and customers, who often get excited when they shop for good, and share their experiences on social media. Consumer enthusiasm for the combined cashback and giving experience creates a key point of differentiation from competitors, and it creates loyalty. Seventy-five percent of consumers will buy only one brand or buy a more expensive brand if the company has a social impact program, according to Edelman's Trust Barometer 2020.[3]

"We help our customers make giving a seamless part of their online shopping experience," explains Jenni Cassidy, vice president of partnerships and revenue at Giving Assistant. "Giving Assistant shoppers feel better about what they buy and the stores they already frequent because they can make a difference with every purchase."

Giving Assistant works with merchants to create cashback deal structures that are interesting to shoppers and also enable companies to obtain their business goals. Higher cashback rates can be offered for new customers or repeat customers, depending on whether companies are pursuing a customer acquisition or retention strategy. But that's not all. "Offering cash back helps brands entice and more meaningfully connect with new and returning shoppers," Cassidy explains. "Customers feel more engaged with a brand that rewards them for shopping, and they feel excited to pay forward their earnings to something meaningful —another positive link that's hard to create otherwise."

Giving Assistant's cross-promotional campaigns give brands the chance to explicitly convey their passion for a particular cause—and then rally their customers and Giving Assistant's membership base behind it. Through email, blog content, and additional touchpoints, Giving Assistant's cross-promotional campaigns encourage shoppers and nonprofit supporters to come together to save and raise money for the designated nonprofit with whom the brand has partnered, acting on their consumer preferences and reflected values.

How much of an impact can a partner like Giving Assistant make? The numbers tell the story. According to Giving Assistant's 2020 Annual Report, membership in the program was up by 10 percent and 30 percent of members made multiple donations. Cashback donations were up 98 percent in the past year, with 260,873 individual donations made. In one month during the holiday shopping season, $27,000 was donated. How do these numbers translate into impact? Consider that $36 can feed 14 New York City children for an entire week through City Harvest. For $36, 15 people living with mental illness can benefit from participation in a recovery support group through the National Alliance for Mental Illness. And a $25 donation sent to General Needs can buy a new pair of sneakers and clean socks for a homeless veteran. "As we strive to be the publisher of choice for giving efforts, this further proves that anyone can make a positive impact and no donation amount is too small," Cassidy offers.

It's a Whole New World

Empowered consumers are shaping the world in many ways. They are demanding value from businesses, and that value increasingly includes purpose and ethics. A recent survey conducted by Cone and Porter Novelli found that 78 percent of U.S. consumers say that organizations must positively affect society, not just make money.[4] This is a seismic shift. It wasn't too long ago that companies were advised to avoid social issues because promoting a cause was seen as being too risky.

Recognizing this shift, in his 2018 letter to CEOs, Laurence Fink, chairman and CEO of BlackRock, the largest money-management firm in the world, brought the business community's attention to this new reality:

> Society is demanding that companies, both public and private, serve a
> social purpose. To prosper over time, every company must not only deliver
> financial performance, but also show how it makes a positive contribution

to society. . . . Without a sense of purpose, no company, either public or private, can achieve its full potential. It will ultimately lose the license to operate from stakeholders.[5]

"Organizations will rise and fall based on their ability to deliver on these new demands," explains Larry Weber, CEO of Racepoint Global, an integrated marketing communications agency, and author of *Authentic Marketing: How to Capture Hearts and Minds Through the Power of Purpose.*

Purpose cannot be a marketing gimmick. It's vitally important that companies are authentic. "This better good must be central to the organization's core mission," Weber explains. "It's a fundamental value that is infused into the company's bloodstream so that it runs horizontally through every facet of the business—from R&D and marketing to finance and HR. Bad behavior will be called out in a nanosecond, with reputations and stock values paying the price."[6]

Marc Benioff, chairman and CEO of Salesforce, couldn't agree more. "The business of business is improving the state of the world," he explains.[7] This isn't just a nice idea for Benioff, it's what Salesforce has actually done. Since its earliest days, Salesforce has looked to leverage its technology, people, and resources to improve communities throughout the world. This is how positive social impact becomes part of a company's DNA.

Performance-Based Partnerships with Purpose

In recent years, companies have begun to employ performance-based partnerships to express their purpose and values. These highly visible partnerships, which are directly connected to customer sales, invite customers to join with them in making a difference. Giving Assistant is one of those companies. The following are some additional examples.

KidStart, Banks and Building Societies, and Thousands of Retailers[8]

KidStart is a U.K.-based loyalty program for parents designed by parents. Over the past 10 years, KidStart has helped thousands of families save millions of pounds for their children. The idea is simple and compelling: build your children's savings whenever you shop. Members shop at more than 2,300 well-known retailers on KidStart's desktop or mobile app, or via the KidStart Savings Prompt browser extension that works on all major web browsers, to find where savings are available. Savings are captured and can be directly linked to the KidSave children's savings account (or any Child Trust account or savings account that accepts electronic payments). Whole networks of families and friends can link their purchases to a given child's (children's) savings account(s)—aunts, uncles, and grandparents can all save for the future of the kids in their lives via the Beanstalk family saving app.

While a large partner network is key to KidStart's success, the company carefully vets potential partners to ensure a solid fit. "We have retailers interested in talking to a particular set of parents who come to us all the time," explains Julieta Lucca, affiliate marketing manager at KidStart.[9] "Of course, we are very protective of who we put in front of our members because we know that they trust us to share retailers worth their while. We take that very, very seriously." Vetting works both ways. KidStart's commitment to helping families save for their children's future is important to many of its partners. "When we launched our savings app, it strengthened our relationships with retailers because they knew that we really care about what we are doing and about helping our members save for their kids," says Lucca.

KidStart listens closely to its membership when considering what new retailers to add to the program. Currently the company is looking to increase the number of sustainable companies with whom it is collaborating, as this is increasingly important to its families. Lucca understands this desire: "Everyone needs to think about how their work is impacting others in the long run," she explains. "As a consumer, I am interested in ethical products, in ethical retailers, but it extends beyond that, because shoppers vote with every purchase and we're an intrinsic part in helping drive change for good."

Subscription Dog Treat Company and Local Animal Shelters

There is a subscription gift box for everyone out there, whether their interest is in self-care, gardening, arts and crafts, mysteries, or grilling. Each subscription box brand is well positioned to partner with organizations that focus on that shared interest: book groups, master grilling communities, and gardening clubs.

One company that makes customized boxes of toys and treats for dogs, for example, worked closely with local animal shelters to introduce new dog parents to the company's subscription program. If the new dog parents purchased a subscription as a result of the local shelter's introduction, the nonprofit received a portion of that purchase in the form of a partnership commission. These partnerships are wins on multiple fronts. Dogs get a monthly box of fun. New puppy parents get to share in the joy they have helped make possible while supporting the shelter that brought their new pup into their lives. And the company has benefited from a highly successful customer acquisition strategy.

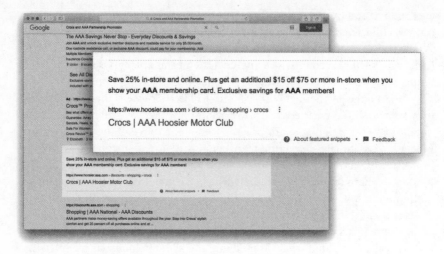

FIGURE 11.2   Crocs and AAA partnership promotion.

Crocs and AAA

Creating partnerships with community groups and associations can be a great way for enterprises to reach potential new customers and for organizations to provide additional value to their members and earn a bit of cash. The footwear brand Crocs, for example, partnered with the American Automobile Association (AAA) of Indiana, offering AAA members an exclusive discount on its boots, flats, clogs, sandals, flip-flops, sneakers, and loafers (Figure 11.2). Members received this discount online when they came through the association's dedicated shopping portal or when they presented a valid AAA membership card at the time of purchase when shopping in-store. AAA provided a useful benefit to its members and received a percentage of each footwear sale. And Crocs gained new customers, additional sales, and a nice brand association from collaborating with AAA.

Microsoft and Local Chambers of Commerce

In its effort to reach and help resource small businesses, Microsoft built relationships with small business influencers such as chambers of commerce, local mentorship organizations, and banks and shipping companies.[10] By collaborating with local chambers of commerce, the software company was able to provide chambers' member businesses a discount on the purchase of its latest software suite. When members ultimately purchased the enterprise's products, the chamber of commerce received an incentive payment—a new revenue stream. This partnership proved to be a very effective way of reaching a large swath of small and mid-sized businesses at scale, while also supporting local communities.

Goodness Takes Effort

Purpose-driven partnerships programs can be complicated because they often involve hundreds of independent, volunteer-run organizations. To be successful, enterprises have to be able to keep track of sales that each of these organizations catalyze, accurately determine the commissions they have earned, keep them informed of the funds they have earned, and cut checks to them every quarter. This can be a time-consuming proposition.

Partnership management platforms can manage this goodness from start to finish. Unique codes can be created for each partner, and when customers use these codes to make a purchase, they can be automatically tracked, commissions can be calculated, and checks generated automatically. What's more, partners can track the funds they've raised in real time, which enables them to budget more accurately.

Tips for Finding Your Impact

For some companies, social impact is so entwined with their products and services and ways of operating that it's hard to imagine what or who they would be in its absence. What would Nike, Patagonia, or Seventh Generation be without environmental stewardship? In their *Harvard Business Review* article, Professors Omar Rodriquez Vila and Sundar Bharadwaj refer to these companies that were built on a foundation of social impact as social-purpose natives. They contrast these players with social-purpose immigrants, companies that have operated without a deep societal purpose.[11] The good news is that it's very possible for organizations to identify, embrace, incorporate, and begin to live out of an authentic sense of social purpose.

Larry Weber offers the following suggestions to companies to identify their impact in his book *Authentic Marketing: How to Capture Hearts and Minds Through the Power of Purpose*:[12]

1. **Explore your values.** Does your company have a founding or current core value that is relevant to your prospects and customers? Can this core value become the driving force of an effort that is a natural extension of your business, which can have a positive impact on the world? What partners also hold this value?

2. **Picture your audience.** Who in the world might benefit if they had access to your products and services? What type of partnerships could provide access to your product or service to those people in need?

3. **Identify customer needs.** What do your customers care deeply about that is aligned with your business? How can you make a true difference in this area? What partners may be able to help?

4. **Evaluate liabilities.** Weber also suggests that you evaluate any potential risks in championing a values-based effort. Does your product or service hold potential to do harm in any way (think security issues, environmental issues, jobs loss issues)? If the answer is yes, what type of effort can you initiate to be vigilant and proactive to ensure that more good than harm comes from your efforts? Can you take a leadership role in this effort? If it's a controversial subject, what risk do you need to assess and where do you need alignment? What partners might be able to help you do so?

As consumers become much more values-aligned in making their purchase decisions, social impact partnerships represent a great way to create a deeper connection. They represent a clear opportunity for brands to align with their customers' desires and purpose, which can create a lasting connection to the brand. Careful consideration of the *right* partners is necessary, but brands that choose to explore this type of partnership should find themselves rewarded with a lasting positive reputation.

The Quick Summary

- Empowered consumers are demanding value from businesses, and that value increasingly includes purpose and ethics.

- Explore your brand's values to see if there is a driving force that can make a positive impact on the world. Then, identify potential partners that share this value.

- Be authentic at every turn. Purpose cannot be a marketing gimmick.

- Explore the potential for performance-based partnerships that express the core purpose and values. These partnerships, which are directly connected to customer sales, invite customers to join in making a difference, which results in a win-win-win.

- Purpose-driven partnerships programs can be complicated and time-consuming propositions. Automated partnerships platforms can manage this goodness from start to finish.

What's Up Next?

This section has covered the many different forms that partnerships can take. At this point, you may have lots of ideas about who you want to partner with, and how those partnerships might look in action. Now it's time to actually get started building those partnerships. The next part, "Get Started in Partnerships," covers the stages of getting a partnerships program off the ground. In the next chapter, you'll learn how to get internal buy-in to actually start testing partnerships.

Notes

[1] "How to Build Deeper Bonds, Amplify Your Message and Expand the Consumer Base," 2018 Cone/Porter Novelli Purpose Study, Cone Comm, accessed May 28, 2021, **https://www.conecomm.com/research-blog/2018-purpose-study**.

[2] Ibid.

[3] "2020 Edelman Trust Barometer," **Edelman.com**, January 19, 2020, **https://www.edelman.com/trustbarometer**.

[4] "How to Build Deeper Bonds" Cone Comm.

[5] "Larry Fink's 2018 Letter to CEOs," BlackRock, January 18, 2018, **https://www.blackrock.com/corporate/investor-relations/larry-fink-ceo-letter**.

[6] Larry Weber, *Authentic Marketing: How to Capture Hearts and Minds Through the Power of Purpose* (Hoboken, NJ: John Wiley & Sons, 2019).

[7] Dan Pontefract, "Salesforce CEO Marc Benioff Says the Business of Business Is Improving the State of the World," *Forbes*, January 7, 2017, **https://bit.ly/3xAz5zy**.

[8] "How It Works," KidStart, accessed May 28, 2021, **https://www.kidstart.co.uk/View/howdoeskidstartwork-main.aspx**.

[9] Daisy-Blue Tinne and Chris Campbell, "EMEA: Partnerships with Purpose," **impact.com**, Partnerships Experience 2021 by **impact.com**, recorded June 24, 2021, video, 34:02, **http://bit.ly/Impact-PX2021-Partnerships-Purpose**.

[10] "Microsoft Services, Tools Help Small Business Compete on a Global Scale," Microsoft, February 12, 2008, **http://bit.ly/tools-help-businesses-compete-global-scale**.

[11] Omar Rodríguez-Vilá and Sundar Bharadwaj, "Competing on Social Purpose," *Harvard Business Review*, September–October 2017, **https://hbr.org/2017/09/competing-on-social-purpose**.

[12] Weber, *Authentic Marketing*.

PART III

Get Started
in Partnerships

CHAPTER 12

How to Get Your Partnerships Program Started

Trust & Will is a digital disruptor in the estate planning industry. It knows that estate planning can be a daunting task, no matter how savvy you are. Its goal: "enabling every American to create a plan that's customized to fit their needs, their life, and their legacy." Trust & Will does this by making the process of setting up a will, trust, or nomination of guardianship as simple and straightforward as possible.

As a relatively new start-up, Trust & Will had not yet entered the partnerships space.

To get its partnerships program established and productive quickly, Trust & Will wanted to work with a partnerships agency that understood the full landscape and had successfully worked with other early-stage companies. It chose PartnerCentric, a leading partnerships agency for start-ups, which has assisted in the IPO or acquisition of over 65 brands.

But before it could jump in, Trust & Will wanted to strategically develop a data-backed program that would reach its target consumer. Working together with PartnerCentric, it delved deep, enriching its understanding of its target audience, and researching and recruiting partners that could successfully reach them. The research revealed a core target customer: recently married parents. These folks tend to think about estate planning later in life, revealing the need for an educational component that could be delivered via partnerships to reach and influence this audience.

PartnerCentric recruited employee perks partners—companies that work with enterprises to create inclusive and equitable employee environments to proactively reach this key demographic and educate them on why early estate planning is so important. The agency implemented dual campaigns: one that tracked sales (for potential customers who know what they are looking for when they come to the site) and one that tracked lead generation (for those customers who need more education before making a purchase) in order to expand publisher breadth and reach people at different stages of the purchase journey. The results spoke for themselves:

- From when Trust & Will's affiliate program launched in October 2018 to February 2021, it saw consistent revenue growth of 58 percent monthly.
- The Trust & Will affiliate program tripled in revenue from 2019 to 2020.
- With the addition of the lead generation campaign, productive publishers grew by 174 percent.

This partnership strategy has proven to be very effective for Trust & Will, and has allowed it to invest additional dollars to scale partnerships. These added investments in the channel, and the positive ROI from those dollars, played a crucial role in the overall growth of the business and, paired with the success of other channels, aided in securing additional venture capital backing.

"Affiliate partnerships are a low-risk way to drive high ROI and not only introduce your start-up to your target audiences while increasing sales, but also help fund future growth plans for your business," said Stephanie Harris, owner and CEO of PartnerCentric. "As long as you are clear on your goals and have a tailored plan in place, this channel will help you grow your business and keep those investors happy. At the end of the day, where else can you find that kind of certainty?"

Getting Partnerships Off the Ground: Taking Stock

An enterprise can successfully employ partnerships as a growth strategy no matter its size, industry, business model, or stage of business life cycle. But actually getting a partnerships effort off the ground within your company takes a bit of planning. While there's no single roadmap for every enterprise, there are some essential steps that every company will need to take in order to launch a successful program. This chapter discusses what it takes to get a program going internally: recognizing the opportunity, identifying the right time to move on it, having in place the organizational commitment, vision, strategy, and partnerships growth engine—people, process, and technology—and then doing it. The chapters that follow will tackle designing your partner experience, which includes everything from your partnerships program to your partner engagement strategy.

Building the Case for Executive Buy-In

You see the opportunity. You're excited and ready to go. Now it's time to build the necessary support to make it happen. While three people sitting around in a conference room may grasp the partnership opportunity and begin to test the waters, a successful partnerships program ultimately needs to be rooted in, and nurtured by, broad and strong organizational commitment. Successful programs become deeply integrated with enterprises' business strategy, products, and customer experience because they turn into fecund sources of revenue; this is only possible when there is buy-in from the top executives. You are also going to need broad support for your program because partnerships are cross-functional endeavors. Your success is highly connected to your ability to build out a strong, positive, and efficient intraorganizational effort with marketing, public relations, product marketing, business development, customer success, finance, legal, and other departments—not to mention with your partners!

It's a good idea to lay the groundwork for internal cross-collaboration from the beginning, identifying what stakeholders in your organization ultimately need to be onboard to ignite a strong partnerships program. Is it your CFO, CMO, head of business development, software engineers, and promotions managers?

Once you have identified the stakeholders, take some time to understand what is important to them. What do they have to gain and lose from your company becoming involved with partnerships? What loyalties or obligations might they have that might affect their ability to lend support? (See Figure 12.1 for a quick way to capture your thoughts.) You may want to verify these perceptions over time and keep any that hold water top of mind in future interactions, and while planning for and evaluating your program's success.

Build the Vision for Partnerships

Securing buy-in from the top is often an educational endeavor because today's partnerships are a different way of doing business for many enterprises. When done well, today's partnerships are collaborative, mutual, and transparent. They make previously impermeable corporate boundaries permeable. Many partnerships are performance-based, and few people initially understand their ins and outs. Others have preconceived notions of partnerships, reaching back to the earliest days of

Stakeholder/ Department	What might they have to gain?	What might be at stake?	What are their performance objectives?	How will we approach them?
Stakeholder #1				
Stakeholder #2				
Stakeholder #3				
Stakeholder #4				
Stakeholder #5				

FIGURE 12.1   Understanding key stakeholders in the partnerships effort.

affiliate marketing when there was "huge opportunity, but little regulation,"[1] during which time some enterprises were burned. Partnerships and performance-based payment models have significantly evolved since then.

"Organizations have to be able to get beyond the assumptions they've made over the years about how things work, because they may no longer be valid," cautions Keith Posehn, former head of performance partnerships at Uber. "We build up layers and layers of experience; unless we tear those layers down regularly and assess them, we will be blind to change. The CEO or CFO has to say, 'I'm willing to throw out my preconceived notions about this, my belief in how this works, because it may not be in line with the reality of the opportunity.'"

The conversation around partnerships starts with the business case. Why are partnerships an important growth strategy for businesses in general, and specifically for your organization? To effectively make the case, do research so you can present good, hard facts that come together as a solid vision. Get specific about how partnerships are enabling enterprises to meet their business objectives, objectives that are similar to yours—whether that is growth by customer acquisition, growth by increasing customer lifetime value, or both—or something altogether different. (Note that you can find plenty of resources to help you make your case—see **thepartnershipsbook.com**.)

Share examples of companies in your own industry and beyond. Spotlight the range of partnership types that enterprises are employing to grow in different ways and suggest several partnerships that may make sense for your company to consider. If nothing else, providing clear examples of partnerships plants a seed. It gets people thinking about the potential of partnerships, and that's enormous, because when leadership starts viewing the landscape with a partnership perspective, more ideas emerge.

Once you have set the stage, explain why partnerships work, how they are built on trust-based, established relationships that enable them to cut through the noise and reach their target customers, often in unique ways that go beyond traditional customer engagement efforts. Describe how partnerships generate and capture demand. Provide specific examples of how partnerships shorten customer and shopping journeys and amplify marketing initiatives. Then flip perspectives and focus on how they improve enterprise customer experience by making it easier for your target customers to find you and get their questions answered. Underscore how having a trusted third-party recommendation in the mix can give customers confidence in their purchase decision.

Be prepared to compare and contrast the basics of performance-based partnerships, fixed-fee partnerships, and traditional cost-per-impression (common in advertising) compensation models. You'll want to be able to talk CPA, tracking, multitouch attribution, and partner incentives. Help management understand that paying for performance is energizing for many partners, as it means that they are paid for the results they generate, and how this same practice can reduce the risk for your own company. But that does not mean you should rule out fixed-fee or hybrid compensation models—what is important is to track your results to ensure that the partnership delivers incremental value regardless of payout model. You may want to share the research findings of the Performance Marketing Association, which found that ROAS for partnerships was 12:1, illustrating the high value of partnerships for "businesses that want the most bang for their marketing buck."[2]

It can be useful to identify where your company is already partnering to dispel the myth that partnering is outside your organization's range of expertise. Most companies are already partnering; they just might not recognize it as such because partnerships are spread throughout many departments, go by a variety of different names, and are likely not tracked in an automated or unified way. You may want to share that some companies, having mastered the art of partnership automation, are looking at the range of partnerships within their organization to see where it makes sense to systematically manage and track them in whole or in part on a singular partnership management platform (PMP).

Discuss what it takes to get a program growing, and that this can be accomplished quickly by working with a partnerships agency that knows the ropes and has the connections, or more slowly by building out your own partnerships organization. In either case, recommend taking an iterative approach. Start small; build wins—maybe even create a very limited test program with a handful of partners. When the program succeeds, you'll come back to the powers that be and show them the incremental wins and the ROI, and share your plan to further scale the program to enable your company to grow faster and further.

But don't stop there. Listen well to people's hopes and concerns, then address them thoughtfully. Hold multiple conversations. Partnerships are a long-term play.

What if the company isn't ready? It never hurts to talk about partnerships. The opportunity is clearly there, but it may not be right for every company right now. Starting the conversation and laying the groundwork will, at the very least, put your enterprise in a prime position for when the opportunity *is* right. When the budget comes in, or the right hire is made, having the lay of the land right now allows you to act when the moment arrives. That said, it's important to realize that for organizations that procrastinate, what is at stake includes loss of revenue growth, loss of competitiveness, erosion of profit margin, and tougher barriers when entering new markets.

Develop Your Strategy

You've got the green light! Yeah! And you still need to work with your executive team to answer a few key questions:

- Who will run and staff your partnerships effort?
- What business objectives will your partnerships program work toward?
- What is your timeline?
- How will you measure your success?

Who Is Leading the Charge?

One of the first questions your company will need to answer is "Who is going to run this partnerships effort?" This person will need to be actively involved in representing your partnerships effort both internally and externally, able to advocate for the partnerships effort, close deals, and secure the necessary resources. Consider the types of partnerships that you hope to put in place both initially and in the future, and then work backward to determine what kind of person you will need to make that happen.

In the past, when traditional affiliates comprised the majority of an enterprise's performance-based partnerships portfolio, partnerships efforts were run primarily by young professionals. As partnerships have become more complex, and as revenue from partnerships has begun to generate a significant share of companies' revenue, different skill sets and more experienced leaders are assuming the helm.

Many of today's seasoned leaders built strong partnerships programs from the ground up, working with traditional affiliates to perfect the ins and outs of the pay-for-performance compensation model. Over time, they broadened the scope of their efforts, addressing a wider range of business objectives with a more diverse set of partners. In doing so, they generated significant growth for their companies, some contributing as much as 28 percent of their company's overall revenue.[3] Today, some of these leaders hold titles that reflect this expansion in remit, including global head of strategy and business development, chief customer officer, chief growth officer, or even chief partnerships officer (CPO).

What does a global leader of partnerships (who I will refer to for simplicity's sake as the CPO) do? Generally speaking, a CPO is tasked with driving productive partnerships that help the organization grow. They oversee the overall strategy, health, and evolution of a company's partnerships ecosystem. A new position, the CPO's remit is still being defined in many companies; however, some of the essential responsibilities include:

- Providing the vision, philosophy, strategic direction, and overall priorities for their partnerships efforts.
- Defining the KPIs and goals that determine the success of their department, and establishing the systems to readily track and measure those KPIs.
- Enhancing the organization's ability to effectively collaborate both internally and externally (including setting the vision and standards for partner experience [PX]).
- Articulating the partnerships opportunity to relevant stakeholders throughout their enterprise, and providing regular data-driven updates regarding the impact of partnerships on overall business results and specific business objectives.
- Growing their partnerships program or ecosystem with valuable partners.
- Effectively advocating for the resources and funding they need to succeed.
- Defining the roles and responsibilities of their subteams and mapping out an optimal organizational structure.
- Championing the partnerships effort within the industry and among the organization's most important partners.
- Identifying emerging opportunities and potential threats to the company in which partnerships efforts can make a difference.
- Being attuned to competitive threats and changes in the external environment that may impact the effectiveness of the organization's partnerships efforts—both positively and negatively—and developing plans to effectively harness or defend against them.

Toward this end, CPOs are responsible for the following deliverables:

- A strategic plan to guide overall growth and maturation of the partnerships program and ecosystem—including partner portfolio mix and vision and standards for partner experience—and its tactical execution.

- Forecasts and assessments on how much revenue or value can be generated from the partnerships effort.

- Budget and resourcing plans for the partnerships growth engine (people, process, and technology) that puts them on the road to hitting their goals.

- Standard operating procedures for managing the full partner life cycle and portfolio optimization.

- A map of organizational structure for the current, near, and longer term along with roles and responsibilities of each subteam.

Does It Make Sense to Work with a Partnerships Agency?

Partnerships programs can get to productivity much more quickly when run by and staffed with people who have been there and done it; in fact, there are several highly successful partnerships programs out there that are run by amazingly small but experienced teams. Other companies look to partnerships agencies to help them get going. This holds true whether they are a start-up or a well-established company.

To be clear, enterprises are still actively involved in their company's partnerships effort even when they hire a partner agency. They still need to provide the underlying business goals and strategy, brand knowledge and guidelines, and creative, and they will need to regularly design campaigns, promotions, and content. Agencies provide plenty of value by crafting the partnerships strategy that will enable the enterprise to achieve its underlying business goals and strategy: identifying and recruiting new partners; managing the day-to-day program operations; nurturing partner relationships; ensuring compliance; measuring and optimizing each partnership and the overall partnerships program; developing best practices; generating new ideas; and securing the underlying PMP that allows for tracking, analytics and reporting, global payouts, and contract management.[4]

Do you have the talent you need in-house or will you need to look outside? I've included a list of questions to help companies assess their internal capabilities, along with a fair amount of information about working with agency partners, in Chapter 14, "What About Agencies? Your Partners in Partnerships." It's important to note that some companies that build their partnerships programs with an agency never bring their partnerships program in-house; others do, in whole or in part.

What resources and skills will you need to run your partnerships program?

Role	Responsibilities
Partnerships Development	Sources new influencers, brand ambassadors, and mass media partners.

Skills/competencies needed	Skill available (Y/N)	Plan to develop or acquire this skill

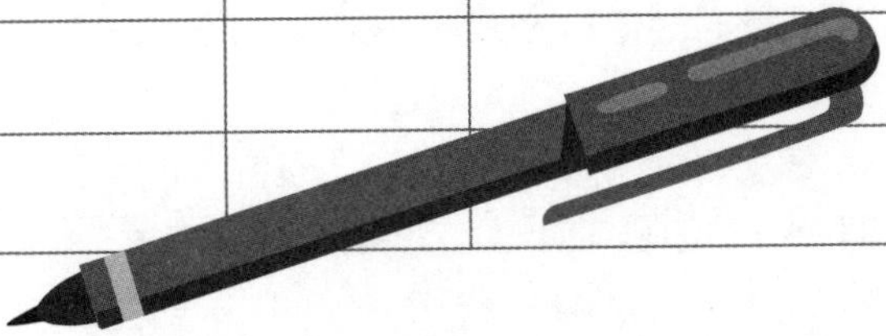

FIGURE 12.2   Partnerships organization roles, responsibilities, skills, and competencies.

Whether you choose to work with an agency or not, it can be helpful to clearly describe the roles, responsibilities, skills, and competencies you will need for your partnerships organization and a plan for how you will get them in place (Figure 12.2).

To Whom Should Your Partnerships Program Report?

Partnerships organizations typically report into several places. The majority of partnerships programs currently report to the CMO (26 percent), which is not surprising given referral partnerships' impact on customer engagement. The second most common home for partnerships is business development (21 percent), which should also not come as a surprise. Here's an important consideration: although partnerships programs are only embedded in product management departments 10 percent of the time, companies that have embedded partnerships in their product organization are 34 percent more likely to have a high-maturity partnerships program.[5] Why is this the case? For many companies, the product department serves as a key part of the brain of the organization—a critical organ for developing strategy and orchestrating cross-departmental collaboration. A partnerships team that is aligned with the product organization means that partnerships can be woven directly into product strategy. This structure also opens up a world of deeper, more tightly knit, integrated partnerships that generate outsized value for both companies.

You want to live where you are loved. Who enthusiastically supports your partnerships effort and wants you to succeed? Another important factor when considering reporting relationships is the culture of each department and whether it's conducive to partnership success. Does each department welcome an entrepreneurial spirit and a test, validate, and learn approach? Partnerships can only succeed if they are transparent, data-driven, and built on both external and internal collaboration. Your partnerships team needs to embody these factors, and it helps if the people it reports to do as well.

What Will Your Program Focus On?

Work with your executive team to determine how your partnerships program will help your company grow. This is where you complete the statement, "We want to drive growth by. . . ." Be sure to align your partnerships effort with critical business needs. For example, if you are focused on growth in market share, as many companies are, what are the branding and profit margin parameters that surround that strategy? Unless you are a discount brand, don't fall into the trap of thinking that you have to offer discounts to build a successful partnerships program. There are many ways to be successful, even on coupon and deal sites, without discounting your brand. Next, consider who is going to make this growth happen. Who are your target customers? Where do they reside? What do you know about them? What do you want these customers to do? Make full price purchases? Download your mobile app and use it? Purchase your excess inventory? Use your product more?

With these questions answered you can begin to build out your go-to-market plan: Who is doing what, when, where, with whom, and with what outcome or result? What are the customer behaviors you want your partners to catalyze—what are the micro and macro conversions that you will pay your partners for prompting? Where along your customer journeys do these behaviors take place? What roles will you be looking for your partners to play (i.e., introduce, influence, close, retain, and reengage?) If this sounds only vaguely familiar, you may want to refer back to

Chapter 3, "How Partnerships Can Help You Meet Critical Business Goals," and its associated worksheets at **thepartnershipsbook.com**.

If You Are a Start-Up Starting a Partnerships Program

Start-up companies face unique challenges when launching a partnerships program. "As natural disruptors in their verticals, start-ups often answer to boards and investors who demand metrics and timetables that wait for no one, and need to impress everyone," explains Stephanie Harris, owner and CEO, PartnerCentric. "Founders of start-ups have ambitious market share objectives as they face well-financed competitors."

Partnerships built on a pay-for-performance model are well poised to drive demand and growth for these brands as they have broad reach and are low-risk. But start-ups have to meet several hurdles to be able to employ partnerships, and when they meet these hurdles, they can get to productivity and begin optimizing their program quickly. Drawing from the company's depth of experience in working with well-funded start-ups, PartnerCentric offers these questions for start-ups to consider before launching a robust partnerships program:

- Have you worked out your value proposition, quantified your total addressable market, and validated your product's desirability with your target customer base?
- Have you identified your competitors and potential competitors?
- How strong is your brand recognition in the marketplace? Do you have a plan to focus on brand recognition initiatives in other channels, as many key players will insist that you have an established footprint?
- Do you have the budget to secure direct placements that will maximize your brand's visibility on top-notch partners' platforms?
- Do you have an editorial and promotional calendar? Have you already developed creative and editorial content?
- Are you open to working with a wide range of partnership types to best meet your business objectives?

What Type of Budget Will You Have?

Your budget will depend upon what you want to achieve and how quickly. Will you be building your effort in-house or working with an agency? When you consider your budget for commissions, remember that partnerships operate differently from many customer engagement initiatives. If your partnerships are run exclusively on a performance basis, commissions will be paid out of revenue that you generate. As long as the quality of your sales is good, you will have already made the money out of which you will pay your commissions. In this case, it's in everyone's best interest to have a flexible commissions budget. A fixed budget will not decrease risk; however, it might constrain your success. You may also want to budget for additional avenues of exposure such as paid placements, performance bonuses, giveaways, branding events, and content creation.

How Will You Measure Your Efforts?

Determine how you will measure your program results. Almost every business initiative today needs to be measured to show the value it has produced based on the investment made and on how it contributes to achieving overall enterprise revenue goals and business objectives. Partnerships programs are no different. Track and measure what is important to your executive team as a whole and to individual stakeholders—you may want to refer back to Figure 12.1 to help you determine this set of metrics. Where possible, make sure the metrics you keep enable your team to proactively optimize your partnerships effort and will enable you to make wise decisions and investments in the future. Chapter 16, "Next Steps: Envision and Plan a Durable Partnerships Program," talks more about measuring the value of your program.

When Will You Show Results?

Get clear on your executive team's expectations for results. Remember that partnerships are a different breed; they do not work like many marketing initiatives, which are likely to be reference points for your executive team.

Partnerships take longer to set up and might not yield an immediate ROI compared to, say, paid search advertising. Here's why: people, not algorithms, comprise partnerships. These working relationships take time to recruit, nurture, and get to productivity. You also will need time to operationalize your strategy: develop your go-to-market plans, design your actual program, develop content and creative to help your partners be successful, and get your partnerships growth engine (i.e., people, process, and technology) in place. If you choose to work with an agency, it will help you with your go-to-market plans, program design, and aspects of your partnerships growth engine.

That having been said—and this is key—partnerships are the gift that keeps on giving. They are always on, you typically only pay out when they deliver results, and although you invested more time in setting up a partnership compared to, say, an advertising campaign, you will see long-running consistent returns on it. Unlike an advertising campaign, which is more like a coin-operated slot machine—insert a coin every time and see if you get a positive ROI—you have to keep feeding the machine.

Establish Your Partnerships Process

It's easy to shoot from the hip, taking an ad-hoc approach to getting your partnerships operation off the ground; however, in **impact.com**'s work with thousands of different partnerships, we have observed a common process that emerges as enterprises and their partners forge, deepen, and optimize their relationships. When companies proactively adopt this simple yet standardized process for their partnerships effort from the get-go, they can save time and effort, are likely to avoid some common mistakes, and don't have to redesign business processes as they grow.

These observations have been codified into the Partnership Life Cycle, a multistage process that can be proactively applied to all types of partnerships (Figure 12.3). Enterprises and their partners cycle through these stages multiple times as they expand their partnership's impact. The six stages of the Partnership Life Cycle are:

1. *Discover and Recruit:* You have identified your needs and generated your ideal partner profile; now it's time to bring your plans to life. This stage is about finding and recruiting partners that are a good fit for your brand and your company's current business objectives.

2. *Contract and Pay:* You and your potential partner are interested. Now it's time to set yourselves up for long-term success with contracts that acknowledge and reward the value you both bring to the table.

3. *Track:* Transparency and trust are hallmarks of modern partnerships and tracking provides full disclosure of partnership activity that enables that trust. In this stage you determine what variables you want to identify (e.g., new or returning customers, customer devices used, incremental sales, product purchases at the category and SKU level) and how to best ensure that partner traffic is being tracked and credited as accurately as possible.

4. *Engage:* Success lies in activating your partners and then keeping them productive over the long haul. Offering training, fresh and engaging content, relevant incentives, and strategic insights into partner performance keeps your partnerships humming.

5. *Protect and Monitor:* To be successful, your partnerships need to generate real results: new customers, entry into new markets, upsells and cross-sells, and mobile installs and usage. Staying vigilant against fraud and ensuring partner compliance with the law and your brand guidelines are key to ensuring that your results are valid.

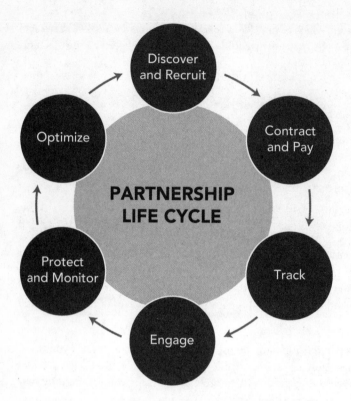

FIGURE 12.3   The six stages of the Partnership Life Cycle.

6. *Optimize:* Successful partnering is iterative. It takes smart experimentation with your partner to bring out the best in your partnership. This stage, which is ongoing, is where all your upfront work is made manifest.

Eventually companies automate this entire process, which enables them to scale and optimize each of their partnerships and their portfolio as a whole. For a deep dive into what this looks like, see **www.thepartnershipsbook.com**.

Select Your Partnership Management Platform (PMP)

In the past, companies often started out scrappy, using several point systems to manage their partnerships programs. These systems might have included Salesforce or HubSpot to track leads and Google Docs or Box to manage documentation and spreadsheets. But these ad-hoc combinations fell short as partnerships programs became more sophisticated.

A good partnership management platform enables programs to get off on their best foot, to not limit their competitiveness because they don't have the underlying capability in place. Today's partnership management platforms enable enterprises to:

- Manage a growing and diverse set of partners (those that exist today and those that have not yet come on the scene) efficiently and transparently.
- Create a system of record for myriad customer journeys by tracking the true source of every sale and lead across multiple channels and partners. The best partnership management systems allow businesses to track accurately, provide insights on partner activity (which creates incremental value), and provide the capability to pay partners uniquely down to the transaction level (which allows enterprises to pay their partners on a performance basis, accurately assess their value, and promote incrementality).
- Streamline and automate all aspects of the Partnership Life Cycle—including discovery and recruiting, tracking, reporting, contracting, and payments—so that their partnerships programs become customizable, optimizable, and scalable.
- Generate performance results and KPI scorecards in real time with hundreds of variables.
- Ensure partner compliance with brand guidelines, consumer privacy regulations, and tax law.
- Enable global partnerships programs with global tracking, local compliance, and the ability to pay partners in local currencies.

Partner agencies work with partnership management systems to get the best results for their clients. Enterprises that manage their programs in-house will want this capability, too.

Spotting Potential Partners

Your program is ready to go; all you need is partners! There are millions of potential partners out there to be discovered, from large publishers to small publishers to influencers to mobile apps to strategic business integrations. The challenge is finding and recruiting the right partners, and bringing them into the fold, with the right amount of effort and in a way that reflects who you are as a partner.

Create an Ideal Partner Profile

It's helpful to create an ideal partner profile to have as the background for your partnership discovery and partner qualification efforts. What are the essential qualities every potential partner must have? What hurdles must be met to even have that partner be considered? These profiles should be generated from your own results: What are you finding to be critical success factors? And they should be reexamined and updated (if necessary) with each partner portfolio review. This profile can serve as a hurdle for any and all new potential partners. Some questions to consider as you work to identify your ideal partner profile: Who is a fit for my brand? Can they endorse my brand with credibility? Do they have access to the types of customers I want to acquire? Do they have access to the right touchpoints to influence their audience or customers (e.g., email, inserts, video, audio, etc.)? Are they interested in a potential partnership for the right reasons? Do they share the same values as my brand?

Jared Saunders, who manages the partnerships team at the online diamond retailer Blue Nile, created "Our Strategy for Determining Partner Mix" to guide his team's efforts in recruiting and managing partners (Figure 12.4). It describes the commitment they have to strategic and purposeful partner selection as well as key "must-haves" to be considered: positive brand exposure, cost efficiencies, positive financial contribution, and product focus. It also recognizes that partners are not created equal and that the cost of building and maintaining a partnership, including relationship management, must be considered when evaluating performance and value.

OUR STRATEGY FOR DETERMINING PARTNER MIX

We conscientiously, strategically, and purposefully select partners:

Based on positive brand exposure, cost efficiencies, potential financial contribution, and product focus.

Keeping relationship maintenance, budgets, and their engagement level in mind.

While using data to help guide mix and direct focus.

FIGURE 12.4   Blue Nile's strategy for determining partner mix.

Cast a Wide Net

In the early stages of looking for partners, it's important to cast a wide net because some potential partners may not be familiar with how partnerships work or share your desire to collaborate. Indeed, the more nontraditional the partner, the more upfront work it may take to unlock the value that is there. As a result, when first getting their programs going, enterprises looking for broad exposure often rely heavily on traditional affiliates, but that doesn't mean that everyone needs to begin there.

One place to start is to ask, "What is our customer doing when they're not shopping with us?" Think about how you can engage with them in other places, when they're doing something else, and whether it will seem natural or helpful for your brand to be part of that. What *kinds* of companies would be good partners? What other brands are attracting your audience? Answering these questions will likely produce some companies that are not competitors but have a strong relationship with your target audience.

Now study those potential partners, what their businesses look like, and how they've constructed their customer experience. Can your enterprise fit into that customer experience and these potential partners' existing relationships with *their* customers? Start hypothesizing ways you can add value to the experience so that the customer gets something from the partnership that is an improvement over what they already receive.

For example, one of the best customer experience integrations is a partnership between Airbnb and Delta. When a Delta customer books a flight to a destination, the Airbnb partnership is presented as part of the booking experience, asking the customer if they'd rather stay at an Airbnb instead of a hotel and offering a link to book accommodations—stated as "Fly there, live there." That's a seamless customer experience, adding value and anticipating a need of the shared customer.

Of course, fitting into the user experience and customer relationship is unique for each business. The best way to start thinking about how to fit is to look at the major kinds of partnerships and hypothesize how you can build relationships, whether that's through coupon, cashback, and deal sites, mobile app integrations, influencers, mass media publishers, or strategic B2B partnerships. Within each of these buckets there's a universe of partnership opportunities.

In building the use case, think about how each of these types of partnerships would help achieve your business objectives. Build a centralized resource (it can even be a spreadsheet at this early point in the process) to map out all of the potential early partnerships. Then, contact these potential partners to discuss the potential. Determine who is the right person on the partner's end and explain the type of partnership you're looking to form. Determine if the potential partner already

Potential partner and type of partner	Business objective(s) for potential partnership	Existing partnership activity	Appropriate contact and role	Actions to take or have been taken
Potential partner #1				
Potential partner #2				
Potential partner #3				
Potential partner #4				
Potential partner #5				

FIGURE 12.5 Create a central database for your partnerships effort.

works with enterprises like yours and gauge whether they are interested in collaborating with you (Figure 12.5). Once that process is complete, you may find that you've found three partners in each bucket that are interested in exploring working with your enterprise. This may only be 9–15 partners, but it's a strong start.

Partnership Management Platforms Simplify the Discovery Process

Partnership management platforms can simplify the partner discovery process and make quick scaling possible. These proprietary combinations of web crawlers, integrations with major web services, social platforms, app intelligence companies, and dedicated teams of in-house partner curators enable enterprises to discover a network of best-fit partners for their current business objectives. There are well-developed marketplaces for coupon, deal, and loyalty sites, influencers, mass media publishers, and mobile apps embedded in today's PMPs. Enterprises can filter by channel, category, keyword, promotional method, geography, reach, audience demographic, engagement quality, traffic directed to competitors' sites, and more depending on their objectives, targeted customer, and potential partner type.

With filtered results in hand, companies can narrow down the potential partners to those that are most likely to succeed.

More advanced platforms generate recommendations for partnerships using data science and machine learning, which simplifies the discovery process in important ways. Leveraging reams of data, they are able to both enhance partner profiles and to better understand what comprises a productive partnership—is it audience match? Product positioning? Shipping, headquarters, and marketing geo categories? Promotional methods used? Performance metrics? Or some combination thereof? This combination means more productive partnerships for you and a faster route to grow your partnerships program.

Get Going

The most successful programs are led by entrepreneurs like Priest Willis, Sr., senior manager, global partnerships strategist at Lenovo, who encourages partnerships organizations to get out there and gain first-hand experience. "Be a guinea pig!" Willis offers. "Especially when you are starting out, don't be paralyzed by the data and the talk you hear. Just jump in, get your feet wet, and learn."

The Quick Summary

- Starting partnerships programs is about recognizing the opportunity, identifying the right time to move on it, having the organizational commitment, vision, strategy, and partnerships growth engine—people, process, and technology—in place, and then doing it.
- The key to beginning any partnerships program is for the executive team to fund the program and set goals, and that's only possible if it's crystal clear what partnerships can do for the business.
- Companies often work with partner agencies to help them establish their partnerships programs quickly and successfully.
- Think about the future when establishing your partnerships team, processes, and technology. Don't be limited tomorrow by the decisions you make today.
- Take an entrepreneurial approach to your initial partnerships. Experiment and don't be afraid to fail or start over. The goal is to demonstrate growth before scaling up, so think outside the box.
- "Jump in, get your feet wet, and learn," says Priest Willis, Sr., senior manager, global partnerships marketing strategist at Lenovo.

What's Up Next?

When you have executive buy-in, funding, staff, and a clear idea of who your potential partners are, it's time to start thinking in more detail about the partnerships program itself, and what it will feel like for those partners. The next chapter is about how to design your program's partner experience.

Notes

[1] Robert Glazer, *Performance Partnerships* (Austin: Lioncrest Publishing, 2017), p. 10.

[2] "2018 Performance Marketing Study: Full Year 2018 Taking the Pulse of Performance Marketing in the US," Performance Marketing Association, August 7, 2019, **http://bit.ly/ PMA-Performance-Marketing-Study**.

[3] A Forrester Consulting Thought Leadership Paper Commissioned by Impact, "Invest in Partnerships to Drive Growth and Competitive Advantage," **impact.com**, June 2019, **http://bit.ly/forrester-impact-invest-in-partnerships**.

[4] "What's New & What's Next with Performance Partnerships," Acceleration Partners, accessed May 31, 2021, **http://bit.ly/future-of-performance-marketing**.

[5] "Invest in Partnerships," **impact.com**.

CHAPTER 13

How Does It Feel? Creating a Beneficial Partner Experience

If you are a creator or publisher looking to promote Walmart's hundreds of millions of products to your audiences, members, or customers, you may find it to be a daunting task. Where do you start and how do you locate what is likely to resonate best?

Walmart created DealFinder to address this challenge. Built on top of the company's partnership management platform, DealFinder is a simple widget that enables partners to easily search through Walmart's extensive inventory of products to find the best options for their audiences. Products include high-turnover items found in Walmart stores, more extensive holdings stored in its warehouses, and third-party seller items available through Walmart Marketplace. Filters allow partners to search Walmart's product catalog by category, product, new arrivals, best-sellers, clearance, exclusivity to Walmart, or theme—for example, Get Your Patio Summer-Ready, Gifts from the Heart, or Perfect Valentine's Day Presents for Everyone and Every Budget. Figure 13.1 shows how easy it is to search Walmart's inventory for televisions.

FIGURE 13.1   DealFinder makes it easy for partners to locate products.

A single click on any item, in this case a television, brings up product descriptions, pricing, customer reviews, and delivery options as shown in Figure 13.2. Partners can easily save items for future use, generate tracking links, and create placements to promote the item on their own sites or social media directly in Deal-Finder. It's that easy.

DealFinder is one of several initiatives that Walmart has undertaken to date to intentionally enhance its partners' experience. Walmart's partner experience strategy also includes helping its partners interact more effectively with their audiences, members, or followers. To be clear, Walmart's partners have to know their audiences or members well—what they are interested in and how and where to interact with them—and they have to be making their audiences' or members' lives better in significant ways in order to be accepted into Walmart's partnerships program. Walmart's value-add is to provide additional insights that are unique to Walmart with which partners can enhance their efforts. For example, by sharing partnership performance data, including how the partner is specifically impacting Walmart's

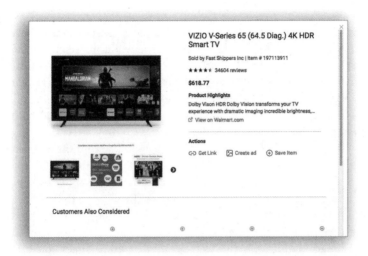

FIGURE 13.2   Partners can easily generate referral links and ads with DealFinder.

shopping journeys and sales, partners can see what combination of product, offer, and messaging works best. With that information in hand, partners can optimize their future activity to enhance conversion. Walmart also shares aggregate-level data—not PII—with its partners that enables them to understand what best-selling products they may want to share with their audiences. Similarly, if a partner is successfully selling laptops, Walmart may suggest that it also market mouses or keyboards to its audiences to better meet their needs, while also increasing average order value and/or customer lifetime value.

"Our best strategy is to help our partners by equipping them with the right insights and data so they can interact even more with their members," explains Aldo Bukit, associate director of marketing, affiliates, and APIs at Walmart eCommerce, whom we met in Chapter 2. "We can't just say, 'here's the link, drive traffic to us.' That was fine and great about 10 years ago, but moving forward, we have to be more engaged . . . [We have to provide them] with the right offers, messaging, and tools."[1]

Enhancing its conversion experience—how easy it is for customers to make a purchase—is another critical aspect of Walmart's partner experience enhancement efforts. Ease of purchase starts with simplifying the purchase process—every additional step increases the chance a customer will walk away without a sale. Toward this end, Walmart has created a software development kit (SDK) to simplify the conversion process for its partner-assisted purchases. A BuyNow button can be placed next to a product offering on a partner's website or mobile app, enabling interested customers to place an item directly into their shopping cart on **Walmart.com**.

What's more, Walmart merged its mobile and desktop partnerships programs, which were originally run on two separate platforms, to ensure that customers are able to search for products and make their purchases on the same device. Now customers interacting with Walmart partners via mobile are automatically directed to the right product page on Walmart's mobile app (if they have it installed) to complete a purchase, rather than its mobile desktop ecommerce site, providing the user with a superior mobile shopping experience. If they don't have the app installed, then the consumer is given a choice: continue their shopping experience on Walmart's mobile website (they get deep linked into the product page the partner was promoting) or install the app. Once the user installs the app and opens it, they are immediately taken to the product page that the partner was promoting—a process called deferred deep linking. In addition to creating a seamless shopping experience for potential customers, this integration simplifies partners' experience in two important ways. First, partners no longer have to decide which Walmart platform (mobile web or mobile app) to direct potential customers to, as a single tracking link automatically directs customers to the right purchase environment. Second, partners only have to join one Walmart partnerships program.

To further enhance its conversion experience, Walmart offers state-of-the-art delivery options for customer purchases. Whereas a few years ago customers were willing to wait up to 10 days for items to be delivered, today online shoppers want fast—and often free—delivery options. To meet this demand, Walmart offers free standard delivery options ranging from same-day in-store pickup to next- and two-day delivery for most items. Expedited pickup and delivery is available to members of Walmart+. These shipping options enable Walmart to better meet today's increased customer expectations for quick delivery. In doing so, it also enhances customer conversion rates, which is music to partners' ears.

A strong internal partnerships team and effective cross-functional collaboration are essential to Walmart's ability to deliver partner experience excellence. "We recognize the importance of our partners and the value they bring to our customers and to Walmart," Bukit explains. "We want to work closer, and continue to become more integrated with our partners in the future." Toward this end, Bukit's team reviews partner performance data daily, sometimes hourly, during peak periods, to see what is working and what isn't and what can be done about it. They funnel insights to their business team and other relevant areas of the organization with whom they determine what insights can be shared with partners. In addition to focusing on daily market activity, the partnerships team, business team, and product engineers meet weekly to discuss strategy, capabilities, and timelines for new partner experience initiatives. Bukit sees his leadership team's job as educating the organization about partnerships—and advocating for them internally.

Be Intentional About Your Partner Experience

Who you partner with matters. And how you partner impacts with whom you can partner. Having a reputation for being a smart, innovative, and trustworthy partnerships team that is easy to work with and deeply committed to its partners' success is a powerful advantage when it comes to recruiting and growing long-term productive relationships with top-notch partners. It encourages partners to work with you and to bring their A game to the effort. It's also its own inbound partner recruitment strategy; being a great partner draws potential collaborators to you and encourages your current partners to be ambassadors, recruiting other exceptional partners for you. This is especially helpful for lesser-known brands that might enjoy collaborating with larger, more established brands but may not otherwise be able to get their attention. Being a great partner has value beyond recruitment. "Brands that provide an enhanced partner experience grow faster than their peers, are more profitable, and drive higher customer satisfaction and retention downstream," explains Jay McBain, principal analyst, channel partnerships and alliances at Forrester.[2]

The stakes are high and the experience you create for your partners—your partner experience—is too important to be left to habit or happenstance. At **impact.com**, we recommend that companies become deeply intentional about their partner experience, defining it, nurturing it, evaluating it, and enhancing it as they do their brand identity and their customer experience. Doing so requires an "outward-in" look at your partnerships effort, understanding what is important to your partners and carefully considering how meeting their needs and expectations can generate business value for your business.

This chapter will explore some of the key aspects of today's partner experience: developing your partnerships vision and partner value proposition (PVP), translating that vision into daily operations, collaborating for partner ongoing success, institutionalizing your learning, and measuring and assessing your partnerships experience.

Develop Your Partnerships Vision

Your partnerships vision is the foundation for your partnerships efforts. It articulates your purpose and why you are invested in these collaborations. It also puts context around your purpose, describing what is important to you when it comes to partnerships and the spirit in which you participate in them. Your partnerships vision informs the decisions your company makes when it comes to partnerships and the way you will help shape the emerging partnership economy. It's not intended to be a playbook that calls all the shots; rather it's a guiding light, a North Star of sorts, to enable everyone within an organization to have a shared understanding of what it means for your company to partner. It sets the standard for your partnerships, regardless of where partnerships are initiated or managed within your organization—business development, marketing, PR, customer service—enabling you to develop best-in-class partnerships at scale with consistency. That same North Star is a strong selling point for potential partners; it enables them to know what they can expect when they partner with you.

Your partnerships vision should be compelling and authentic, an expression of your deepest convictions and core values. It should reflect your partnerships' brand personality and voice—who you are as a partnerships organization. And it must be in sync with your overall corporate brand essence and guidelines.

The partnerships vision that governs Jared Saunders' partnerships team at the online diamond retailer Blue Nile, "Our Goal as a Performance Marketing Team," can be found in Figure 13.3. The statement is clear that success for Saunders' partnerships team is achieved by actively cultivating and strengthening individual partnerships. This is not a "set it and forget it" operation. Toward this end, team members play multiple roles—creators, participators, counselors, and enablers—and are expected to do so with professionalism and tact. The guidelines make clear that while profitability is important, positive brand exposure is primary; trading off brand risk for brand profitability is not an option. Finally, financial responsibility

---

Our Goal as a Performance Marketing Team

Our goal and intent as the Affiliates and Partnership team
   is the ultimate success and profitability of our company.

While our methods adapt to each situation,
   we strive to build positive brand exposure and drive profits.

We cultivate and strengthen partnerships;
   acting as brand ambassadors with professionalism and tact.

We test and prove our methods
   with insightful data and creativity.

Practicing strict fiscal responsibility thru optimization.
   Acting as creators, participators, counselors, advocates, and enablers.

FIGURE 13.3 Vision statement for Blue Nile's partnerships team.

is paramount and will be achieved through a combination of testing, analysis of data-based insights, and a fair amount of creativity.

As you think about your partnerships vision, it's important to consider how you will partner in good times and in difficult moments. In fact, how you show up in both moments is the ultimate statement of your partnerships philosophy. During the COVID-19 pandemic, Brian Marcus, former director of eBay's Global Partner Network, encouraged enterprises to be mindful of how they treated their partners during this unusual time. "This new normal presents you with the opportunity to be a partner in a way that has not been seen, that is unprecedented," Marcus explained. "This means adjusting your program to reflect the reality of today, and it also means that actions you take now will outlive this period of time in the future, so be real careful about how you treat your partners."[3] (Full disclosure, Marcus now works at **impact.com**.)

Similarly, Keith Posehn, former head of performance partnerships at Uber, encourages enterprises to be "trust forward" about how they will handle mistakes. As an example, he cites a time when Uber had a problem tracking commissions for a partner for a period of time. Recognizing that it was Uber's problem, Posehn took action. "I told them that we screwed up," Posehn recalls, "and that we were going to fix it and make it worth their while to give us their trust." And then he did. Posehn took the partner's average earnings-per-click result, applied it to the time period of the outage, and paid its commission accordingly. He also gave it a 10 percent bonus for its trouble. "It was a small gesture that made a difference in our relationship for years to come," Posehn recalls.

Posehn also recommends that enterprises be consistent when it comes to enforcing their program rules. "Don't make exceptions, like giving partners three strikes," Posehn offers. In his experience, "You've got to hold your partners to account. If your rules don't apply consistently, then no one is going to be able to trust the rules. They won't believe you when you say you have a rule." Clear is kind.

Articulate Your Partner Value Proposition

Your PVP is rooted in your partnerships vision and is a summary statement that explains why a potential partner would want to invest its time, resources, and reputation in you. How would working with you contribute to its success? Why are you uniquely qualified to deliver that value? Your PVP is different from your customer value proposition, which describes the benefits a customer will receive when purchasing your product or service. Figure 13.4 shows an example of a PVP from eBay.

Increasingly we expect to see companies broadening the scope of their PVP to include how they actually partner—the type of experience partners can expect

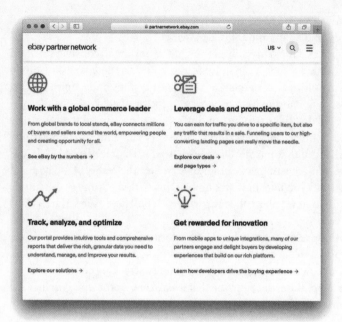

FIGURE 13.4   eBay's partner value proposition.

when they come on board. For example, we imagine companies acknowledging what their partners are trying to achieve:

> *We know you want to continually increase the value of our products and services in your audience's eyes, while also making a fair profit, and we want to help make that happen. Toward this end we will provide you products that are desirable and easy to sell. We will run relevant campaigns and provide you with tested content and partner resources (e.g., DealFinder) that will facilitate your success. We will offer you a competitive commission and compensate you fairly for your influence on our customer journeys, even if you are not the last touch. To enable you to optimize your partnership results, we will give you access to our sales and performance data and relevant customer and product insights. And we will be excellent partners, who are committed to working with you in a collaborative, transparent, and mutually rewarding way.*

Develop your PVP and then employ it in your partner recruitment efforts as a meaningful way to differentiate yourself from other enterprises' partnerships efforts. Keep it and your partnerships vision statement front and center, within eyeshot of every member of your partnerships team, as a reminder of what comprises partnership success for your organization.

Live Your Vision

Developing your partnerships vision and PVP are important first steps toward building an excellent partner experience. However, they won't make a speck of difference if your partnerships team doesn't live by them. If you claim these values and principles to be the foundation of your program and you don't deliver on them, you are likely to do more harm than good to your partnerships experience.

Translating your partner philosophy and value proposition down to the operational level is where your partner experience aspiration becomes reality. It's incumbent upon your partnerships team to determine the most important aspects of your partner experience from your partners' point of view—which may extend beyond what you consider your partnerships "program"—and to distinguish yourself from your competitors on those points. Key areas to consider include the products you offer, your conversion and post-conversion experiences, your overall program and incentives, your recruitment process, and the way you support your partners' success—topics that are explored next.

Offer Great Products

Partners are interested in the desirability and marketability of an enterprise's products, services, and experiences, and whether they are a good fit for their audiences, members, or customers. Once desirability and marketability are established, partners are also interested in how easy it is for them to access up-to-date product information and product-level tracking links. This is why DealFinder was such an important partner experience investment for Walmart.

Not every enterprise needs, or is able, to create its own DealFinder widget; however, companies can continually update their product information for their partners via interfaces like their product feed or API. Useful interfaces include essential information about products, performance, inventory, pricing, and any other data needs that your partners may benefit from. Be sure to enrich your product feeds or APIs to promote the products, brands, or categories you want to highlight and that will work well for each of your partners. It's a good idea to talk with your partners frequently to accurately understand their appetite for your offerings and to glean new insights into your potential customers.

Focus on Your Conversion and Post-Conversion Experiences

The ease with which potential customers can actually purchase your products is also important to your partners. If your products are too hard to purchase, customers will walk away before making a purchase. Eighty-seven percent of online shoppers say they would abandon their shopping carts during checkout if the process was too difficult, according to a recent study conducted by the payments company Splitit, and 55 percent admitted they would abandon their carts and never return to the retailer's site.[4] If partners lead customers to you but you cannot successfully convert them, your partners will not be able to make money via your program. To be blunt, they will not be your partners for long. As seen with Walmart, ease of purchase means simplifying the purchase process with a BuyNow button, a congruent conversion experience—partners being able to direct potential customers to the right enterprise experience: app to app, desktop to desktop—and state-of-the-art delivery capabilities.

Your post-conversion experience also matters. A recent Pitney Bowes Global Ecommerce Study found that 61 percent of consumers were unhappy with their online shopping experience in 2018—and this number is accelerating. The rate of dissatisfied shoppers in the United States is accelerating even faster, with 56 percent dissatisfied—up from just 36 percent in 2017. The reasons cited by consumers include delivery delays, costly shipping, inaccurate tracking, confusing return policies, and lost or incorrect items.[5] The cost of a poor post-purchase experience is high to you and your partners. The same study found that in response to a bad post-purchase experience, 90 percent of online shoppers in the United States will act in a way that will hurt an enterprise's brand. These actions often include sharing their frustrations on social media, potentially impacting their entire social network's perceptions, and never purchasing from the enterprise again.[6] This doesn't reflect well on your partners or their credibility.

"More and more, consumers are telling us that the post-purchase experience—what happens after the order—is every bit as important, if not more, than the shopping experience that occurs before the order," said Lila Snyder, president of commerce services at Pitney Bowes. "The silver lining for retailers: consumers are giving you the blueprint for how to get it right, and those who get it right will be rewarded with customer loyalty and revenue growth."

Provide a Motivating Program

Incentives are an important part of modern partnerships. It's important that your incentives are competitive, so that your partners choose to work with you and direct traffic to you rather than to your competitors. Incentives alone are not enough, however. Your ability to adequately track traffic and attribute value so that partners are accurately compensated provides a critical foundation for a motivating partner program. Today's PMPs enable you to track your myriad shopping journeys to see where partners have actually influenced your customers, allowing you to pay them accurately for their impact. Fairness goes a long way toward creating an excellent partner experience.

There are times in every partnerships program that commission structures need to be changed. Sometimes these changes benefit some or all of your partners, other times they may not, or they may not appear to initially. In every case, it's important to talk over changes with your partners so they can understand your rationale and see how it is likely to impact them, and to identify ways they can be successful under this new commission structure. (For more information on partner incentives and tracking, see **www.thepartnershipsbook.com**.)

Partnerships programs do not exist in a vacuum. Keep an eye on your competitors and their partnerships programs to spot trends and changes in strategy, and to uncover opportunities for your program to differentiate itself. Don't be afraid to try new approaches. Segmenting your partners according to their appetite for new initiatives, and taking care to nurture those partners who are enterprising, can enable you to quickly take advantage of opportunities for you to push the market, your partners, and your program forward as they present themselves.

Collaborate with Partners for Ongoing Success

Enabling your partner's success begins in your very first interaction. Taking the time upfront to get to know them, their business, and what they are looking to accomplish in a potential partnership is time well spent. It helps assure fit and alignment, and gets your collaboration off on the right foot. Consider using the Partnership Design Canvas (PDC) when structuring your partnerships to ensure that your mutual understanding is translated into your partnership agreement. (See Chapter 5 for more information on the PDC.)

Establish Your Partner Web Presence

Make it simple for your potential partners to find you and find what they need. One way to do this is to create a destination for them on your website. This section of your website is the home for your partnerships program, and includes your PVP; descriptions of your partnerships program, policies, and procedures; details about the types of partners you want to collaborate with; information about how to apply to your partnerships program; and information about your partnerships team.

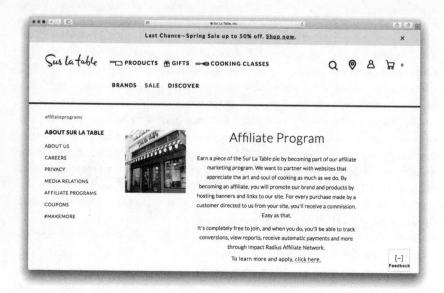

FIGURE 13.5   Sur La Table's description of its partnerships program.

Your partnerships program page can also be the entry point to a partner portal: a microsite specifically for partners that have already been accepted into your program to access training, brand assets and content, and more. The goal is to enable partners and potential partners to get what they need, when they want it, without involving you—although, of course, you're there, ready to help, if they can't find the answers they need.

There are plenty of great examples out there from which companies can draw upon when deciding what might work best for them. Figure 13.5 shows an example from Sur La Table, the retailer that sells cookware and dinnerware and offers cooking lessons.[7]

When potential partners click through the referral link, they find an application as well as the basics of Sur La Table's partnerships program: its default commission structure (4 percent), its payout restrictions (when it will not pay commissions such as on sale items and its cooking classes), and a link to its program terms and conditions (Figure 13.6).[8]

Increasingly, enterprises are forming private partner communities that enable members to directly connect with each other. Shopify, for example, has a community hub, which is accessible via its partner web pages, that allows its partners and developers to ask and answer questions, get recommendations, collaborate, and, in their own words, "learn from each other's triumphs and failures, and ultimately thrive, together" (Figure 13.7).

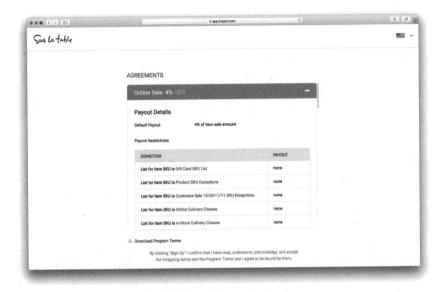

FIGURE 13.6   Sur La Table's basic partnership agreement.

FIGURE 13.7   Shopify connects its partners and developers via a dedicated community.

Welcome Aboard!

Nothing else tastes like success. Do what it takes to get your partners productive quickly. What do they need to represent your company and your products well to their audiences, to make money in your program, and to work well with you? And what do you need to know about them to help them be successful? Remember, their success is your success. You are in this together.

Kickoff calls are a great way to begin the onboarding process. They provide a perfect opportunity to better understand your new partners, including their hopes, concerns, questions, and expectations, and to assess their level of knowledge and experience with your products, industry, and program. Not enough enthusiasm? Give them reason to be excited. Looking for too much too soon? Help them be realistic, while not dampening their spirit.

Follow up this conversation with a series of customized onboarding emails. These emails should reflect your kickoff conversation, describe your products and program, identify the resources that are readily available to them (educational materials and marketing assets) and where they can be accessed, and address new partners' most frequently asked questions and challenges. At **impact.com**, we recommend that these emails (three to five) take place within the first month of your partnership. Be sure to monitor partners' progress and make a phone call or send an email when they hit certain milestones. Know that when partners are becoming significant enough to your performance, they warrant regular phone consultations about their performance. More complex partnerships, such as product integrations, will require more upfront interaction among your respective teams.

Teach Your Partners Well

Ask your partners about their learning needs and goals upfront—and then deliver. Make training about your products and your program readily available and largely self-service for partners. Take eBay, for example. Its partner network site includes details about its program and access to resources, as well as training on building ads and campaigns, driving traffic to increase revenue, and monitoring performance and optimizing results via its partner web pages (Figure 13.8).

Supply the Right Content at the Right Time

How can you stay top-of-mind, continuously drawing your partners back in to promote you? How do you keep them informed and excited about your products and program? Ongoing engagement is the heart and soul of successful partnerships.

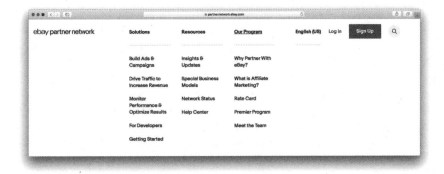

FIGURE 13.8   eBay offers training to enable its partners' success.

Like any strong relationship, partnerships need connection. Partner blogs, newsletters, and email are simple and cost-effective ways to provide updates about your company and promotions and to share partner resources and stories. Partner communities offer a more interactive vehicle for engaging partners; however, they are more expensive and require community management.

There must be substance behind this engagement to have it bear fruit. Enterprises with successful partnerships programs create a steady stream of fresh, relevant promotions, campaigns, and content to give their partners a reason to act on their behalf—now. They experiment with a variety of types of content—trend reports, best-seller lists, customer testimonials, case studies, reviews, templates, and so on—and with different formats: articles, videos, webinars, and social posts. And they are careful to ensure that customer-facing assets work on the devices and platforms on which their partners are active. Influencers, for example, are likely to need shortened deep links that save potential customers time and energy by sending them directly to specific in-app pages rather than to a general website or store, as well as assets that work on social media platforms. Most importantly, they keep their links up to date and functioning.

It's super helpful to plan out your partner promotions, campaigns, and content in advance, in an editorial calendar. As an actionable tool, an editorial calendar facilitates advanced planning. It helps organizations think strategically about the content and campaigns they need to create and ensure that they have relevant content for all of their partners. It can also help teams allocate responsibility, manage and meet deadlines, and evaluate the success of their efforts. Editorial calendars are working documents; they can be added to as needed, allowing you to take advantage of unexpected moments that the marketplace creates for your brand to be relevant and delightful.

There are many ways to create content and campaign calendars; the right choice for an enterprise reflects its own priorities and workflows. It starts with a time period—a quarter or a year—whatever your focus. The next step is to block out time on your calendar for key promotions, seasonal or holiday campaigns, and any other events such as new product launches that your partners should hear about from you first. What content and brand assets will you need to develop in support of each? Next, add the regular content pieces that you create to the calendar—your monthly best-selling lists or quarterly trends sheets—the features your partners count on. Then begin filling in your calendar with other items. What content do you need to generate to keep your business moving forward? What assets do your partners need to represent your company, brand, and products to their audiences? What do you need to create and what can you adapt from marketing and public relations? Last, consider what content you might create to help your partners work better with you or market better to their customers—newsletters, blogs, email updates? Wade Tonkin, director of global affiliate marketing at Fanatics, has a rule of thumb: when two or more partners ask the same question, it's probably time for content to be created.

We at **impact.com** recommend that you create a partner coverage map based on your editorial calendar (see Figure 13.9). The map simply describes the content and format, the device and platform for which it's created, the partner for which it's intended, and the scheduled dates for the content to be available. This coverage map will help ensure that your partners have what they need, when they need it, to be successful.

What Content Are You Providing for Your Partners?

The following sections describe **impact.com**'s scheduled partner content.

Share Insights and Brainstorm Opportunities

At **impact.com**, we highly recommend making it a priority to offer your partners customized insights into your partnership's performance so they can work together with you to optimize your mutual results. Access to this information is a key selling point for potential partners—note that it's one of the top features in eBay's PVP (Figure 13.4). During your planning process, work with your partners to set achievable performance goals and then share your partnerships data with them—most partners don't have any idea how their efforts are impacting enterprises' results. Turn the lights on! When both parties have access to the same data about a partner's traffic and customers, it enables productive in-flight adjustments.

What Content Are We Providing for Our Partners?
Here is our scheduled partner content:

	Content	Format	Device and platform	Date for release
All partners	Update on upcoming promotions	Partner newsletter	Distributed through partnership automation platform	January 2
Partners reaching household enthusiasts customer segment	Seasonal item liquidation	Product feed	Partner websites and mobile apps	January 10
All partners	Quarterly trend report	Report	Distributed through partnership automation platform	January 15

FIGURE 13.9   Partner coverage maps ensure that partners have the content they need to be successful.

Sharing knowledge of trends that you are seeing across your shared customers and audiences can significantly lift partner results. For example, you might share your observation that leisure suits have been trending for men 21–30 or that traffic your partner sends from its Editors' Picks tends to convert really well. As long as you talk in generalities (i.e., you can't say "<email address>" likes to shop for leather boots), you can share insights that can positively impact their results, without violating any privacy laws.

Standardize and Automate Your Partnerships Process

We recommend adopting a standardized partnerships process and automating as much of it as possible as part of your partnerships experience strategy. This includes everything from partner discovery and recruitment to contracting, tracking, engagement, compliance and fraud detection, and optimization. This will enable you to build ease into your partnerships process, providing you with a strong backbone around which to build a smart, consistent, and efficient signature partnering style. Importantly, this will also free up your team's time to focus on higher-value-added activities that make a difference to your partners.

Broaden Your Circle

Delivering an excellent partner experience is part of many people's jobs because partnerships are cross-functional in nature. They often require input from marketing, branding, promotions, legal, finance, mobile, public relations, and product strategy. At **impact.com**, we recommend that partnerships teams map these dependencies and proactively build, and regularly nourish, relationships with people relevant to the partnerships effort across their whole organization so the people who need to work together can do so seamlessly. Be mindful that a fair amount of education about partnerships in general, and performance-based payment models more specifically, often takes place early on.

Be mindful of the two-way nature of these working relationships. Understand what your partnerships organization needs from these other functional areas to succeed, what they need from you, and how the partnerships effort impacts them. We often hear of the benefits of sharing partnerships performance data—conversion rates, new customers won, unique contributions to the customer journey, and profit margin—with branding to show how partnerships are building awareness and consideration with prospects and are leading to nondiscounted sales. Ensuring that finance understands how performance partnerships work and how they differ from advertising—commissions are paid only for success and out of revenue generated—is reassuring and heads off discussions of fixed budgets that will only hinder results.

Capture Your Partnerships Learning

As enterprises gain experience in partnerships, priceless knowledge gets created but, all too often, it remains in a few people's heads. When partnerships organizations are running fast and looking forward, it's hard to take the time to institutionalize learning. Putting knowledge sharing on the back burner is a missed opportunity for enhancing the partnerships experience as best practices remain undefined and unimplemented. And it puts organizations at risk as learning can easily walk out the door.

To avoid this leakage, many companies hold weekly planning meetings where they bring each other up to speed and set priorities and tasks for the team. They circle back later in the week, or at the next planning meeting, to capture new learnings and see what progress has been made. Some are adopting aspects of the agile movement, holding regular meetings to discuss not what the team is doing but how they are doing it, what is going well, and what can be improved. Capturing this learning in playbooks, shared working documents, or other evolving artifacts acts as a forcing function for reflection, conversations, and knowledge dissemination. Taking the time to learn in this way is not a luxury when your partnerships experience matters. It's at the very center of your partnerships experience efforts as long as the spirit is one of enablement, not control. Remember that the goal is to facilitate an excellent partnerships experience, not create cumbersome tasks for already busy people.

Assess Your Partnerships Experience Regularly

What is measured gets attention—so if you are truly committed to building an exceptional experience for your partners, you want to identify key partnerships experience performance metrics for your partnerships effort. And you are going to have to hold yourself accountable for your performance on these metrics with the same rigor you do your financial metrics. To be meaningful, these metrics should reflect what is important to your business success and to your partners' ability to do business with you. They should also be forward looking and actionable: How will they help you make better decisions for the future? Your metrics should also help you assess whether you are living up to the expectations you set with your partnerships vision and PVP.

Metrics can be designed to evaluate the success of your program, your efforts to support your partners, and your partnerships process. Is your program competitive? Are your products desirable and marketable? Are your campaigns and content useful? How does your conversion and post-conversion process help or hinder your partners' efforts? Are you providing your partners with the data they need to optimize their performance in a timely manner? Are there tools and widgets (e.g., Walmart's BuyNow button or DealFinder) that might enhance your partners' ability to succeed? Where is there friction, and therefore opportunity, in your partnerships process—recruiting, contracting, onboarding, training, and optimization?

We know this is a large ask—it's far easier to talk about establishing metrics than it is to generate them, much less live by them. Useful metrics require quality underlying data, which is derived from your own and your partner's experience. Ultimately it involves aligning incentives with these new measurements.

Ask Your Partners About Their Experience

Being regularly curious about your partners' experience—being intentional about flipping perspectives to see your partnerships efforts through your partners' eyes—enlarges your company's perspective, provides you with insight into overall trends, and empowers you to focus on the areas for enhancement that are most important to partners. A structured partnerships experience assessment process can be just the tool to make this happen.

Why is a regular process necessary? As it turns out, organizations are not always good at self-assessment. Consider the findings of a survey conducted by the management consulting firm Bain & Company about how companies perceive the service they provide to their customers. Eighty percent of the 362 firms surveyed believed they were giving "superior service" to their customers—but only 8 percent of their customers agreed.[9] That is a significant mismatch that would have gone unnoticed had a feedback loop with the firms' customers not been initiated. If firms can be that off-base in understanding the experience of the customers they've been charged to understand, it's easy to imagine that they might be off-base in understanding their partners' experience.

There are three essential steps in the Partnerships Experience Feedback Cycle—ask, synthesize, and act (Figure 13.10).

Asking partners for feedback can be accomplished in several ways. Enterprises can employ simple diagnostic tools such as a thumbs-up—our experience was great—and a thumbs-down—we had issues—throughout the partnership life cycle to identify where there is friction, and therefore opportunity, in an enterprise's partner recruitment, contracting, onboarding, and optimization efforts (Figure 13.11). This same tool can be used to garner partners' feedback about the value of specific content and enterprise communications—was this content helpful?

Enterprises can ask more extensive questions and solicit partner suggestions via surveys and ongoing suggestion boards. Partner surveys can be easily created and distributed; the key is to keep them short and useful—every question asked

FIGURE 13.10 Employ the Partnerships Experience Feedback Cycle.

How was your experience:

Great   Had Issues

Was this answer helpful?

FIGURE 13.11   A simple thumbs-up or thumbs-down can garner valuable high-level feedback.

should be linked to an actionable insight. Digital suggestion boards are also useful ways to crowdsource partner input on an ongoing basis. Partners can submit ideas and build on the ideas of others. Enterprises can prompt partners for feedback and suggestions in general and on specific topics that can help them achieve greater impact. Partner communities can represent fecund opportunities for gathering suggestions and feedback either directly or indirectly. Be sure to regularly monitor the conversations that are taking place for insights.

Gathering partner input is important, but it's only the first step in the Partnerships Experience Feedback Cycle. The next step is to derive meaning and insights from the data your partners took the time to provide. To facilitate synthesis, it can be helpful to divide partner insights into categories that make sense for your business. These might include products, conversion pathway, commissions, promotions, specific stages of the partnership life cycle, or people issues. Once your suggestions are categorized, the focus turns to thoughtful consideration of how partner suggestions may enhance your partnerships experience and create business value for you. You may want to prioritize your partners' recommendations (listed as opportunities) and estimate the investment required to pursue them, as in Figure 13.12.

Establishing a simple yet effective governance structure to manage this process is important so that your partners know you truly care about what they have to say and so your program benefits from their ideas. The cost of not completing the entire process can be high, potentially doing more damage than if you had not initiated the feedback process at all. Finally, partners should be thanked for going through the effort of offering feedback and included in solution design where possible.

The Quick Summary

- Be intentional about your partnerships experience. Exceptional partnerships experience is a powerful advantage when it comes to recruiting and retaining top-notch partners.
- Your partnerships vision should provide the philosophical foundation. Anyone reading or hearing your partnerships vision should be able to readily understand

Evaluate Our Partners' Suggestions

Here's our ranking of our partners' suggestions:

Priority Ranking	Description of PX Opportunity (including benefits)	Estimated Investment Required

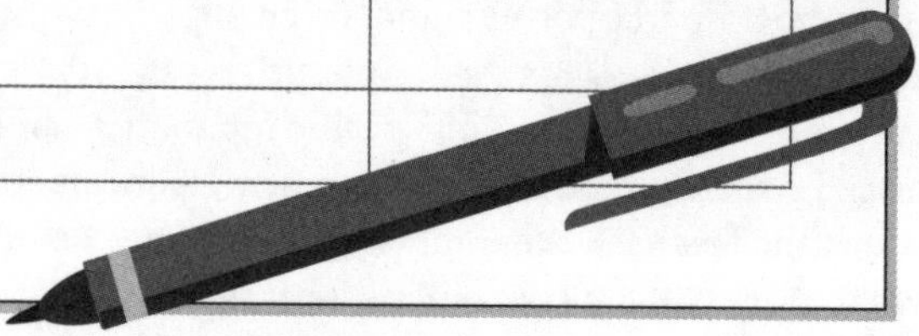

FIGURE 13.12 Evaluate your partners' suggestions.

why you are committed to these types of collaboration, what's important to you when it comes to partnerships, and the type of partner you want to be.

- Translate your partnerships vision into your partner value proposition (PVP) and share it with potential partners so they know why you believe they should invest their time, resources, and reputation in you.

- Create an ideal partner profile to guide your partnerships discovery and recruitment efforts. This profile sets the bar for who is an acceptable partner for your program.

- Translate your partnerships vision into your daily operations. Identify others within your organization who impact your partner experience and work with them to deliver. Find ways to regularly share your learnings.

- Collaborate with your partners to ensure your mutual success.

- Develop metrics that enable you to measure and assess your overall partnerships experience performance. Evaluate these metrics along with your financial measures in your ongoing program review process.

- Flip perspectives often. Work with your partners to determine what is important to them. In addition to ongoing discussions, implement a formal feedback mechanism to gather your partners' assessment of your partnerships experience. Establish a governance structure to manage the feedback cycle to ensure it meets the expectations it creates.

What's Up Next?

When you've got your program essentials in place, you're ready to build a roadmap for your partnerships program's development. As the old adage cautioned, "failure to plan is planning to fail." I've got your back and will look at envisioning and planning a durable partnerships program in the next chapter.

Notes

[1] Aldo Bukit, **Walmart.com**, "The Fast and the Reliable: How Walmart Leveraged Transparency and Data to Build Better Partner Relationships," interviewed by Mike Head, **impact.com**, video, 7:14, **http://bit.ly/Impact-interview-Aldo-Walmart**.

[2] Jay McBain, "Channel Data Is a Competitive Differentiator," Forrester, blogs, January 11, 2019, **http://bit.ly/Forrester-Channel-Data**.

[3] "Prioritizing Performance: Affiliate Marketing Predictions for 2021," Acceleration Partners, November 11, 2020, **https://www.youtube.com/watch?v=GamTXoo2hPU**.

[4] Jacqueline Renfrow, "Most Shoppers Abandon Their Purchase If Checkout Is Too Hard," *Retail Dive*, Brief, August 13, 2018, **http://bit.ly/hard-checkout-leads-to-abandoned-purchases**.

[5] "Pitney Bowes Global Ecommerce Study Finds We Are Shopping Online More Frequently and Frustrated More Often," Pitney Bowes, October 24, 2018, **http://bit.ly/press-release-ecommerce-study**.

[6] Ibid

[7] "Affiliate Program," Sur La Table, accessed May 28, 2021, **https://www.surlatable.com/affiliateprograms.html**.

[8] "Sign Up," Sur La Table, accessed May 28, 2021, **http://bit.ly/surlatable-affiliate-sign-up**.

[9] James Allen, Frederick F. Reichheld, Barney Hamilton, and Rob Markey, "Closing the Delivery Gap," Bain & Company, 2005, **http://bit.ly/Bain-Company-closingthedeliverygap**.

CHAPTER 14

What About Agencies? Your Partners in Partnerships

DMi Partners is a full-service performance marketing and growth marketing company based in the United States and the mastermind behind the Rastelli's and Sunbasket partnership I described in Chapter 1. As you may recall, Sunbasket and Rastelli's have enjoyed a fruitful long-term relationship, with Rastelli's providing fresh protein for Sunbasket's D2C prepackaged meals.

Sunbasket is one of several strategic business partnerships that DMi Partners has arranged for Rastelli's. Two years ago the company began talking with Rastelli's about potential strategic partners it might be able to work with in the food industry. The concept was straightforward: develop a D2C business by entering into referral partnerships with companies like Sunbasket that provide high-quality food to consumers. The pitch to potential partners: let us be the butcher for your customers. The idea was well received and Rastelli's and DMi Partners were in the midst of highly productive conversations when the COVID-19 pandemic happened. Overnight those companies saw that their customers needed a high-quality source of meats and seafood delivered directly to their homes now, not in the future, and several extraordinary partnerships were quickly launched.

Facilitating strategic brand partnerships is one of the many services DMi Partners provides for its clients. "We start at the very beginning with branding and ideation, thinking what we want the brand to look like online, all the way through full execution of all digital campaigns," explains Patrick McKenna, founder and CEO of DMi Partners. "From affiliate and other partnerships, to social media, search engine marketing, and full service ecommerce integration. Occasionally we get to engage with our clients in really in-depth, top-down partnerships—Rastelli's is one of those relationships."

When it comes to facilitating strategic brand-to-brand partnerships, DMi Partners looks to bring together brands that have similar target customers but aren't competitors. "We want to help both brands leverage each other's audiences to grow both of their businesses," explains Christina Nolan, vice president of affiliate marketing at DMi Partners. "We are looking to secure unique angles and get ahold of unique audiences to grow our brands."

DMi Partners also looks for companies that offer high-quality products. "That's what lies at the center of being able to leverage this partnership economy," McKenna explains. Partners have to be able to see the value that the potential partner brings. "If Rastelli's wasn't producing high-quality products, there is no way we could have gone to Sunbasket and gotten them to agree to have this partnership with us."

Rastelli's works with a range of partnership types. Ninety-two percent of Rastelli's partnerships revenue is content-based—DMi Partners has secured over 200 placements for Rastelli's, year-to-date, with mass media publishers. The company also works with coupon and deal sites, which it employs to close the conversion funnel. "A consumer may have been educated about Rastelli's from a content partner; however, in doing the research, they realize there are many places to get meat delivered," Nolan explains. "When they realize they can get cash back through a rewards partner like Ibotta, they end up pulling the trigger on Rastelli's. We leverage these partners in tandem with each other to make sure we have a really tight conversion cycle for the consumer."

DMi Partners is highly committed to its clients' success. "We try to make sure that our incentives are totally aligned with our clients," explains McKenna, "because then we're able to really become true partners with our clients, to sit at the same side of the table with them, and be responsible for driving their growth." Those incentives can take the form of revenue or profit shares, or doing joint ventures or equity partnerships with clients.

Go It Alone or Go with an Agency

Enterprises have three options when it comes to creating, managing, and growing their partnerships portfolios: manage everything in-house, hire an agency, or operate under a hybrid model where some portion of their portfolio is managed internally and some externally. Collaborating with agency partners is common practice. Enterprises of a variety of sizes, business models, and levels of partnerships program maturity work with agency partners.

Why do enterprises choose to work with agencies? Companies look to their agencies for expertise and efficiency. Some enterprises are looking to create a partnerships program from the ground up, while others are looking to expand their existing portfolio in a different region or direction. Others are looking to agencies to handle the tactical and operational aspects of their program or to conduct a one-time audit. And there are many variations that fall in between these two endpoints. The common denominator is the need for resources—capability, capacity, relationships, and/or tech expertise—that enterprises currently don't have, or don't have enough of. A few examples of how enterprises are using agency partners follow.

Perform[cb] Agency and a Pet Essentials Brand

Perform[cb] Agency is a performance marketing agency specializing in the cost-per-acquisition marketing model. In March 2020, a well-known pet essentials brand came to Perform[cb], looking to scale its partnerships program.[1] The program had 15 active partners, eight of which were performing well.

Perform[cb] performed a program audit through which the team identified several opportunities for growth and optimization. This included onboarding new partners based on competitive insights and client KPIs, reengaging dormant partners, and implementing a tiered payout system to better incentivize upper-funnel partners while maintaining an efficient return across the program. Within the first month of launch, this pet essentials brand's partnerships program grew significantly, with a 286 percent increase in revenue. Over a 12-month period, the agency was able to drive a 354 percent increase in order volume overall.

OtterBox, Gen3 Marketing, and Content Publishers

Gen3 Marketing (Gen3) is a full-service marketing agency specializing in all aspects of digital marketing, including affiliate marketing, SEO/search engine marketing (SEM), social media, and digital public relations. OtterBox, which designs protective and stylish phone cases as well as premium coolers and accessories, works with Gen3 to manage and grow its partnerships program.[2]

In April 2020, Amazon instituted a large decrease in its commission rates for its partnerships program, which dramatically reduced the earnings of many publishers.

This created a perfect opportunity for brands like OtterBox to build direct relationships with publishers that had previously only promoted OtterBox through Amazon. Working with Gen3, OtterBox instituted an outreach strategy to strengthen partnerships with a select group of content publishers through customized content, enhanced exposure, and adjusted compensation models. The primary goal was distribution of quality content, ideally focused on top-selling products.

The results were quick and significant. In the first few weeks, revenue from just two of the targeted publishers created notable results. Specifically, OtterBox received excellent exposure from CNN Underscored through posts such as "Shop these brands offering special discounts for workers on the front lines of COVID-19," which featured OtterBox's 40-percent-off promotion for front-line workers, and the "Guard your new iPhone SE with a new screen protector" article, which showcased OtterBox's three most popular screen protectors for the iPhone SE. This additional exposure increased CNN Underscored–sourced visits to **otterbox.com** by more than 13,000 percent year-over-year and revenue by more than 16,000 percent.

Assessing Your Internal Capabilities

The starting point in any company's decision about whether to hire an agency is an honest assessment of its in-house team's capabilities. Does it have what it takes to build, manage, and grow the partnerships program that the company needs and wants? Is there a market disruption, such as Amazon decreasing its partnership commissions, that, with the right assistance, can be turned into a market opportunity? Other questions to consider, organized by phases of the partnership process, follow (Table 14.1).[3]

Types of Agencies That Create and Manage Partnerships

There are three basic types of partnerships agencies: full-service digital marketing agencies, partnerships type–specific agencies (e.g., traditional affiliates, influencers, strategic business development), and a combination of the two (e.g., an agency that manages multiple partnership types, but not all).

Just like partnerships teams have traditionally operated in silos within most companies, so has agency management of various partnership types. While most full-service agencies have focused primarily on the larger search and display advertising budgets, smaller agencies have focused on just one or more partnership types: traditional rewards affiliates, influencers, commerce content publishers, and strategic business development partnerships. Part of the reason for this focus

TABLE 14.1   Assessing Your Internal Partnership Capabilities

Phase of partnership life cycle	Questions to consider	Why consider this question
Planning	Are you able to develop go-to-market strategies, track your customer and shopping journeys, create customer coverage maps, and perform partner gap analysis?	Creating, informing, and delivering a go-to-market strategy is the most important capability for high-maturity partnerships programs.
Discovery and recruitment	Are you able to define your ideal partner profile, define standards for partner acceptance, and find and recruit the types and quality of partners you want?	To recruit high-quality partners, you have to be able to articulate what you want and don't want, utilize lookalike and propensity models to find potential partners, and bring them into your emerging partnerships ecosystem.
Tracking	Are you able to effectively track relevant micro conversions and macro conversions? Are you able to future-proof your tracking solutions?	Partners need to have full confidence in your ability to assess impact. Your tracking ability needs to create a clear link between desired customer behaviors, partner activity, and micro conversions and macro conversions moments. Privacy is a key consideration, and you need to be able to ensure that your tracking solution meets current and future privacy initiatives across every platform.
Engagement	Are you able to effectively onboard, train, and provide partners with a steady stream of content, promotions, and campaigns in order for them to reach their full potential?	Ongoing partnership engagement is critical to the success of every partnership.
Protect and monitor	Are you able to effectively manage fraud and other overpayments? Can you ensure regulatory and branding compliance?	Fraud is expensive—and so is noncompliance with local laws and branding guidelines, such as bidding on trademarked words.
Optimization	Do you know which combination of partners, incentives, content, campaigns, and products brings out the best in each of your partners? Do you know how each partner impacts your customer and shopping journeys? Can you build partner KPI scorecards and a partner program dashboard to learn how you are performing at any moment and time, and what can be done to further enhance results?	Being able to measure and assess current and future performance for individual partnerships and for your portfolio as a whole is critical to any partnerships program's success. It builds organizational commitment, enables more effective allocation of resources, and determines future partnerships program strategy.

Source: Adapted from "A Buyer's Guide to Partnership Success: Evaluating Services and Technology,"
Forrester, November 2020.

and specialization is the unique approach each type of partner typically requires. However, as the category of partnerships has become more well known in the past few years, more agencies are developing more skills for the different partnership types. And with the rising importance of being present and relevant inside the daily information of modern consumers' lives, along with rising ad prices due to the new limitations placed on marketers regarding targeting, tracking, and measurement of ads, full-service digital marketing agencies have recently gotten into the partnerships business as well.

As partnerships and partnerships programs have increased in complexity, sophistication, and value to enterprises, companies' expectations for their agency partners have changed. In addition to ensuring that their partnerships programs run smoothly, many enterprises are looking to their agencies for strategic thinking, innovation, and partnership matchmaking. They want their agencies to have a solid understanding of their company's business objectives, their partner value propositions, and the partner landscape so they can co-create customized, innovative, and data-informed strategies to help companies generate incremental growth. And they want their agencies to help them proactively identify and mitigate risk to ensure that their programs are working within the bounds of their brand guidelines and the law. Rather than outsourcing their partnerships programs, these enterprises are effectively calling in resources, hiring agencies to work as part of their partnerships team (even if the team is only one person). This is a significant shift—much more than semantics. It's about truly partnering with agencies to address enterprises' most critical business objectives.

The rise of influencers has created influencer talent agencies that work with influencers to help them find the best enterprise partners and negotiate the best deals for themselves and their audiences. Most influencers with sizable followings work with talent agencies. Among them are Gen Z's media heroes and more traditional celebrities in film, television, music, and sports.

When Hiring an Agency

Today, companies can avail themselves of agency expertise in marketing strategy and program design, search engine optimization, paid social, programmatic, social media monitoring, compliance testing, fraud mitigation, and more. They can work with agencies that approach enterprises' business holistically, weaving partnerships into an overall customer engagement strategy. They just need to find and hire the agency that best fits their needs and then work well with them.

If you are considering hiring an agency for your program, **impact.com** recommends that you interview several agencies to learn about their partnerships philosophy, experience, expertise, and the quality of their results, and to explore what it might be like to work together. Take your time and get your questions answered. Read reviews, case studies, and testimonials, and speak with existing and former clients. Attend industry conferences and events, and ask around about various firms. Address any issues these conversations surface with any potential agencies that make the final cut. Commit when you are convinced that a potential agency partner has what you need, that it is able to deliver, and that you want to work with that partner. Most agency contracts run a minimum of 6–12 months and that is too much time to waste.

Be Clear About Your Objectives

When exploring working with an agency, be prepared. The clearer you can be about who you are, what you are hoping to achieve, and what you bring to the table, the better off everyone will be. In a recent blog post, Acceleration Partners, a global partnerships agency, warned that this "is not the right place to work out a company's value proposition. Affiliates invest time and money in promoting companies and companies need to be respectful of that or they run the risk of losing those partnerships forever."[4]

Be able to articulate your strategic business goals, how you envision your partnerships program addressing them, and your time frame for results. And if you are planning to expand your partnerships program globally, you'll want to make sure that any agency that you choose has the expertise and contacts to help you move forward.

Understand the Scope of Your Potential Engagement

What is inside and outside a scope of work? Robert Glazer, founder and CEO of Acceleration Partners, recommends that you clearly articulate the responsibilities that enterprises and agencies assume when working together. Generally speaking, in his experience, enterprises are responsible for their internal business knowledge, overall program goal and strategy, branding guidelines and creative, and origination of campaigns and promotions. In terms of creative, this includes any assets you want (or don't want) to be used, details about requirements, your marketing and promotional calendars, and information about new product features and launches. Enterprises also need to attend regular meetings, provide approvals, and pay the bills. Agencies are generally responsible for customer strategy, program operations, new ideas and best practices, partner recruitment and engagement, fraud monitoring and compliance, and measurement and optimization.[5]

The success of partnerships as a customer engagement tool means that its remit is expanding into areas that have been previously managed by other functions and agencies. An example of this is mass media partners, whose editors can often have relationships with both an enterprise's PR and partnerships teams. Lacie Thompson, founder and CEO of the marketing and consulting firm LT Partners, recommends that enterprise partnerships teams work closely with their internal and external PR firms to coordinate their efforts with publishers or take on similar efforts if a PR firm or team is not a part of the equation. In Thompson's experience, this intentional effort reduces confusion and maximizes impact. As an example, Thompson shares her firm's experience in building out a partnerships program with the jewelry company Made by Mary. When the partnerships team began pitching commerce content managers at digital publications, similar to how a PR team pitches to editors, the impact was significant. It was able to secure 16 press mentions for the jewelry company within three weeks, resulting in an increase of 465 percent in month-over-month (MOM) clicks and 174 percent in MOM revenue.[6]

Know What You Bring to the Table

The best agencies have their pick of enterprises with which they can work, so it's helpful to know what you bring to the table when exploring taking on an agency partner. Why should this agency work with you over other potential enterprises? Most agencies like to see a strong organizational commitment to partnerships as a growth strategy when choosing to work with companies. Agencies do their best work when they have context for the work they are doing, an understanding of the larger needs of the organization, and confidence in the organization's commitment to partnerships as a growth strategy. Do you have the support of your CMO, chief strategy officer, or chief partnerships officer or investors? What's important to them? What hurdles do they need your program to meet?

What Is Your Market Position?

Are you an established brand with a strong reputation and highly marketable products? Or are you a well-funded start-up that is committed to employing partnerships as part of your customer acquisition strategy? As a rule of thumb, Acceleration Partners suggests that if your company has annual sales of less than $8 million, it will be difficult for you to break even after you pay agency management fees.[7]

What Is the State of Your Portfolio?

Have you been paying your partners based on who had the last click and is in need of a commission reset? Do you have a strong partnerships program and are you looking to enhance your revenue by diversifying partner types, potentially collaborating with content partners and/or other brands?

What Is Your Mindset?

Consider how holistic and innovative a program you want to have and what your organizational structure and leadership will realistically allow. Are you looking to grow your portfolio via well-proven strategies, or are you eager to explore new territory together, testing novel approaches with different partners?

How Big a Budget Do You Have?

Companies must also be clear on what they intend to spend on their partnerships program and how they will measure performance. Knowing this information enables agencies to understand the type of results they will need to generate for you and at what level of compensation. Upfront clarity eliminates miscommunication and sets a strong foundation for the relationship.

What Are You Like to Work With?

How you partner matters. Are you a "set it and forget it" client or do you see a potential agency partner as an extension of your team? Do you treat your agency partners professionally and respectfully or as vendors or expendable resources?

When Assessing Potential Agencies

What is important to consider when it comes to interviewing and selecting an agency partner?

Do They Have What You Need?

Perhaps the most fundamental criterion is the agency's expertise and the scope of its offering. Does it have the expertise and experience that you need and are willing to pay for? Take the time to talk with the agency about its business, clients, and its experience in your vertical. Does it have a solid grasp of your company, business goals, products and services, target customers, and the regions in the world in which you operate? Does it understand the nuances and language of your industry? Be sure to inquire about the results the agency has achieved for clients with similar business objectives as yours. And if it works with your competitors, carefully explore potential conflicts of interest and how they might be handled.

Get personal. How does a potential agency partner envision driving results for your partnerships program? "Every business is different," explains Thompson. "You can't take a playbook from one customer and apply it like peanut butter to another, even if they are in the same industry." You want to find agencies that will custom design a partnerships program to match your business goals and your situation in the marketplace. What does your potential agency envision as top priorities for your program and what is its rationale? What types of partners is it recommending for you and why? Are these partners likely to generate incremental value for you? How deep is the agency's bench of relevant partner connections? What tools does it use to recruit potential partners?

What Can You Expect?

What is the process that the potential agency will take you through to determine ongoing strategy and optimize your results? Each agency has its own signature strategic process and they are not all the same. Have the agency walk you through the process and explain what is involved in each stage. How does it define success? What is its timeline for success? Figure 14.1 shows JEB Commerce's strategic roadmap as an example. As you can see, its process includes an audit of the enterprise's current state and a vision for a future state; a strategy for selecting potential partners, launching, and optimizing individual partnerships and the portfolio as a whole; and strategies for building a mature partnerships portfolio and long-term growth.

What Type of Insights Do You Want?

How robust is a potential partner's reporting? Consider the partnership management platform that potential agency partners prefer, as it ultimately determines

FIGURE 14.1   JEB Commerce's roadmap to partnership success.

what is possible with partnerships programs, and there is considerable variation among various platforms. If you have already made an investment in a partnership management platform yourself, make sure that the potential agency is well trained, certified, and proficient on the platform. If you have not already made a tech investment, or if you are looking to make a change, evaluate the platforms it uses and recommends. How good and comprehensive are the data, insights, and predictive capabilities of its platforms? What will the technology it recommends to you enable and what will it preclude? Drill down a bit to see what capabilities are already available in the technology and what's in development. Is it able to offer multitouch attribution? If not, you won't have the insights into partner activity across your customer journeys, which is necessary to understand the value your partners provide and compensate them accurately. Inquire about the upfront and ongoing fees associated with a given platform.

How Good Is the Agency's Compliance and Fraud Monitoring?

Compliance is important for every brand, and especially for companies operating in highly regulated industries. How familiar is the agency with key regulations in the regions in which your business operates? How will it monitor for brand, trademark, and Federal Trade Commission compliance?

What are the tools the agency will use to monitor fraud in your program? What type of tools does it use to identify fraud? Does it have people on staff who specialize in fraud prevention?

What Will This Relationship Cost You?

There are three general compensation models for agencies—flat fee, a variable amount that is entirely performance-based, or a combination of a retainer and performance. Most agencies work on a combination of retainer plus performance model. The compensation structure that is ultimately negotiated should reflect the type of work that agencies are doing for you. If agencies are able to impact your performance, not just execute on your behalf, they are more likely to agree to some or all of their compensation being performance based. Whatever compensation structure is put in place, it's important to be very clear that your desired outcomes are the specific customer behaviors—micro conversions and major conversions—that are necessary to generate those outcomes. Build your metrics around those behaviors.

Is This the One?

Consider the level of transparency and integrity with which a potential partner operates. Your agency partner is meant to be exactly that, your partner. It should have your best interests in mind, protect your brand, be transparent, and be performance-oriented. With today's partnership management platforms, partner performance is trackable, making transparency possible and desirable. If a potential agency claims to be an expert in the field and wants you to turn the keys over, be wary. Robert Glazer warns, "If agencies were more transparent about the outcomes they're producing, you probably would have fired many of them years ago."[8] Insist on transparency into your program's performance and into how the agency's time and budget are spent.

Jake Fuller, director of acquisition at JEB Commerce, recommends that you explore a potential partner's level of commitment to you. How interested is it in working with you? What types of resources will it commit to your partnerships program? Who will be working with you? What is its team structure? How skilled and experienced are the people who will be dedicated to your program? How does it determine its program caseload for account managers or teams? Are they dedicating and managing their time to your program each week in relation to your main and supporting objectives? Fuller says that it's quite common to see managers in the industry responsible for 25–35 accounts, which allows for a "putting out fires" strategy at best. He recommends asking about the partner turnover experienced on a team level and the institutional knowledge that goes with it. You don't want your partnerships portfolio to be managed by individuals who are continually getting up to speed on your account.

Finally, in the end it's important to ask yourself if you are comfortable taking on this agency as a partner. Even if it meets your qualifications, you still want to work with the people who will be managing your program. Do they feel like a good fit? Do you feel as if you can trust them? Why or why not? If you don't, pay attention. What else do you need to know to get comfortable? And if you find yourself talking yourself into working with a potential agency, keep looking.

The Quick Summary

- Enterprises have at least three options when it comes to creating, managing, and growing their partnerships portfolios: manage everything in-house, hire an agency, or operate under a hybrid model. Collaborating with agency partners is common practice among companies of all sizes, business models, and levels of partnerships program maturity.

- Partner agencies come in two basic varieties: partnerships type–focused agencies and full-service digital marketing agencies. Outsourced program management (OPM) agencies are designed to help enterprises with the day-to-day management of their affiliate partnerships programs. In addition to ensuring that their partnerships programs run smoothly, enterprises look to full-service digital marketing agencies for strategic thinking, innovation, and partner discovery and recruitment.

- The starting point of any enterprise's decisions about hiring an agency is an honest assessment of its in-house team's capabilities. Do you have what it takes to build, manage, and grow the partnerships program that your company needs and wants?

- When hiring an agency, enterprises should be clear about their objectives. Why do you want to work with an agency? What is the scope of a potential engagement? What would success look like for you? Understand what you bring to the table and why an agency may be excited to work with you.

- When assessing a potential partner agency, consider its expertise, experience, and partner relationships. Does its vision for your program and its recommendations for types of partners make sense for you? What resources will it commit to your partnerships effort?

- What can you expect when working with an agency? What is the process it will take you through? What is its timeline for success? What type of performance reporting will you have access to and how often? How much transparency will you have into how your team's time and budget are spent? Does it have any potential conflicts of interest?

- Consider the underlying compensation model for your collaboration. Does this seem fair and motivating?

- In the end, enterprises and their agency partners need to be able to work well together and want to do so. Can you imagine them being an integral part of your partnerships team day in and day out? Do you trust them? Do they want to work with you?

What's Up Next?

In the next part, "Unleash Your Partnership Potential," we'll turn our attention to how enterprises can further unleash their leadership potential, with discussions of various partnerships program maturation strategies.

Notes

[1] "In-House vs. Agency Affiliate Program," Perform[cb], case study, accessed May 28, 2021, **https://www.performcb.com/case-studies/in-house-vs-affiliate-agency-case-study/**.

[2] "Recruiting Meaningful Content Publishers in a Mature Program," Gen3 Marketing, case study, May 28, 2021, **https://gen3marketing.com/case-studies/recruiting-meaningful-content-publishers-in-a-mature-program/**.

[3] Adapted from an **impact.com**-commissioned study conducted by Forrester Consulting, "A Buyer's Guide to Partnership Success: Evaluating Services and Technology," Forrester, November 2020.

[4] "Is an Affiliate Management Agency Right for You?," Acceleration Partners, accessed May 14, 2021, **http://bit.ly/accelerationpartners-am-agency**.

[5] "The Ultimate Guide to Affiliate Marketing Partnerships," Acceleration Partners, online course, accessed May 14, 2021, **http://bit.ly/acceleration-partners-partnerships**.

[6] Lacie Thompson, Founder and CEO of LT Partners, interviewed by Lisa Leslie Henderson for **impact.com**, November 17, 2020, audio, 59:58.

[7] "Is an Affiliate Management Agency Right for You?," Acceleration Partners.

[8] "The Ultimate Guide to Affiliate Marketing Partnerships," Acceleration Partners.

PART IV

Unleash Your Partnership Potential

CHAPTER 15

What Is Partnerships Program Maturity and How Do I Get It?

I f you have ever purchased an official jersey, hat, or other memorabilia of a favorite collegiate or professional team, it probably came from Fanatics, the largest online retailer of officially licensed sports merchandise. Partnerships are vital to Fanatics' growth. The company works with a portfolio of nearly 1,000 modern partners to sell over 500,000 products from over 500 different teams, and this number is growing.

Fanatics began its partnerships program 15 years ago. Coupon and cashback sites originally comprised the majority of Fanatics' partnerships, as they did at the time for most companies. Today, Fanatics' partners include influencers, bloggers, and affinity-based communities, as well as sports content aggregators like SB Nation, news publishers such as the *Chicago Tribune* that are located in towns with beloved sports teams, and large media companies such as CBS Sports. Together these partners comprise a profound customer acquisition and retention engine for Fanatics.

Diversifying its partnerships portfolio. Fanatics became intentional about diversifying its partnerships portfolio several years ago, following a senior management change at the company. "Our new leadership was more data-driven in their decision making," explains Wade Tonkin, director of global affiliate partnerships at Fanatics. "When we got deep into the numbers, we realized many of our affiliates were not bringing in incremental revenue. They were bringing in sales, but they were sales that were likely to have happened anyway. As a result, we were paying sales commissions when we didn't need to be, which decreased our overall profitability."

The company revamped its partnerships strategy to capture more value. First, it revamped its commission structure to encourage affiliates to promote items that had more incremental value to Fanatics. Second, it began to recruit partners that were able to influence the top of the sales funnel, partners that generated demand for Fanatics' products, rather than just closed sales. Influencers, bloggers, and affinity-based communities were a natural fit. These partners already enjoyed trusted relationships with Fanatics' prospects: passionate sports fans. What's more, they had high levels of ongoing engagement with these fans; many fans would visit partners' sites daily to keep up on the latest news. When these sports-based partners chose to feature Fanatics' products on their blogs, social media, websites, or boards, it was a match made in heaven.

"Our partners give people a reason to shop," Tonkin explains. "Fans come through their sites directly to ours, where they find what they want, check out, and then a portion of the sale goes back to the original sports site in the form of a commission. We've had some huge wins, working this way. Several content partners have driven six-figure sales numbers on specific events, like a Super Bowl or college football national championship."

Importantly, these are incremental sales for Fanatics. The customers who come to Fanatics via these partners are often outside the reach of its other marketing efforts. In other words, in the absence of these partnerships, the resulting sales would have been lost. What's more, 90+ percent of the time, these partners close deals faster than the company's other marketing efforts. "Customers that come in via these partners don't comparison shop or go to coupon sites to get further discounts," Tonkin explains. "They send them and we close them."

Recruiting these sports enthusiasts partners to work with Fanatics can take time and education. In most cases people have built these sports communities out of a love for a team, not out of a desire to drive revenue, and they can be apprehensive about merging the two. In these situations, Tonkin encourages potential partners to query their audiences directly about monetizing the site in this limited way. In his experience, fans are usually quite enthusiastic about their favorite blogger being compensated for the research they do and the content they create. This form of monetization doesn't compromise the integrity of the writer or the site; it actually enhances it, as it provides fans with an easy and reliable source of official team merchandise.

Optimizing partnerships performance. Tonkin's goals for Fanatics' partnerships portfolio go beyond recruitment of diverse partners; he wants to make each of his partners as productive as possible. He understands that when his partners win, Fanatics wins.

"We've got a good brand and great products, so what matters is figuring out what success looks like for each partner and each partnership type, and doing it, and then replicating that success with as many potential partners," Tonkin explains.

A great PMP is essential here. Fanatics tracks all of its partner interactions and shares that data directly with its partners via an email report or an API that will enable them to put sales data into their own dashboards. This information allows partners to see the impact of their efforts and to identify opportunities for improvement. Working with shared data from actual results, Fanatics and its partners can roll up their sleeves, test different initiatives, see what works, and learn from the results.

In some cases, optimization included moving partners from operating via co-branded websites to having partners send traffic directly to the Fanatics of League Store ecommerce site. This move enabled partners to have access to the full range of League products and promotions—the Leagues often restrict product mix and promotions on co-branded sites—which allowed many to drive more sales and commissions. The move also simplified life on Fanatics' end, as operating parallel ecommerce sites was labor-intensive and did not have the tracking and reporting capabilities that enable performance optimization.

Getting the right PMP in place. A mature partnerships program isn't run on a spreadsheet. Nor was Fanatics able to run its program on a traditional affiliate network. The network charged Fanatics a percentage of each partnership payout, which became prohibitively expensive. Migrating to a software as a service (SaaS) platform brought six-figure savings on platform costs alone and allowed the company to be more flexible and aggressive with its commission offering to bigger partners by virtue of the network/platform commission not being based on a percentage of the affiliate commission spend.

Organizational changes: form follows results. Until recently, Tonkin's group has operated as its own siloed entity: affiliate marketing. As people from other departments have come to understand how performance marketing works, and seen the revenue it generates, they have begun to tap into the affiliate marketing group's expertise and PMP. Several key traditional publishing relationships have been transformed into full or hybrid performance partnerships. "It's been a big win, putting a different perspective on some of these relationships that we have had for years," Tonkin explains. "Our slowest growing [newly converted partner] is growing at a rate of 2.5x year over year and some are doing substantially more than that."

Responsibility for several of these partnerships has been moved under Tonkin's remit, freeing up other areas, such as those that focus on sponsorships, to focus on nonperformance-based partnerships. Tonkin is careful to keep everyone throughout the organization up to speed about these partners now that they have converted to a performance basis, so that people continue to understand that they made the right move.

Although Tonkin's group is still referred to as affiliate marketing, this name is being revisited to more accurately reflect the enlarged scope of its efforts. "A lot of what we do within our program has evolved past that," Tonkin explains. "This is much more than semantics at work here. People have different connotations in their heads about affiliate relationships versus partnerships. When I think of an affiliate, I think of somebody who joins a program, gets approved, and does what they do, making a few hundred bucks a month posting links on their sites. When I think of partnerships, I think of bigger operations and more complex deals. I think of two-way relationships with people who are on the phone every week, sharing ideas, making things happen."

Tonkin's group manages both affiliates and partnerships, although it does separate them. Within the partnerships group there are both business development people and relationship managers. "We have hunter-types who can readily identify a prospect and bring in the deal," Tonkin explains. "They hand new partners off to another group that focuses on nurturing those relationships, working closely with them to get the performance out of them."

Tonkin is clear that building and nurturing relationships is essential to the success of diverse partners. Partnerships with influencers, bloggers, communities, publishers, and media houses are long-term investments, not one-off transactions. While it takes time and energy, this level of commitment enables partners to quickly identify and tap into opportunities that arise over the course of a sports season or several seasons. Sometimes these opportunities are predictable: preseason sales, Father's Day sales, or Mother's Day promotions. Other times, they are last-minute surprises such as a new uniform release for a team or a Super Bowl or Sweet Sixteen win. "We have to be able to move on a dime in these situations and that is only possible when an established relationship is in place," Tonkin explains.

Institutionalizing partnerships learnings. Tonkin and his group are entrepreneurs. When opportunities arise, they thrive on having the freedom to figure out what will work best, to act, to learn, and to apply their learnings to other partnerships. That having been said, they also have a combined 40-some years of partnerships experience under their belts that they want to be able to share more broadly with their team. As a result, they are actively working to institutionalize their learning in useful ways.

"We don't want to be telling people that this is the way they have to do things," Tonkin reassures. "We just want to give people guidelines, tips that have worked well for us in the past, that can empower them to run with it. There are so many moving parts, it's hard to stay on top of everything all of the time." Toward this end, they have set up an internal wiki to capture learning, playbooks to facilitate "hot market execution," and are working on a mission statement that puts forth the company's partnerships philosophy. They are also considering various ways of seeking partner feedback, perhaps a net promoter score, to assess "whether people are feeling the love and getting their time and money's worth out of our relationship."

"Life is good at Fanatics," concludes Tonkin.

**What is the difference between
full potential and partnerships maturity?**

A company is operating at its **full potential** when it has an
active and diverse partnerships portfolio that consistently
creates value for itself, its partners, and their shared customers
and audiences. It does so by operating in a collaborative,
transparent, and mutually beneficial way with each of its partners.

Maturity is an assessment of a company's overall capacity:
Does it have what it takes to reach its full potential?

FIGURE 15.1   The difference between full potential and partnerships maturity.

Maturity Is a Good Thing

Partnerships are a winning strategy. Companies can derive positive results with partnerships whether they are just getting started or have been at it for a while; however,
enterprises that are building the necessary underlying partnerships architecture and
capabilities now will be the real winners in the future. Partnerships program maturity
allows for companies to reach their full partnerships potential (Figure 15.1). Already,
firms that have the highest-maturity partnerships programs generate a greater share
of their revenue from partnerships, drive faster revenue growth from their partnerships and at the overall company level, and are more likely to exceed stakeholder
expectations of business metrics than companies with less mature partnerships programs.[1] This chapter explores some of the primary strategies that companies are
currently pursuing to realize their potential. To explore each of these strategies in
more depth, enjoy the resources available at **www.thepartnershipsbook.com**.

Key Activities Along the Path to Full Potential

What is the path to a successful partnerships program? While every company
develops its own definition of its full potential, and charts its own path to get there,

patterns can be seen among their strategies. At present, these activities include taking a more strategic approach to partnerships, becoming more intentional about their partner experience, adopting and automating the partnerships process, diversifying their partnership types, expanding globally, optimizing their partnerships and their overall partnerships program, and building their partnerships organization to support their current and future growth.

Take a Strategic Approach to Partnerships

In the past we have observed that as companies gain traction, they become more strategic and less ad-hoc in their partnerships efforts. Today we are seeing companies being deliberate and strategic from the get-go, building on the experience and infrastructure of those who have been at it for a while, several of whom have shared their knowledge with us for this book.

As discussed in Part III, this involves creating a vision for their partnerships efforts. This vision describes at a high level how partnerships will enable enterprises to meet their most critical business objectives and the philosophy that underlies their partnerships efforts. This vision is translated into a strategic plan that describes what the partnerships organization will achieve over several time frames and links those outcomes to critical business objectives. The strategic plan is rooted in a comprehensive analysis of current partner and competitor performance and includes forecasts developed with the input of enterprises' modern partners and relevant internal stakeholders. It identifies where growth will come from—existing and new partners—and plans for discovering, recruiting, and nurturing new partners to productivity. It also recognizes the products, content, promotions, incentives, and people resources that are necessary to realize the anticipated results.

Partnerships planning looks beyond the actual portfolio to the capability and capacity of its supporting growth engine. Does the program have the right people, processes, and technology in place to carry out this year's plans and to be ready for what is coming down the pike? What is the best way to manage partnerships across an entire organization? How do partnerships skills and capabilities need to grow to generate and manage an increased number of global and strategic business-to-business partnerships? Is there strong organization support for necessary organizational shifts and investments?

To recruit quality partners, enterprises begin to think of their partnerships experience as a product or service that they offer their partners. They develop partner value propositions that articulate why potential partners would want to collaborate with them, how they will contribute to their success, and why they are uniquely qualified to deliver that value. Many begin to standardize and automate their partnerships process, adopting tools like the Partnership Design Canvas and standardized contracts, creating ideal partner profiles and clear guidelines for partner acceptance in order to streamline, not limit, their partnerships experience. Branded partner portals and partner Facebook groups offer fecund self-service resources for partners. Real-time API-enabled partnerships reporting—combined with ongoing direct consultation and collaboration between an enterprise and its individual partners—enables partners, and therefore enterprises, to meet and exceed their goals. Finally, enterprises develop standardized ways of eliciting partner feedback to improve their way of doing partnerships and of being partners.

Adopt and Automate the Partnerships Process

In the past, when companies began partnering they often operated on a wing and a prayer, piecing together different processes, practices, and technology, the majority of which are not specifically designed for partnerships. Today enterprises that are working toward their full potential recognize that they cannot manage their partnerships in a makeshift way and on spreadsheets. They know that partnerships portfolios that generate almost a third of companies' overall revenue, and that reside in multiple departments, require specially designed technology that automates the entire partnerships process, allows for customization, and brings the wisdom and truth of data science to bear.

These companies adopt technology that supports all of their current and anticipated partnership types so they can cost-effectively and cost-efficiently simplify and consolidate their global partnerships efforts. They look for platforms that provide visibility into all of their partner activity and enable them to accurately track, value, and compensate partner influence across their entire omnichannel and global customer journeys. This allows them to determine whether their partners are providing incremental value, offer their partners real-time insights into their performance so they can self-optimize, and often structure partnerships on a performance basis. They also want their PMP to spot abnormalities and accurately predict future partner performance, uncover fraud, and identify compliance issues. Many companies are also looking for their PMP to help them discover and recruit high-quality partners around the world and to engage with them on an ongoing basis in order to build productive, long-term relationships. And, of course, they want to be able to simply and easily pay their partners, wherever they operate globally, on time and in their preferred local currency.

Increasingly, companies are looking to separate their PMP from partner program strategy and management services, just as they have previously done with their advertising programs. Affiliate networks have traditionally married the two, which has limited enterprise choice and ability to select the best technology and the best agency partners to meet their unique needs. Further, as companies consolidate their partnerships efforts across their organizations, increasing the volume of activity that takes place in their partnerships program, they are increasingly opting for platforms that charge a flat fee for managing their partnerships, rather than a percentage of partnerships payouts, so that they can effectively fix their costs and not be directly penalized for growth.

Diversify the Company's Partnership Types

As companies' partnerships efforts mature, they expand and diversify their portfolio of partnerships to unlock more value. In the earliest phase of partnership maturity, companies tend to work with a small group of partners, perhaps 10–25, most of which are affiliates. This makes sense: these modern partners have well-established partnerships processes and influence customers at the point of sale to drive conversions. As companies gain more experience, they increase the number of partners in their portfolio. However, they lack diversity in their partner types: 90 percent of revenue is driven by 10 percent of their partners. This leaves enterprises highly vulnerable to a handful of their partners' results. A shift in partner focus or loyalty can take down a partnerships program.

Scaling and finding the right partner mix becomes a priority as companies continue to mature. Enterprises begin to segment their partnerships portfolios in terms of their target customers and their customer journeys, as well as by geography, product, and market vertical, and look to a broader swath of partner types to enable them to meet their goals. They will look to some partners to help them attract new customers and to others to catalyze ongoing shopping journeys. By the time companies are operating at the highest level of maturity, they have developed a more balanced portfolio that includes a sizable number of partners across a range of partnership types. Having proven the success of the pay-for-performance compensation model for partnerships, at this point companies often begin to explore its applicability to a wider variety of partnerships located in various departments.

Expand Globally

Partnerships enable companies to have an expanded and engaging presence in a highly fragmented marketplace. The global digital marketplace has vastly multiplied consumer purchase options. Partnerships enable companies to expand their presence to a potentially infinite number of storefronts around the world.

Global expansion typically takes place through enterprises' existing partnerships programs. It's too complicated for partners to join multiple programs for different regions if the products offered around the globe are essentially the same. And it's far easier for enterprises to run their programs on a single PMP, assuming the platform supports local language contracts and can make payments in local currency. Yet global expansion remains complex. It requires in-country expertise and support and solid compliance with local laws and practices. This is not the place to move forward enthusiastically, making up the rules as you go and asking for forgiveness from local authorities later. It takes careful upfront planning, expertise, and strong relationships with local partners. Many companies elect to work with partnerships management agencies to establish and manage their programs in areas in which they wish to expand.

Optimize the Company's Partnerships and Its Partnerships Portfolio

As partnerships become responsible for a significant and increasing portion of overall corporate revenue, more people within enterprises become interested in partnerships efforts and performance. Optimization of individual partnership performance, and of overall partnerships portfolio results, becomes critical.

Optimization of individual partnerships and of an overall partnerships portfolio involves measuring and assessing past performance, using predictive analytics to forecast future results and reduce incidences of fraud, and proactively designing new combinations of product, promotions, content, and incentives to enable partners to grow. Being able to track each partner's influence on customer journeys becomes table stakes. To do so, companies use a state-of-the-art PMP to track customer action across every device and channel. With this data, they can better understand their actual customer journeys and see how their partnerships efforts interact with and influence other marketing activities.

To more fully understand and assess partner impact, companies are broadening their perspective on measuring partner value to include both partner efficiency and partner effectiveness metrics. In addition to looking at CPA, ROAS, and revenue, they are looking at partner-assisted revenue—revenue they may have helped to generate but that they didn't close—partner profitability, partner ability to reach new customers, and partner results by product categories, geography, device, and SKU. These insights enable enterprises and their partners to assess incrementality and right-price their activities, paying partners for the actual value they bring.

Enterprises are pulling multiple levers to help catalyze their partners' growth. Sharing performance insights directly with partners who don't generally have access to enterprise sales data to see the impact of their efforts allows partners to proactively optimize their results. Testing various combinations of product, content, promotions, and incentive structures gives enterprises and their partners the opportunity to determine what makes a difference to their partnership results. Providing fresh brand assets that support partner success, promoting partners across their broader marketing efforts, offering personalized training and certification, and mentoring key performers also help move the needle.

Build the Partnerships Organization

Most enterprises are knee-deep in partnerships; they just may not recognize it as such because their partnerships have many different names and are developed and managed in different departments across their organization. As enterprises begin to build a track record of successful performance partnerships, and as their leadership begins to understand that partnerships have the potential to generate as much or more revenue than sales and marketing, interest in partnerships grows across organizations. Senior-level management is installed—please extend a warm welcome to the new chief partnerships officer—and intentional collaboration across departments engaged in partnerships begins. This collaboration is often accompanied by a gradual migration of partnerships to one PMP. With the ability to track each partner's influence on an enterprise's business now possible, enterprises begin to evaluate when and where it makes sense to convert other partnerships to a performance model. In some cases, performance partnerships efforts are consolidated under one roof.

Prepare for the Future

Partnerships are fast becoming a critical lifestream for enterprises. Hundreds of innovative enterprises are stretching the boundaries of what "partnership" means, spawning new types of partnerships, experimenting with how those partnerships are designed, optimized, and scale, and learning what it takes to effectively collaborate across organizational borders. What's happening here is not just a rebranding of affiliate marketing, it's the birth of the partnership economy. Although we are in the early days of fully realizing the full partnerships potential, we see it already infusing all aspects of customer engagement, and in the not-too-distant future, partnerships ecosystems will be the foundation upon which highly successful businesses are built.

The Quick Summary

- Every enterprise defines what full potential is for itself and charts its own path to get there. However, successful partnerships programs share the same essential foundations: a strong and broad organizational commitment to partnerships as a growth strategy; a clear yet evolving vision for how partnerships can achieve critical business objectives; a strategy for realizing that vision; and an enabling partnerships growth engine.

- What is the path to reaching full potential? Companies are taking a more strategic approach to partnerships. They are adopting and automating the partnerships process. They are expanding and diversifying their partnerships portfolio and taking their programs global once they have experienced success in their home market. They are using advanced techniques to value and optimize their individual partnerships and their partnerships program and portfolio. As their remit expands and they begin to manage a greater portion of enterprise partnerships, converting them to a performance basis, they are building stronger and more experienced partnerships organizations. In every way they can, they are preparing for a bright future through partnerships.

What's Up Next?

The next chapter explores the partnerships planning process, which enables enterprises to both maintain and optimize their current partnerships program while putting a strong foundation in place for the future.

Note

[1] "Smooth Your Partnership Journey by Learning from High Maturity Companies: How to Make Tactical Improvements to Your Partnership Program," **impact.com**.

CHAPTER 16

Next Steps: Envision and Plan a Durable Partnerships Program

P riest Willis, Sr., senior manager, global partnerships strategist at Lenovo, is developing the technology company's global partnerships strategy for the coming year. It's a big job—the $20 billion company has a robust global growth strategy and partnerships operations in more than 35 countries.

"I've heard it said that strategy is the clouds and how that strategy gets translated into day-to-day operations is the dirt," Willis explains. "My job is to be able to take us from the clouds to the dirt." Drawing from the company's ecommerce strategy for the next year, which identifies Lenovo's revenue goals and areas of focus (i.e., customers, products, and regions of the world), Willis and his global partnerships team begin to chart their course.

"I have a strong team that I rely on that really knows their local businesses," Willis explains. Great talent is vital to his partnerships team's success. Willis believes that, at their core, partnerships are a people business; you can't do business in distant markets from faraway headquarters. The daily blocking and tackling takes place with local partners on the ground. A strong distributed partnerships team is also essential because although 90 percent of the company's overall partnerships strategy for the coming year will be similar across the globe, how that strategy plays out locally will differ significantly. Customers are different. Product preferences are different. Holidays are different. Business customs and regulations are different. Global operations require local understanding and capability.

In addition to figuring out how the partnerships team will reach its revenue goals for the year, the planning process also includes an assessment of Lenovo's partnerships portfolio. Who are they each reaching, both individually and collectively, and where along their customer journeys? Are there gaps that need to be filled? Are partners being paid accurately for their impact? And is there balance in the portfolio—is the company too dependent on any partners? What new partners does it want, and need, to bring onboard and what is its plan for making that happen? Can it discover and recruit them itself using the tools embedded in its partnership automation platform? Will it need to hire a partnerships agency to help it get established in new regions?

As part of this assessment, Willis seeks formal feedback in the form of an annual email survey from Lenovo's portfolio of thousands of partners. The goal of the survey is to understand Lenovo's partner experience, what's important to partners, and what Willis, and his team, can do to be a better enterprise partner. Willis reads through all the surveys and weighs each comment on a variety of factors when considering what enhancements they will make to Lenovo's partner experience.

Willis complements Lenovo's internal analysis with a solid external look at competitive partnerships programs, companies that include HP and Dell. His team studies strong partnerships programs in unrelated industries, such as companies like Uber, to learn what they are doing, why they might be doing it, and how that may apply to Lenovo. Willis also actively builds and nurtures relationships with others in the field, generously helping each other by sharing ideas and observations.

Annual planning goes beyond figuring out how the partnerships team will reach its revenue goals this year—it's also about planning for the future. "You have to be thinking about the business and what it will look like three to five years out, so you have what it takes to make it happen," Willis explains. That means setting up the infrastructure to support expansion into new lines of business, ways of doing business, and regions of the world. What kind of technology, people, and process will the future require? "You have to open your thoughts up and not be afraid to pivot where necessary," Willis says.

Planning also means being mindful of how the changes that are taking place in partnerships are impacting other important stakeholders in Lenovo. "Partnerships can be a lot more than what people thought in the past, and that is putting pressure on other departments within companies," Willis explains. "We are starting to push the boundaries of what this role really means. It's fun and it's challenging at the same time."

Designing Your Partnerships Strategy

Developing your partnerships program strategy is essential to the success of partnerships efforts. It's how companies go from vision to revenue. It's also one of the most challenging aspects of running a partnerships program, second only to the discovery and recruitment of potential partners, according to research conducted by Forrester.[1]

This chapter considers why people experience partnership planning as complicated. It also introduces the Partnerships Program Planner (PPP) and the Partnership Maturity Roadmap (PMR), tools that enterprises can use to guide their planning process. The PPP and PMR incorporate many of the concepts and frameworks that have been introduced—and will continue to be introduced—throughout this book. You may want to have them nearby as you work your way through this chapter.

Planning Is Challenging and Critical

Planning your partnerships strategy is important. It brings everything you have done and hope to do together in one forward-looking process. But it can be complicated. Why is this the case?

Planning takes place on several levels. It involves managing ongoing program operations while simultaneously creating and implementing a viable growth strategy. Ongoing program management is complex on its own. Forrester estimates that there are over 90 distinct components to manage in a partnerships program.[2] Add keeping a finger on the pulse of the market, understanding and recruiting new partners and new partner types, identifying and testing out new approaches and tactics, developing and growing your partnerships organization, and building organizational commitment to partnerships, and you get a sense of the complexity. Strategy development also includes multiple time frames. What do you need to do this week, in the next few months, and two to four years out to keep your present business humming and ensure that you are generating more revenue that is of better quality and coming from more diversified sources? Keeping your eye on the opportunity and the potential rewards for going for it can turn complexity into adventure.

Partnerships are collaborative. Strategy development isn't an isolated activity. It's a collaborative undertaking among senior management, partnerships program leaders and managers, and an enterprise's myriad partners. Generally speaking, the business unit determines its revenue target business objectives, and then, as seen with Lenovo, partnerships program managers translate those growth targets and related business objectives into partnerships program goals and activities. They do this by collaborating with each of their partners to determine their individual growth targets for the year. What is each partner willing and able to do? What does each partner need from the enterprise partner managers to realize its goals? The gap between what existing partners are able to do and what an enterprise is expecting in terms of growth is where new partners come in.

Planning looks different across industries and around the world. Software and financial services companies, for example, report that their top planning tactic is defining a go-to-market strategy, whereas retail and travel companies spend most of their time evaluating partnership readiness and experience.[3] Companies operating in North America and Europe, the Middle East, and Africa (EMEA) also cite go-to-market strategies as a top tactic; however, their colleagues in Asia-Pacific (APAC) countries emphasize channel readiness and partner experience.

It's a dynamic marketplace. Planning in rapidly evolving marketplaces, and in markets that are subject to disruption, introduces a fair amount of uncertainty into a process designed to create certainty. While planning for existing operations has an established structure and past results and experience upon which to build, new initiatives need structure to be put in place and data to move from hypothesis to experience. Taking an entrepreneurial approach, building certainty through deliberate experimentation provides companies with relevant structure to create the reality that is needed. Building testing into your partnerships process so your partners can learn with you builds trust and certainty.

The Partnerships Program Planner

The Partnerships Program Planner provides a simple framework to assist enterprises in developing their own partnerships program planning process (Figure 16.1). The PPP has five key components:

1. What you plan to accomplish: the headline, a summary of what you plan to accomplish with your partnerships effort in the coming year.

2. Current state of your partnerships effort: a description of how your partnerships program is presently performing.

3. Future state of your partnerships effort: a summary of where your business is headed in the next one to three years and the type of partnerships program you will need to bring that vision to life.

4. The plan: a description of how you are going to close the gap between the current state of your partnerships portfolio and its future state. It includes key activities, milestones, time frame, and resources needed.

Partnerships Program Planner

Time Period:

What We Plan to Accomplish:
The headline, a summary of what you plan to accomplish over this time period.

Current State of Your Partnerships Effort:
Description of how your partnerships program is currently performing.

Future State of Your Partnerships Effort:
Summary of where your business is headed in the next one to three years and the type of partnerships program you will need to bring that vision to life.

The Plan:
Description of how you are going to close the gap between the current state of your partnerships effort and your desired future state.

Potential Challenges:
Account of what might get in the way of your success and what you will proactively do to mitigate these risks.

FIGURE 16.1 The essential components of the Partnerships Program Planner.

5. Potential challenges: an account of what might get in the way of your success and what you proactively will do to mitigate these risks.

What You Plan to Accomplish

I've said it before, and at the risk of being redundant, I'm saying it here once more: business strategy informs your partnerships strategy. When you know the revenue that your company wants you to achieve, the growth strategies it would like you to employ (i.e., new customer growth; an increase in customer lifetime value, profit margin, and/or market share), the customers you are meant to target and the geographic regions in which they reside, and the products with which you have to work, you have what you need to begin to plan your partnerships strategy.

This initial section of the PPP is essentially your elevator speech, a brief summary of what you plan to accomplish with your partnerships effort in the coming year. It includes your revenue goal and accompanying business objectives and key initiatives you will undertake, as well as the KPIs you will use to measure your success. It paints a broad picture that is more fully detailed in the remaining sections of the PPP.

Current State of Your Partnerships Program Effort

Strategy is about starting where you are and knowing where you want to be. A solid and honest look at your current partnerships performance and portfolio provides a starting point for your efforts. Think of it as the starting place of a run. Where you want to be is the finish line.

Start with an overall look at how well your program is performing. Where are you in your ability to capitalize on the partnerships opportunity that you originally identified and presented to your management team?

How much revenue are you contributing? How significant is your effort to your organization at this moment in time? Many companies look first at the revenue they are generating for the enterprise. What percentage of your overall corporate revenue is derived in whole or in part by your partnerships effort?

What business goals are you meeting? Next consider how partnerships are enabling your company to meet its business objectives. It can be helpful to take the perspectives of the key stakeholders you identified earlier on when considering how partnerships are enabling your company to meet its secondary business objectives because partnerships do not exist in a vacuum; they influence enterprises' customer journeys and financial results. (See Chapter 12, "How to Get Your Partnerships Program Started.") How are your partnerships efforts helping your CFO, Chief Growth Officer (CGO), and CMO achieve their goals?

Take your CMO, for example. In many companies the CMO is the custodian of their customers and their extended customer journeys. How are partnerships enabling your company to better serve its customers and improve their experience? Partnerships often shorten customer journeys, enabling customers to more quickly and easily find what they need. Interjecting a trusted voice into the shopping journey enables them to feel more confident in their purchase decision and their ability to get the most from their purchase. Another way that partners shorten customer journeys is by directing potential customers to enterprises' mobile sites or apps, where they can "get things done." In many regions of the world, people's smartphones are their most trusted resource—a recent Google study found that 96 percent of people use a smartphone to "get things done."[4]

Shortening customer journeys increases the efficiency of enterprise customer engagement efforts, enhancing enterprise financial results. Partnerships can also help enterprises achieve their customer acquisition goals by reaching quality customers that are outside of the reach of their other customer engagement initiatives. They may introduce, influence, close, or reengage customers—or all of the above! And partners are able to nurture those quality prospects into customers with strong lifetime values via ongoing engagement, often inspired by chained compensation structures that enable them to share in future revenue that they help to generate.

Next, consider your partnerships efforts within the context of your CFO. At **impact.com**, we often hear that mature partnerships programs are able to enable companies to create more predictable revenue streams on an ongoing basis and in moments of market disruption. A diverse portfolio of partners, combined with well-designed and targeted promotions and campaigns, enables enterprises to generate revenue quickly, with or without discounts.

Switch perspectives for a moment to think strategy. How are partnerships building your company's capacity to enhance or develop new products, expand into new marketplaces, and pivot based on current or potential market changes? What about public relations? How are your relationships with influencers and mass media publishers increasing brand awareness—and how does compensating them on a performance basis impact their enthusiasm and results? Don't forget business development—have you been able to develop productive partnerships from leads that don't meet their deal size hurdles and/or test out potential partnerships for them before looking to scale? And then there is customer service: Are they able to send people looking for samples to review on their sites to you as potential influencers? Or to direct enthusiastic customers to you as potential brand ambassadors?

When you combine your overall revenue numbers with your performance in helping your company meet—or exceed—these secondary business objectives, you have a more complete sense of the value your partnerships effort brings to your enterprise. Most companies find that the impact of partnerships across organizations and their KPIs is significant.

How efficient is your program? Next let's consider the costs and efficiency of your partnerships effort. What does it cost to run your partnerships program? When you know your costs and the revenue your effort brings in, you can calculate your efficiency. Enterprises use several different metrics, including ROI, ROAS, and contribution margin after marketing (CMAM). Use whatever metrics make sense for your business and help you proactively make smart decisions and investments. Be sure that among them are metrics that are used to measure the effectiveness of other functions that partnerships may impact or be compared with, such as marketing and business development. Metrics can be calculated in multiple ways and with different data sources, so know when and where apples are being compared with apples and when they are being compared with spinach.

Is your program healthy? Next assess the overall health of your partnerships program. What are your program KPIs and how are they trending? Let's consider growth first. How many partnerships do you currently have? Is your program growing? Remember, the goal here is not growth for the sake of growth, but growth in productive partnerships. What percentage of your partners are productive? Is this increasing over time?

Keep an eye on overall portfolio balance to assess potential revenue volatility. Are any of your partners responsible for more than 25 percent of total revenue? If any one of your partners left, how exposed would you be in terms of target customer coverage? If any one partner is responsible for too much revenue or customer influence, you may want to reduce that risk by tapping the capabilities of other existing or new partners. This may also be an indication that you need more resources dedicated to partner optimization and new partner development.

Next, take a deeper dive into the partners that share responsibility for your success.

Which partners are your top performers? Which ones are your top-performing partners and partner segments and how are they contributing to each of your business objectives? Which partners are bringing in the most revenue? Which are attracting new customers? Which partner is bringing in the highest revenue from new customers? Which has the highest profit margins? Which has the highest average order value? Which provides incremental value to you? What is each partner's expected lifetime value? Which partners are performing better on each of the metrics associated with these business objectives compared to last year and which are performing worse? Why?

How are your new partners doing? Take a special look at your new partners. Which partners are new to your program? Which have performed well and which have not performed as expected? What is your understanding of why this is the case? Don't forget partners that may have performed well in the past but whose performance now is lackluster. What are the reasons for this change? What can be done? What are the key learnings here?

Who are your partnerships reaching? It's a good idea to study your collective partners' audiences from time to time and the profile of the customers that they are bringing to you. Use the same method you did to understand each individual partner's audiences, but consolidate them into a customer coverage map like the one shown in Figure 16.2. Look for gaps and redundancies in coverage by each target customer segment.

Where and how are partnerships impacting your customer journeys? Study your journey maps to see how partnerships in general, and each partner segment specifically, are contributing to your conversion pathway. Are your partnerships shortening the number of interactions people need before they are able to make a decision? What roles are partnerships playing in these customer journeys—are they introducing, influencing, closing, and/or reengaging? What devices are your target customers using when they interact with your partners? Are some better able to engage customers on mobile devices? Are your partnerships lifting the performance of your marketing efforts?

Who are our partnerships reaching?
Here's where our partners impact our customer journeys:

	Target Customer Segment 1	Target Customer Segment 2	Target Customer Segment 3
Awareness	Names of partners	Names of partners	
Consideration	Names of partners	Names of partners	
Close			
Re-engage		Names of partners	
Drive to Mobile			Names of partners

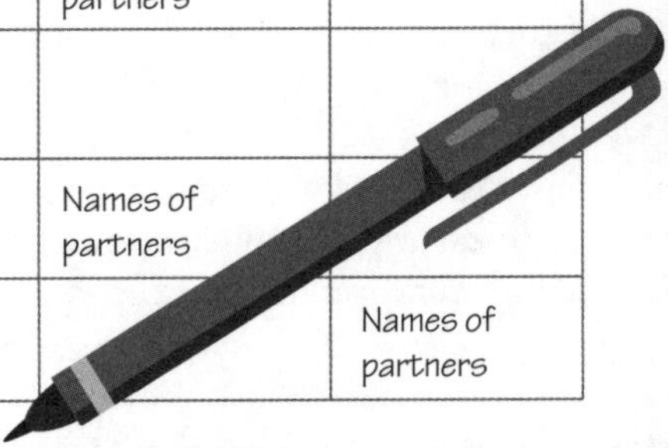

FIGURE 16.2   Who are your partnerships reaching?

Know What Your Competitors Are Doing

In addition to knowing what you are doing, it's important to understand what your competitors are doing—and not doing. Regular assessment of their programs and practices provides companies with helpful insights and many companies are not undertaking this process regularly. In fact, 40 percent of B2C content marketers only look at their competitors' performance once a year (or not at all).[5] Be sure to evaluate your competitors' actions over time to avoid interpreting a fixed-point-in-time strategy as something other than what it is.

Start by taking a look at their partnerships program itself. What are its goals and how is it structured? How is it paying its partners, what are its program terms, and how competitive is it? What can you glean about its overall partner experience? What type of training and resources does it provide? You might have to do a bit of research to uncover this information. Partner pages on enterprise websites are great sources, as is FMTC.co, which crawls the web to find and consolidate partnership information. While you are researching, find out who is leading their partnerships effort and, using tools like LinkedIn, how they have resourced their partnerships program.

Next, explore which partners are sending traffic to your competitors. You can use third-party analytics tools like **similarweb.com** to see which websites are driving traffic to competitors. You can also find competitors' key search words that you can use to identify partners. Who shows up when you conduct a search using these words? Should they be your partners? You may also want to study rankings on product ranking and review sites—where does your competition show up, and where are you? The partnerships agency PartnerCentric found that the top three positions on these sites receive more than 90 percent of ongoing traffic.[6] If you are not in the top three, it's hardly worth your effort. Dig deep into why your competitors are receiving the higher rankings so you can learn what you need to do to be in the top three.

Identify a handful of enterprises that you believe are leaders in partnerships and study them as well. They are not your competitors, they are your teachers. They are pushing the limits of what's possible today and defining tomorrow's table stakes. Like Willis asks his team, consider what you can learn from them, what they are doing, and why. Attend conferences to keep your eye on the overall partnerships landscape. It can help you anticipate market shifts, identify key trends, strategies, and tactics, and uncover untapped opportunities.

Future State of Your Partnerships Effort

When you know what you want to accomplish, you are more likely to get there. This section of the PPP asks you to consider where your business is headed over the next one to three years and what type of partnerships program you will need to meet this vision and enable that growth. Will your program need to expand to include new target customers, new partner types, new behaviors, and new regions of the world?

You may also want to consider whether the scope of your partnerships program will change during this time period. Is this the time to begin to identify partnerships and advertising relationships that are distributed throughout your organization—in marketing, public relations, business development—that may be good candidates for conversion to a performance model? In many cases, when these partnerships are redesigned to be on a performance basis, the revenue they generate for the partner and the enterprise increases significantly. This partnership conversion process and the internal readiness to undertake it often requires time, patience, education, a solid technology platform, and a well-proven track record. So if conversion of partnerships is part of your ultimate strategy, it's time to plan for it.

The Plan

This part of the PPP is where you describe the specifics of how you will fill the gap between where you are and where you want to be. To borrow a phrase from Willis, this is where clouds and dirt meet. The plan is a description of how you will manage and grow your existing partnerships portfolio, as well as how you will enhance your partner experience and build a mature partnerships program.

How are you going to sustain and grow your current partnerships effort? What are your go-to-market plans for this year? Stated differently, who is doing what, where, with whom, and with what outcome or result? You may want to refer back to Chapter 3, "How Partnerships Can Help You Meet Critical Business Goals," and to the accompanying worksheet to help you nail down this part of the PPP.

What portion of this activity will come from your existing partnerships? I highly recommend that you work with your partners to answer this question. Share your revenue goals for your partnership with them, compare your revenue forecasts and understand any differences, and ask them to commit to a revenue goal with you. Make note of what your partners indicate they will need from you to accomplish their goals and include this in your resource and capacity planning. Ask your partners what might get in the way of their success and begin to create contingency plans.

Next consider how much growth you will be looking to your new partners to generate. Are your goals both motivating and realistic? Remember, it can take time to get to productivity. Are your new partners ready? What can you do now to nurture and develop these nascent partnerships? How many new partners will you be looking to recruit? How will you discover and recruit new partners? Who is in your pipeline and who needs to be? You may want to explore the discovery and recruitment capabilities of your PMP. Some worksheets offered by **impact .com** that can be helpful for identifying nontraditional business partners are available at **www.thepartnershipsbook.com**. It can be helpful to establish recruitment timeline goals; for example, you will onboard 10 new partners during the next 10 weeks. Keep track of response rates and analyze invitation success using A/B testing models. Finally, consider whether there are any important enhancements you need to make to your partner portal, partnership management platform, or training efforts to attract, recruit, and onboard new partners to get them up and running and productive.

What will you do to enable your partners to be more successful? What does your promotion calendar look like for the year? What are key dates, holidays, and new product launches around which you'll plan campaigns? What is the state of your partner experience and would your partners agree with your assessment? What are key areas of improvement? Products? Commission structures? Conversion and post-conversion experience? You may want to refer back to Chapter 13, "How Does It Feel? Creating a Beneficial Partner Experience" and the accompanying worksheet to bring this dimension of your program back into focus.

Create Your Partnership Maturity Roadmap

How are you going to enable your partnerships to reach their full potential? Can your program benefit from adopting and automating your partnerships process?

Have you optimized your partnerships and your overall partnerships portfolio? Are there new partnership types that may make sense to bring into your partner network—technology partners or new strategic business collaborations? Are you ready to explore being a potential partner for another brand, introducing it to your customers? Is it time to invest in your partnerships organization or to work with a partnerships agency to move your program forward? Where do you want to focus your efforts internally to enhance your partnerships efforts and strengthen your organization's commitment? How will you capture and share your learnings about your customers, products, and markets from your partnerships efforts? Having mapped your partnerships organization's dependencies with other internal functional areas, how will you proactively nurture relationships with these colleagues to your mutual benefit?

I imagine this list of questions may have caused you to tune out and think that this whole partnerships thing is much too much to try and do. Trust me, it's not—if you break the list down, note where you already have taken a given action or developed a capability, then identify which of the remaining activities are relevant to your partnerships program now and in the next one to four years. The PMR (and a downloadable worksheet) was created by **impact.com** to facilitate this process for you (Table 16.1). Once you have run through this list, work with your colleagues to create an impact and effort matrix to prioritize these remaining activities. Then you will be ready, and able, to build out your roadmap.

TABLE 16.1 Partnership Maturity Roadmap

Action/Capability	We already do this/have this capability	We'll work on this. . . .			
		in the next 1–6 months	6–12 months from now	1–2 years from now	2–4 years from now
Define our program vision, mission, goals, and go-to-market strategy (including ideal partner profiles, routes to market, contract strategy, etc.)					
Establish more rigor in forecasting, pipeline generation, and quota setting from our partners					
Establish monitoring processes for our competitors' programs					
Establish cadence for evaluating partner mix, partner gap analysis, and recruitment goals					

(Continued)

TABLE 16.1 Partnership Maturity Roadmap (CONTINUED)

Action/Capability	We already do this/have this capability	We'll work on this....			
		in the next 1–6 months	6–12 months from now	1–2 years from now	2–4 years from now
Establish and enhance the partner experience through more systematic communication and collaboration					
Build out system integrations and APIs to empower partners with real-time access to our data so they can optimize the partnership					
Develop partnerships experience measurement and feedback system					
Adopt, standardize, and automate our partnerships process					
Establish and enhance the partner experience through robust partner dashboards and portals that provide real-time performance insight					
Establish our inbound partner recruitment presence and processes					
Establish and enhance our partner contracting and onboarding experience					
Streamline partner payment and crediting processes					
Expand the scope of tracking to include properties beyond our website (app, marketplaces, etc.)					
Reduce instances of partner fraud, noncompliance, and gaming					
Diversify our program with coupon, loyalty, and deal sites					
Diversify our program with influencers and ambassadors					
Diversify our program with strategic B2B partnerships					
Diversify our program with mass media partnerships					

(Continued)

TABLE 16.1   **Partnership Maturity Roadmap (CONTINUED)**

Action/Capability	We already do this/have this capability	We'll work on this. . . .			
		in the next 1–6 months	6–12 months from now	1–2 years from now	2–4 years from now
Diversify our program with mobile app partners					
Diversify our program with community, affinity, and cause-based partnerships					
Expand our program globally					
Track customer journeys and measure partner incrementality to optimize our partnerships and overall portfolio					
Increase revenue per partner and reactivate dormant partners					
Measure customer and partner lifetime value					
Build out and expand our partner organization					
De-silo the different partnerships teams throughout the organization					
Convert legacy-structured partnerships into tracked partnerships that reward on value delivered					
Consider working with a partnerships agency to expand our presence and capability					

Employ an Impact and Effort Matrix to Prioritize Your Activities

If you have never created an impact and effort matrix, you are in for a treat, because it's a fun and super clarifying process. Find a large whiteboard or large piece of paper that you can draw and adhere Post-it notes to. To set the stage, draw two perpendicular lines (as shown in Figure 16.3). Label the vertical axis "Impact" and the horizontal axis "Effort." Place a minus sign (–) at the end of both lines, close to where they intersect, to indicate a low level of impact. Then place a plus sign (+) at the far end of each of these lines to indicate a high level of impact.

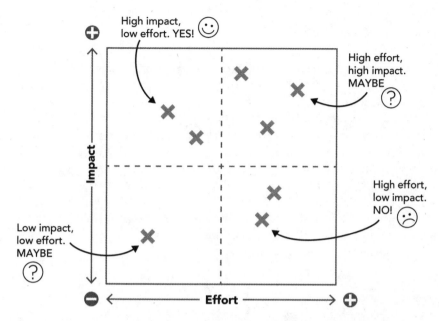

FIGURE 16.3   An impact and effort matrix is a simple way to evaluate and prioritize partnerships activities.

Next, write each activity that made it to your shortlist on a Post-it note, one idea per note. Divide the Post-its among your colleagues and ask them to place them on the matrix—each on the spot they believe is an accurate assessment of the impact that implementing the idea would have and the effort required.

It's a rare moment when everyone agrees, so the next step in this process is to discuss as a group the location of the Post-its on the matrix to better understand their placement and make any necessary adjustments. When the exercise is complete, each of the portfolio maturation strategies will be "properly" located on the matrix according to the group's best thinking. Notably, activities that have high potential impact with low effort fall into the "YES!" category; those that have high effort with low impact fall into the "NO!" category. Those in the middle are strong "maybes." By undertaking this process, your partnerships team will have more thoroughly fleshed out the potential impact and effort of each activity, and developed a shared understanding of the options that will serve as a strong foundation for your partnerships program maturity roadmap.

Last but not least, it's time to develop your timeline. Working from the shared understanding you have built, you can begin to establish a timeline for undertaking each action or capability. What will you work on in the next 6 months, 6 to 12 months, 1 to 2 years, and 2 to 4 years?

Identify Any Potential Risks

The last section of the PPP can be summed up in four words: "what if?" and "here's what." Take the time to identify what might get in the way of your success. What are potential derailers and disruptors to your plan? What are you proactively doing to mitigate these risks? For example, how are you diversifying your portfolio so it isn't too heavily weighted on any particular type of partner or any single partner? What other types of adjustments can you make? How is the external environment changing? What challenges may be on the horizon? Think of new competitors or shifts in competitors' strategy, public health challenges, extreme weather patterns, shifting economic conditions, changing government officials and geopolitics, new technology, and social media platforms. What pivots in strategy might partnerships enable to keep your company and its performance strong?

And then it's time to make it happen.

Complete Your Partnership Maturity Roadmap

Best-in-class partnerships programs are intentional about building program maturity. Use Figure 16.1 to create a roadmap for getting your partnerships program to full potential by plotting out what activities and capabilities you plan to light up in the next 1 to 6 months, 6 to 12 months, 1 to 2 years, or 2 to 4 years.

The Quick Summary

- Developing your partnerships program strategy is essential to the success of partnerships efforts. It's how companies go from vision to revenue.
- Planning is one of the most challenging aspects of running a partnerships program.
- We have created the PPP, a simple framework to assist enterprises in developing their own partnerships program planning process. The PPP has five key components: what you plan to accomplish, the current state of your partnerships effort, the future state of your partnerships effort, the plan, and potential risks to your plan.
- The plan is a description of how you will manage and grow your existing partnerships portfolio as well as how you will expand your portfolio, enhance your partner experience, and build a mature partnerships program.

- The Partnership Maturity Roadmap is a tool that enables partnerships teams to plot out how they will get their program to its full potential over the next six months to four years.
- Take the time to identify what might get in the way of your plan's success. What are potential derailers and disruptors to your plan? What are you proactively doing to mitigate these risks?

What's Up Next?

What does the future look like for partnerships? The next, and final, chapter shares some of my thoughts on where I see the partnership economy evolving.

Notes

[1] A Forrester Consulting Thought Leadership Paper Commissioned by Impact, "Smooth Your Partnership Journey by Learning from High Maturity Companies: How to Make Tactical Improvements to Your Partnership Program," **impact.com**, August 2020, **http://bit.ly/tactical-improvements-partner-program**.

[2] Jay McBain, "Partner Relationship Management (PRM) Comes of Age," Forrester, November 2, 2018, **https://go.forrester.com/blogs/partner-relationship-management-prm-comes-of-age/**.

[3] "Smooth Your Partnership Journey," **impact.com**.

[4] Lisa Gevelber, "Mobile Has Changed Intent and How People Get Things Done: New Consumer Behavior Data," September 2016, **http://bit.ly/mobile-search-intent-consumer-data**.

[5] "Protect Your Brand Integrity and Open New Opportunities with Content Monitoring," Partnercentric, accessed May 31, 2021, **https://partnercentric.com/control-suite/content-monitoring/**.

[6] "TopRank," PartnerCentric, Inc., accessed May 28, 2021, **https://partnercentric.com/control-suite/toprank/**.

CHAPTER 17

What's Next? Prepare for the Future

When Brian Halligan and Dharmesh Shah founded HubSpot, they thought they were starting a software company, but as it turns out, they sparked a movement. The movement, otherwise known as inbound marketing, is a marketing methodology for building relationships with customers and other stakeholders. It was born out of the observation that people are tired of "push" marketing strategies—marketing that pushes products out to a target audience, whether members of that audience have indicated an interest or not. People don't want to be constantly interrupted by advertising or salespeople selling something; instead, they want help in meeting their goals or they want to be left alone. Inbound marketing is an answer to that desire. A "pull" marketing methodology, inbound marketing was designed to help customers meet their goals at every stage of their journeys with enterprises and their brands. It attracts and retains customers by creating valuable and often personalized content and experiences that enable people to find what they are looking for—when they are looking for it. It's enterprises doing what their referral partners do naturally.

To be clear, in addition to starting a movement, Halligan and Shah did start a highly successful company that enables inbound marketing strategies. HubSpot's original product offering, circa 2006, took the form of marketing automation software. Over the years, its product offering expanded to include a full platform of products that enabled enterprise customer interactions across the entire customer journey, including marketing, sales, operations, and customer service. Today, the

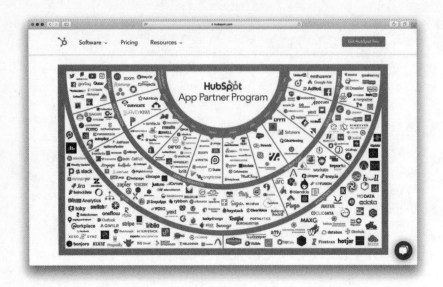

FIGURE 17.1   The HubSpot app ecosystem is continually expanding.

company is continuing to build its platform, with an ecosystem of over 800 app partnership integrations (Figure 17.1). This ecosystem of partners significantly extends the capabilities of the HubSpot platform to include the genius and capability of many others.

The HubSpot app ecosystem is more than a marketplace of applications; the HubSpot platform integrates and coordinates how these apps work together. "You can picture a platform as a hub, with spokes connecting other products to its center," explains Scott Brinker, HubSpot's vice president, platform ecosystem. "The hub binds those disparate products together and orchestrates them in a common mission."[1]

Brinker offers three ways that HubSpot's platform simplifies marketing technology (martech) integrations for its ecosystem customers. First, it establishes an organizing model for the data exchanged between apps in a company's martech stack so there is one centralized "source of truth" for the platform. Second, it creates a "home base," an integrated user interface, where users can accomplish the majority of their work, rather than switching between applications. Third, the platform established a trusted certification process for apps in the ecosystem that ensures that the apps integrate at a meaningful level, although with a searchable directory that enables users to find the right app for their needs. The goal, in Brinker's words, is to "build a truly lovable platform."[2]

And that it is. Today, HubSpot enjoys relationships with 113,000-plus customers in 120 countries. It has sparked more than 150 User Groups in 21 countries, has drawn 70,000 attendees to its annual INBOUND event, and has trained and certified more than 350,000 inbound professionals through HubSpot Academy, its digital learning academy for marketing, sales, and service professionals. The company has developed a Solutions Partner Program for its growing ecosystem of thousands of partner businesses that offer marketing, sales, web design, and customer relationship management (CRM) implementation services. The company is also committed to helping marketing and admissions staff of educational institutions employ inbound marketing to attract and convert prospective students through its Education Partner Program. It also invests in companies in communities that have traditionally had limited access to capital and senior-level coaching via HubSpot Ventures.

The Future of Partnerships Is Ecosystems

As this brief glance at HubSpot's evolving business strategy suggests, the partnerships program of the future will expand beyond many one-off relationships between enterprises and their partners into robust, integrated, and collaborative ecosystems. Enterprises will form these multisided or "n-sided" ecosystems, inviting hundreds, if not thousands, of partners to work together to best meet their shared target customers' existing, emerging, and latent needs and desires. Drawing upon the experience, resources, and imagination of many, these ecosystems will be powerhouses of influence and innovation, crossing industries and verticals, creating value in many ways at a speed and scale not previously possible.

Sound like a pipe dream? It's not. These ecosystems are already here, disrupting and redefining industries, business models, and management practices. Think Amazon, Google, Apple, Alibaba, HubSpot, and others. We're about a decade into this latest way of creating value, which is often considered the fourth major economic revolution in the United States since the nineteenth century (Figure 17.2).[3] Even at this early stage, these ecosystems are powerful and pervasive. A recent Accenture survey of 1,252 business leaders found that 76 percent of them believe that their current business models will be unrecognizable in the next five years because of the influence of ecosystems in the marketplace.[4]

While we often think of ecosystems as a strategy for only the biggest and most sophisticated companies, it's actually a strategy for every company that wants to be around in five years. Indeed, the same Accenture study found that 84 percent of business leaders surveyed believe that ecosystems are important to their strategy.[5] These leaders believe that ecosystem participation allows businesses to innovate (63 percent), increase revenue growth (58 percent), access new markets (55 percent), and access new customers (55 percent).[6] How else will companies compete against ecosystems, which are playing the game with seemingly unlimited resources? As the adage goes, "If you can't beat 'em, join 'em."

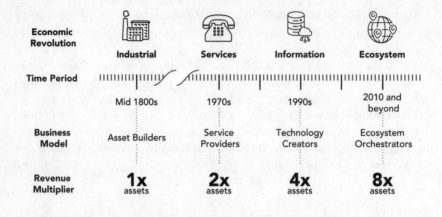

FIGURE 17.2 The four major U.S. economic revolutions and their associated revenue multipliers.

Source: Adapted from Omar Hoda, Joseph Vitale, Jr., and Craig A. Giffi, "The Revenue Multipler Effect," Deloitte, accessed May, 27, 2021, https://www2.deloitte.com/content/dam/Deloitte/us/Documents/manufacturing/us-mfg-the-revenue-multiplier-effect.pdf.

While executives understand that their future involves partner ecosystems, many don't believe they have the experience and capabilities to design and execute them. The good news is that companies that are engaged in partnerships are already on their way because ecosystems are a natural progression of today's partnerships programs.

There are two stages in this progression to partnerships ecosystems (Figure 17.3). The first stage, which is the most common form of today's partnerships programs, is an enterprise-focused network of one-off partnerships. This stage gives way to a more connected partnerships structure where multiple partners work together, integrating their products with that of the underlying enterprise. As collaboration deepens, these enterprise-focused ecosystems become increasingly decentralized, with partners freely interacting and collaborating with each other.[7] Essentially, at a mature state, there are actors magnifying the impact of other partners, creating a flywheel effect.

Partnerships Ecosystems—They Are Not Your Father's Oldsmobile

Although ecosystems are a natural evolution of today's mature partnerships programs, there are important differences, which are captured in Table 17.1 and briefly discussed in the following pages.

Mature Partnerships Program   **Emerging Partnerships Ecosystems**

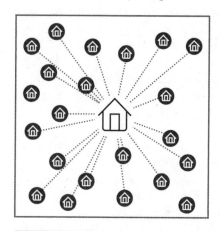 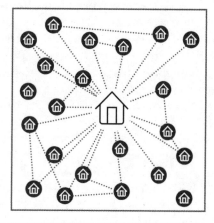

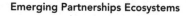

FIGURE 17.3   The evolution from partnerships programs to ecosystems.

Source: Adapted from Michael Lewrick, Patrick Link, and Larry Leifer, The Design Thinking Playbook: Mindful Digital Transformation of Teams, Products, Services, Businesses and Ecosystems *(Hoboken, NJ: John Wiley & Sons, 2018), p. 242.*

Purpose of collaboration. Value creation is at the center of today's partnerships programs. Designed to be a "win-win-win" for customers, the enterprise, and its partners, today's collaborations focus on creating a compelling customer experience around the purchase of enterprise products, services, or experiences and finding opportunities for incremental revenue. Value creation is also at the center of partnerships ecosystems; however, there is an additional win in the equation: a win for the whole ecosystem. This win occurs when the ecosystem works together, in whole or in part, to find a way to better meet its target customer needs than would otherwise be possible.

Enterprise and partner roles. Enterprises are the builders of their partnerships programs and they will be the builders and orchestrators of these *n*-sided partner ecosystems—at least initially. Eventually these ecosystems may morph into entities without an enterprise at the center. Note that some enterprises will build multiple ecosystems simultaneously to meet the needs of their various customer segments and focus areas. HubSpot, for example, is building partner ecosystems around the apps that integrate with its platform and others around its solutions partners (for partner businesses that offer marketing, sales, web design, and CRM implementation services, among others).

Partnership types. An increasingly diverse array of partnership types comprise current partnerships programs and this will surely hold true for tomorrow's partnerships ecosystems. Partners with established audiences or customer bases will continue to be referral partners for the enterprise at the center as well as for other various members of the ecosystem. There will be a stronger showing of strategic brand-to-brand partnerships, as partners play more extensive roles as co-creators of value that transcend corporate and industry capabilities and boundaries.

Target customers. Customers are at the center of today's partnerships and they will be at the center of emerging partnerships ecosystems. Members of the ecosystem will be dedicated to these customers in some way. They may be a member's current customers or audiences, a similar or desired market segment, or an entirely new opportunity altogether. As a result, the ecosystem's overall target customer base is likely to be larger and extend into more markets than would be possible for any one player, or handful of players, acting on their own.

Receptiveness will be another feature of this customer base. We have already seen how referral partners are able to catalyze new customer and shopping journeys between brands and their target audiences because of the authentic, trusted relationships they have established. These relationships create a porousness—a willingness to listen to what specific partner members in the ecosystem say and recommend. As long as partner members remain authentic and committed to their audiences or customers first, this receptiveness is likely to remain, and even grow, as partners work together, harnessing their shared insights, resources, and capabilities in service of their shared customers.

Customer engagement. Responding to consumer preferences for third-party research and recommendations to begin their shopping and customer journeys, enterprises currently cede major portions of their early-in-the-journey customer interactions to their partners. When appropriate, these partners bring enterprises into crucial conversations with their target customers, generating and capturing demand for enterprise product offerings. This influence will be magnified in ecosystems, whose omnipresent nature will enable them to interact with their target customers any time and place, in multiple native and trusted settings. What's more, each member of the ecosystem will be free to both drive and receive referrals and recommendations from other members for their own value propositions as well as for integrated value propositions made possible by multiple members working together.

Customer value proposition. Today, referral partners primarily work with the enterprise's value propositions, offering their unique perspective on it based on the audiences they reach or the use cases they support. Partners also bring new features and capabilities to enterprise existing value propositions or create joint value propositions together. As collaboration deepens, multiple ecosystem members will work together to create integrated value propositions, incorporating members' resources, capabilities, experience, and intellectual property. The goal of these collaborations will be to better meet customer needs in whatever shape that takes, answering a larger call than simply enhancing the enterprise's current value proposition.

Source of innovation. Innovation in today's partnerships programs is centralized, involving a collaboration between the enterprise and each of its partners. They ask themselves, "What can the two of us create together that we cannot make happen on our own?" and move forward from there. Innovation is more distributed in a partnerships ecosystem. Partners will collaborate whenever the opportunity arises, bringing together their many capabilities, resources, intellectual property, and experience in order to best meet the needs of their target customers. Each of these elements is considered a rentable building block of future products, services, and experiences that the members of the ecosystem can combine and recombine to create new and meaningful value for their shared customers. This new world of partnerships ecosystems will be asset-light, as partners plug into each other's capabilities.

Data openness. Although performance data is shared between an enterprise and each of its partners in high-performing partnerships programs, generally speaking data is mostly closed. The enterprise controls the data assets its partners receive and can selectively push it out via marketing promotions or with simpler, non-real-time structures such as product data feeds. As partnerships programs morph into ecosystems, data becomes more open among members, as each treats its unique data assets as a value proposition. Working together, members of the ecosystem are able to leverage insights derived from their data to better understand customer intent, sentiment, and preference and be able to act on it. Partners will provide access to selected data in real time through APIs.

Competitive outlook. Enterprises and their partnerships programs generally see themselves as competing against their well-known, immediate competitors' direct and indirect sales channels. The truth of the matter is that every company is currently, or will soon be, competing against large ecosystems like Amazon. Partnerships ecosystems are built on this understanding, and are designed to be able to compete effectively against these deeply resourced players.

Market valuation. Each of the four economic revolutions previously mentioned had its own signature business model, and each of these business models changed the market's perception of value. Deloitte, the global advisory and consulting firm, studied these changing business models through the lens of the revenue multiplier, a fundamental indicator of value based on an enterprise's overall revenue. It found that each new economic model had a revenue multiplier worth twice the value of the previous model, a phenomenon that has come to be known as the Revenue Multiplier Effect (RMx).[8]

The primary reason for this increase in value is the enterprise's ability to generate more revenue from fewer assets. Deloitte observed that industrial companies are the most physical asset-dependent; physical assets are key determinants of performance and value. As such, industrial companies have the lowest revenue multipliers, with revenue multipliers of 1× assets. Service providers, such as consultants and financial services, which rely more on human assets rather than physical assets, enjoy revenue multipliers of 2× assets. Technology creators, such as biotech companies and software companies, employ their capital to develop and sell intellectual property, which enables them to better scale their offerings. As a result, they have revenue multipliers of 4× assets.

Network and ecosystem orchestrators, which derive their value from creating, influencing, and connecting, enjoy the highest potential revenue multiplier of 8× assets, according to Deloitte's findings. These entities benefit from network effects; their value continually increases as others join the network or ecosystem. For example, the value of Airbnb increases as more people sign up to rent out their dwellings. Additional supply (as long as it's on-brand and of the same quality) begets more demand, which leads to more supply. As a result, ecosystems have the opportunity to realize a revenue multiplier of 8× assets. A quick glance at the top-valued firms of the S&P 500—Apple, Microsoft, Facebook, Alphabet (Google), and Tesla (is it a car company or a technology company?)—shows this connection between how assets are deployed and overall market valuation.

Think back for a moment to the Forrester study that documented the enhanced financial results of companies with mature partnerships programs relative to those of companies with the least developed programs.[9] Companies with high-maturity partnerships experience 2.3× faster revenue growth, are more profitable, and enjoy higher valuation than their early-phase peers. As high-maturity partnerships programs continue to scale their efforts to the level of a partnerships ecosystem, reaching more of their target customers with better solutions to their needs, and faster, how might their financial results continue to improve? How close will they get to reaching an 8× assets revenue multiplier?

TABLE 17.1	Comparing high-maturity partnerships programs and partnerships ecosystems.	
	High-Maturity Partnerships Programs	Partnerships Ecosystems
Purpose of Collaboration	Value creation: "Win-win-win" for customers, enterprises, and partners by selling a specific product or service and by finding opportunities for incremental revenue.	Value creation: "Win-win-win-win" for customers, enterprises, partners, and for the whole ecosystem by creating whatever is possible to best meet customer needs.
Enterprise and Partner Roles	Enterprises are the builders that live at the center of partnerships programs.	As collaboration deepens, these enterprise-focused ecosystems become increasingly decentralized, with partners freely interacting and collaborating with each other.

	High-Maturity Partnerships Programs	Partnerships Ecosystems
Partnership Types	Enterprises employ an increasingly diverse array of partnership types.	Ecosystems employ a diverse array of partnership types, with a stronger showing of strategic brand-to-brand partnerships-focused innovation.
Value Proposition	Partners often work with the enterprise's value propositions and offer their unique perspective on it, based on the audiences they reach or the use cases they support.	Integrated value propositions that incorporate members' resources, capabilities, experience, and intellectual property to better meet customer needs.
Source of Innovation	Centralized. Innovation involves a collaboration between an enterprise and each of its partners—what they can create together that they cannot create on their own.	Distributed. Ecosystem members will collaborate whenever and wherever the opportunity arises.
Data Openness	Mostly closed. Enterprises control the data assets their partners receive.	Open. Enterprises treat their unique data assets as a value proposition.
Competitive Outlook	Goal is to outcompete current competitors.	Goal is to compete against other ecosystems.
Market Valuation	Experience more enterprise growth from their partnerships effort and 2.3× faster revenue growth, are more profitable, and enjoy higher valuations than their early-phase peers.	Potential to reach valuations of 8× revenue.

Build Your Organization's Future Today

Ecosystems are exciting and complex. The success of partnerships ecosystems like Amazon and Alibaba can be daunting, which is why some executives who believe ecosystems are tomorrow's business model are on the sidelines and slow to engage. This is also why some executives, who want to write the rules and succeed in the partnerships ecosystem game, are already investing heavily in modern partnerships. They believe that companies that are late to the game will not be authors of the game, or know how to play the game, if they remain in the game at all. What can organizations do to begin to make the transition from a high-maturity partnerships program to a partnerships ecosystem?

Stay focused on your target customers. Partnerships ecosystems will only be successful if they are customer-obsessed, firmly committed to identifying, understanding, and helping their target customers meet their current, emergent, and latent needs. In the midst of changing business models, operating structures and processes, and cultures, not to mention rapidly changing marketplaces, it can be easy to lose sight of who drives your success. How might you create the conditions that will ensure that your emerging ecosystem remains committed to, and effective in, deeply understanding your changing target customers and solving their most important needs and desires? What rituals and practices might help you continually listen to customers with a fresh ear and capture and share those learnings?

Keep building your partnerships portfolio. To succeed in building partner ecosystems, enterprises need to move into the realm of deep collaboration, employing all types of partnerships to achieve a variety of purposes. How are you employing partnerships to generate and capture demand? How are you working with partners to enhance your value proposition and to co-create new value propositions? Stand back regularly to see what makes for an effective partner. How can you spot them in the wild and bring them into your emerging ecosystem? Take note of meta trends; how is your partnerships program evolving as a whole? What new types of collaboration are being enabled?

Reimagine your business model as an ecosystem. Although most global companies are considering adopting an ecosystem business model, 37 percent of business executives are unable to balance the current business while exploring the new.[10] How can you begin to imagine your new business model? It can be helpful to think of your company's own internal customer engagement and product marketing efforts as an ecosystem—what enables them to work together successfully and what doesn't? How does that change as you cross company borders? What would be your key target customers, activities, value propositions, and partners? What is your partner value proposition? What would be key revenue streams and value exchanges?

Explore what it means to orchestrate a partnerships ecosystem. What does it mean to be a builder and orchestrator of a vibrant and enduring partnerships ecosystem? What resources do you bring to the table that enable you to assume this role? What are the shared values and commitments that would govern your ecosystem? How do you develop and maintain shared purpose, develop and scale ideas, and learn across organizations? How will you incentivize and balance collaboration and competition?

Learn what trust means in an ecosystem whose goals are larger than your organization's bottom line. Enterprises are the trust keepers and builders of partner ecosystems. As such, it's absolutely vital that enterprises and their leadership understand what that means in the context of an ecosystem. This is no small undertaking, as most companies have not figured out how to build trust within their own organizations! In its global CEO survey, PwC found that 55 percent of CEOs think that a lack of trust is a threat to their organization's growth.[11] What are the new rules and expectations for trust when collaborating across organizational borders?

Learn to safely share and protect data and intellectual property. Data and intellectual property are key sources of competitive advantage, but only if enterprises and partners use them to create value. What is the highest and best use of each members' resources? How much needs to be shared? In the midst of sharing intellectual property, how can each player define and protect their "competitive essence"?

How can the risk of data sharing be managed? Sixty-three percent of respondents in the Accenture survey say that technology is the most important thing to get right in an ecosystem.[12] What technology, systems, and guardrails need to be put in place to keep track of the data, ensure that it's governed well, and that it's used properly—not in violation of policies and regulations? And what about cybersecurity?

Get On Board!

Partnerships are the key to creating and maintaining competitive advantage both now and in the future. Enterprises that are committed to developing their partnerships capabilities and portfolios are already developing a deep source of competitive advantage. As they develop and test different partnerships growth strategies and combinations of people, process, and technology, they are learning what it takes to collaborate, to create formidable new business models, and to disrupt industries. These are the companies to watch, to own, to partner with, and to become.

Notes

[1] Scott Brinker, "Why HubSpot's Building a Centralized Platform," **medium.com**, January 25, 2018, **https://bit.ly/hubspot-centralized-platform**.

[2] Ibid.

[3] William Ribaudo, "The Future of Partnerships in Ecosystems," Deloitte, SNS Subscriber Edition 21, no. 16 (May 2, 2016), **http://bit.ly/Affiliate-Ultimate-Global-Guide**.

[4] Michael Lyman, Ron Ref, and Oliver Wright, "Cornerstone of Future Growth: Ecosystems," Accenture Strategy, Research Report, May 11, 2018, **http://bit.ly/Cornerstone-future-growth-ecosystems**.

[5] Ibid.

[6] Ibid.

[7] Michael Lewrick, Patrick Link, and Larry Leifer, *The Design Thinking Playbook: Mindful Digital Transformation of Teams, Products, Services, Businesses and Ecosystems* (Hoboken, NJ: John Wiley & Sons, 2018), p. 224.

[8] Omar Hoda and Joseph Vitale, Jr., "The Revenue Multiplier Effect," **Deloitte.com**, **http://bit.ly/The-Revenue-Multiplier-Effect**.

[9] A Forrester Consulting Thought Leadership Paper Commissioned by Impact, "Invest in Partnerships to Drive Growth and Competitive Advantage," **impact.com**, June 2019, **http://bit.ly/forrester-impact-invest-in-partnerships**.

[10] Accenture, "Cornerstone of Future Growth: Ecosystems," Accenture Strategy, Research Report, May 11, 2018, **https://accntu.re/3xKwsLo**.

[11] PwC, "Redefining Business Success in a Changing World: CEO Survey," **pwc.com**, 19th Annual Global CEO Survey, January 2016, **https://pwc.to/3wClRAU**.

[12] Accenture, "Cornerstone of Future Growth: Ecosystems."

About the Author

David A. Yovanno is the CEO of **impact.com**, the leading global standard partnership management platform that makes it easy for businesses to create, manage, and scale an ecosystem of partnerships with the brands and communities that customers trust to make purchases, get information, and entertain themselves at home, at work, or on the go. With this, **impact.com** has created a third channel for scalable and resilient revenue growth next to sales and marketing.

Dave has provided strategic leadership to SaaS companies in the technology vertical for more than two decades, serving previously as CEO of Marin Software, a San Francisco-based global leader in paid search SaaS technology; as President, Technology Solutions of Conversant, a diversified marketing services company; and as CEO of Gigya, a customer identity management platform. He has also served on the board of the Interactive Advertising Bureau and as a lieutenant and CIO in the United States Navy.

Index